THE GOVERNANCE OF
GENETIC INFORMATION

This volume maps the areas of ethical concern in the debate regarding the governance of genetic information, and suggests alternative ethical frameworks and models of regulation in order to inform its restructuring. Genetic governance is at the heart of medical and scientific developments, and is connected to global exploitation, issues of commodification, commercialisation and ownership, the concepts of property and intellectual property and concerns about individual and communal identity. Thus the decisions that are made in the next few years about appropriate models of genetic governance will have knock-on effects for other areas of governance. In short, the final answer to 'Who decides?' in the context of genetic governance will fundamentally shape the ethical constructs of individuals and their networks and relationships in the public sphere.

HEATHER WIDDOWS is Professor of Global Ethics at the University of Birmingham, where she teaches moral philosophy and bioethics.

CAROLINE MULLEN is a research officer at the Centre for European Law and Legal Studies, School of Law, University of Leeds.

This series of books was founded by Cambridge University Press with Alexander McCall Smith as its first editor in 2003. It focuses on the law's complex and troubled relationship with medicine across both the developed and the developing world. In the past twenty years, we have seen in many countries increasing resort to the courts by dissatisfied patients and a growing use of the courts to attempt to resolve intractable ethical dilemmas. At the same time, legislatures across the world have struggled to address the questions posed by both the successes and the failures of modern medicine, while international organisations such as the WHO and UNESCO now regularly address issues of medical law.

It follows that we would expect ethical and policy questions to be integral to the analysis of the legal issues discussed in this series. The series responds to the high profile of medical law in universities, in legal and medical practice, as well as in public and political affairs. We seek to reflect the evidence that many major health-related policy debates in the UK, Europe and the international community over the past two decades have involved a strong medical law dimension. Organ retention, embryonic stem cell research, physician assisted suicide and the allocation of resources to fund health care are but a few examples among many. The emphasis of this series is thus on matters of public concern and/or practical significance. We look for books that could make a difference to the development of medical law and enhance the role of medico-legal debate in policy circles. That is not to say that we lack interest in the important theoretical dimensions of the subject, but we aim to ensure that theoretical debate is grounded in the realities of how the law does and should interact with medicine and health care.

General Editors
Professor Margaret Brazier, *University of Manchester*
Professor Graeme Laurie, *University of Edinburgh*

Editorial Advisory Board
Professor Richard Ashcroft, *Queen Mary, University of London*
Professor Martin Bobrow, *University of Cambridge*
Dr Alexander Morgan Capron, *Director, Ethics and Health, World Health Organisation, Geneva*
Professor Jim Childress, *University of Virginia*
Professor Ruth Chadwick, *Cardiff Law School*
Dame Ruth Deech, *University of Oxford*
Professor John Keown, *Georgetown University, Washington, DC*

Dr Kathy Liddell, *University of Cambridge*
Professor Alexander McCall Smith, *University of Edinburgh*
Professor Dr Mónica Navarro-Michel, *University of Barcelona*

THE GOVERNANCE OF GENETIC INFORMATION

WHO DECIDES?

Edited by

HEATHER WIDDOWS

and

CAROLINE MULLEN

CAMBRIDGE
UNIVERSITY PRESS

CAMBRIDGE UNIVERSITY PRESS
Cambridge, New York, Melbourne, Madrid, Cape Town, Singapore, São Paulo, Delhi

Cambridge University Press
The Edinburgh Building, Cambridge CB2 8RU, UK

Published in the United States of America by Cambridge University Press, New York

www.cambridge.org
Information on this title: www.cambridge.org/9780521509916

First published 2009

Printed in the United Kingdom at the University Press, Cambridge

A catalogue record for this publication is available from the British Library

Library of Congress Cataloguing in Publication data
The governance of genetic information : who decides? / [edited by]
Heather Widdows, Caroline Mullen.
p.   cm. – (Cambridge law, medicine and ethics)
Includes bibliographical references.
ISBN 978-0-521-50991-6 (hardback)   1. Genetic screening–Moral and ethical
aspects.   2. Genetic screening–Government policy.   3. Privacy, Right of.   4. Medical
records–Access control.   I. Widdows, Heather, 1972–   II. Mullen, Caroline.   III. Series:
Cambridge law, medicine and ethics.
[DNLM: 1. Genetic Privacy–ethics.   2. Decision Making–ethics.   3. Genetic Privacy-
legislation & jurisprudence.   4. Public Policy. QZ 21 G721 2009]
RB155.65.G68 2009
362.196′04207–dc22
2009018067

ISBN 978-0-521-50991-6 hardback

CONTENTS

NOTES ON CONTRIBUTORS

ROGER BROWNSWORD is Director of the Centre for Technology, Ethics and Law in Society (TELOS) and Professor of Law, King's College London, and Honorary Professor in Law at the University of Sheffield.

RUTH CHADWICK is Director of the Economic and Social Sciences Research Council (ESRC) Centre for Economic and Social Aspects of Genomics (Cesagen), Cardiff University. She also holds a Link Chair between Cardiff Law School and the School of English, Communication and Philosophy (ENCAP). She was editor-in-chief of the award winning *Encyclopedia of Applied Ethics* (1998), of which a second edition is now being prepared, and co-edits the journal *Bioethics* and the online journal *Genomics, Society and Policy*. She is Chair of the Human Genome Organisation Ethics Committee and has served as a member of several policy making and advisory bodies. She is an Academician of the Academy of Social Sciences and a Fellow of the Hastings Center, New York; of the Royal Society of Arts; and of the Royal Society of Medicine. In 2005 she was the winner of the World Technology Network Award for Ethics for her work on the relationship between scientific developments and ethical frameworks.

ANDREW EDGAR is Director of the Centre for Applied Ethics, Cardiff University. His research interests include the philosophy of medicine and German philosophy. He has recently published books on Habermas. He is currently the editor of *Health Care Analysis*.

SØREN HOLM is Professorial Fellow at Cardiff Law School, Cardiff University. He is also a permanent visiting Chair at the Section for Medical Ethics, University of Oslo.

KATHRYN G. HUNTER is the Standing Researcher at the Arts and Humanities Research Council Research Centre for Studies in Intellectual Property and Technology Law (AHRC/SCRIPT) at the University of

ix

Edinburgh, and is currently completing her PhD on the governance of genetic databases.

GRAEME T. LAURIE is Professor of Medical Jurisprudence in the School of Law at the University of Edinburgh. He is currently Director of the Arts and Humanities Research Council Research Centre for Studies in Intellectual Property and Technology Law (AHRC/SCRIPT), also in the University of Edinburgh.

NEIL C. MANSON is a senior lecturer in the Department of Philosophy at Lancaster University and is the co-author (with Onora O'Neill) of *Rethinking Informed Consent in Bioethics* (Cambridge University Press, 2007).

CAROLINE MULLEN is a research officer at the Centre for European Law and Legal Studies, School of Law, University of Leeds. Her research interests and publications are in areas of ethics and political philosophy.

HEATHER STRANGE is a research assistant at the Economic and Social Sciences Research Council (ESRC) Centre for Economic and Social Aspects of Genomics (Cesagen), Cardiff University.

HEATHER WIDDOWS is a senior lecturer in the Department of Philosophy at the University of Birmingham. In 2005 she was awarded a visiting fellowship at Harvard University, where she worked on issues of moral neo-colonialism. She serves as a member of the UK Biobank Ethics and Governance Council and she is Lead Editor of the *Journal of Global Ethics*. Her publications include a monograph on *The Moral Vision of Iris Murdoch* and an edited collection on *Women's Reproductive Rights*, and articles and book chapters on all her areas of interest from bioethics to moral theory.

SARAH WILSON is a research associate in ethics at the School of Pharmacy and Pharmaceutical Sciences, University of Central Lancashire. Her current projects include ethics and professionalism in pharmacy practice, innovations in pharmacy practice around public health initiatives, and the implications of new technologies for the pharmacy profession. She has previously worked on projects looking at the ethical, legal and social dimensions of genetic technologies, including issues of social justice as they relate to human genetic research databases. She is author of several articles on ethical aspects of genomic technologies.

PREFACE

Heather Widdows and Caroline Mullen worked together as the lead investigators of the Property Regulation in European Science, Ethics and Law (PropEur) project, an EC funded project that ran for three years and finished in 2007. This volume is not an outcome of that project, but it was the experience of working on the project that provided the inspiration for it. In particular, the dearth of critical theorising which spoke to practice became abundantly clear, as did the need for comprehensive thinking which crossed disciplines and governance jurisdictions and interrogated the foundational assumptions of such governance. It is hoped that this volume, which was conceived as a concept volume with all its chapters commissioned, goes some way to addressing this gap. While it may not definitively answer 'Who should decide?', it does challenge existing practices and suggest alternatives.

We would like to acknowledge the Philosophy Department at the University of Birmingham for welcoming the PropEur project, and particularly to thank Helen Harris, Donna Dickenson, Dita Wickins-Drazilova and Louise Jelf, for their work on the project. The editors would also like to thank Phil Champion and Matthew Hilton.

~

Introduction

HEATHER WIDDOWS AND CAROLINE MULLEN

The governance of genetic information is relevant to issues of health, welfare, privacy and of personal and communal identity. This volume seeks to map this complex and difficult terrain and move beyond it by making positive suggestions for the restructuring and design of ethical frameworks for governance in this area. It sets out the key areas of ethical concern in the governance debate in a way which clarifies the significant features of genetic information and the problems of how it is ascribed, controlled and regulated in order that the complexities of genetic governance can be understood. This book seeks not merely to describe the areas of controversy and ethical dilemma but to drive the debate forwards and break new ground. It offers suggestions and alternatives, in terms of ethical frameworks and models of regulation, which it is hoped will inform the theory and practice of good governance. Accordingly this book intends to speak not only to academics, but to practitioners, participants in research and, perhaps most importantly, to policy makers. For genetic governance is not merely an interesting philosophical problem – although undoubtedly it is this – but more importantly it is an issue at the heart of medical and scientific developments and governance and one that touches on governance in general and globally. For example, issues which are connected to the governance of genetic information include issues of global exploitation, issues of commodification, commercialisation and ownership, conceptions of property and intellectual property and concerns about individual and communal identity and notions of public good. Thus the decisions that are made in the next few years about appropriate models of genetic governance will have knock-on effects for other areas of governance; in particular they will profoundly affect views about the proper units of ethical concern and ethical priorities. In short, the final answer to 'Who decides?' in the context of genetic governance impacts on governance more generally and thus fundamentally shapes the ethical constructs of individuals and their networks and relationships in the public sphere. In order to address these most important questions of governance this volume is divided into three sections: 'Problematising governance of genetic information'; 'Ethical frameworks of governance'; and 'Redesigning governance'.

Section One: Problematising governance of genetic information

This first section of the volume problematises the governance of genetic information, highlighting the key issues of controversy and concern which must be addressed if comprehensive and effective governance mechanisms are to be developed. The chapters in this section, by Neil Manson, Søren Holm and Caroline Mullen, serve to set the scene and map the central concerns of this volume. Each of these chapters focuses on one key aspect of genetic governance and problematises it, revealing its complexity and thus the challenge of such governance.

In the first chapter of the section, 'The medium and the message: tissue samples, genetic information and data protection legislation', Manson systematically examines what is meant by genetic information and the scope of the governance of genetic information. In so doing he seeks to clarify the underlying tensions and dilemmas which surround the acquisition, possession and use of genetic information. Manson begins with the regulation regarding the storing of human tissue containing genetic information. He asks whether the current consent-centred forms of regulation are appropriate means of regulating such tissue (and while his focus is on the UK his argument is applicable to all forms of consent-centred regulation). Having set the scene Manson critically assesses what, if anything, is ethically valuable and significant about human tissue and genetic information and explores what it is that we are seeking to protect. Manson interrogates the nature of information by asking a series of questions, 'What is personal data?', 'What is information?', 'What is genetic information?', suggesting that information is not as simple as is often assumed in the genetics debate. In so doing he reveals the similarities and dissimilarities between these categories in order to critique current practices of genetic governance.

In the light of such discussion he criticises current regulatory practices of data protection which he considers are based on misleading assumptions regarding the similarity of genetic information and other types of information and which have resulted in a distorted and inappropriate expansion of consent-thinking. He concludes by suggesting that clarity about what is at stake in the ethics of communication and information in the genetic debate aids assessment of current governance mechanisms. His hope is that even though such analysis is out of fit with current regulatory practices, it is nevertheless useful in the eventual construction of a robust and justifiable system of governance.

The nature of genetic information and current consent-based thinking having been problematised, the second chapter in the volume, 'Me, myself, I – against narcissism in the governance of genetic information' by Holm, considers whether it is the individual, the family, or society who should be considered to be the decision-making actors within the governance of genetic information. The first option, which grants rights only to the individual, is the most commonly endorsed position in current (Western) practice. Holm argues that this position, which gives the individual primary legitimacy to control the information, is only able to account for some of the moral concerns of the governance of genetic information. For example, the individual has commitments and obligations to others, including family members, which may override individual concerns but which are invisible on the individual model. The second position is the traditional understanding that the family is the unit of ethical concern rather than the individual. Holm is critical of this view for a number of reasons, which include confusions between biological and social understandings of family, and practical difficulties of establishing family decision-making mechanisms. Holm maintains that the third position, although rarely addressed directly, nevertheless underlies arguments about using patient information and by-products for research. He argues that any claim for the state to control genetic information would also apply to other types of information and that to restructure the current system so profoundly would need to produce significant benefits to be justifiable. He argues that there are areas where the state has a strong claim for control of health information, but that these are limited. Holm therefore concludes that none of these actors should be granted primary and sole control, but appropriate governance requires more complex mechanisms with sensitivity to differing specific circumstances.

The final chapter in this section, 'Decisions, consent and expectations of the individual' by Caroline Mullen, brings together themes from Manson's and Holm's chapters as she considers the current emphasis on the individual in governance. Mullen addresses the choices available to the individual donor and the constraints on those choices when considering whether or not to participate in genetic research. She explores what moral considerations individuals might be expected to take into account when deciding whether or not to participate in research and what, if any, obligations the donor has to participate in such research. Mullen's starting point is the current focus on informed consent – which suggests that ethical standards rest on the question of whether the individual is able to give informed consent when deciding whether to participate in research. She maintains that this focus on informed consent excludes further considerations of whether people have responsibilities to consider benefits to others that might arise from research.

Mullen asks whether the potential risks and benefits of medical genetic research challenge this standard of informed consent. Having outlined current presumptions regarding the expectations and responsibilities of the individual, Mullen proceeds to consider arguments that medical research benefits all and thus we have a duty to participate in research (at least when it is not overly burdensome). She suggests that if we follow such reasoning, then there is a general obligation to support genetic health (given its prospect of helping to improve basic health which, she argues, should be prioritised). However, Mullen claims that this obligation to participate in medical genetic research is not straightforward. The reasoning which leads to the claim that we should have concern for one another also suggests that we should interpret this responsibility with respect for people's differing circumstances and with regard to issues of distributive justice. Furthermore, Mullen argues that in some instances there is no obligation to participate in research (and even an obligation not to): for example, when research is presented as an alternative to measures being put into place which might better meet basic health needs. Therefore, what we can expect of potential participants in medical genetic research is not that they recognise a simple obligation to contribute, but that they give consideration to the relative benefits of the research to themselves and others. While she maintains that it is ultimately for the potential donor to judge the relative value of research, she argues that in making this decision they should take into account forms of democratic debate and institutions which are accountable to such democratic processes.

Section Two: Ethical frameworks of governance

The first section of the volume served to problematise and map the key issues in the governance of genetic information. The second section begins to address them. It suggests possible ways that current systems of governance can be adapted, modified or restructured in order to meet the dilemmas presented in the first section. Thus it begins to offer suggestions as to how ethical frameworks should be constructed and interpreted if comprehensive and equitable systems of genetic governance are to be established. The chapters in this section by Heather Widdows, Roger Brownsword and Sarah Wilson all speak to the key tension of genetic governance: that of balancing the rights of individuals and the rights of communities, or in other terminology the need to respect and protect the individual (which, as we saw in Holm's and Mullen's chapters, is the current focus of ethical concern) balanced against the public good. In an effort to address this fundamental tension, Widdows, Brownsword and Wilson all put forward alternative frameworks and, despite the differences in the solutions they suggest, all argue that the over-dominance of the individual (found particularly in current practices of bioethics) must be reassessed if good models of genetic governance, which are capable of tackling the relevant forms of injustice, are to be established.

In the first chapter of this section, 'Constructing communal models of governance: collectives of individuals or distinct ethical loci?', Widdows explores the recent move from individual models towards communal models of ethical governance. She draws on thinking about group rights to explore what conception of groups is necessary for an effective ethical framework. In particular, she is concerned with whether it is sufficient to regard groups as collectives of individuals – with their moral status and attendant rights dependent on the rights of individuals – or whether a more robust conception is necessary to establish the ethical protections required. Widdows begins with the conviction that whether or not one's ethical framework is capable of taking account of group interests and rights fundamentally affects the ethical issues that can be recognised and addressed. Accordingly she suggests that these conceptual concerns about groups and their rights speak directly to the practice and policy concerns of governance addressed in this volume: from the structure of benefit-sharing and stakeholder models to political concerns regarding what counts as participation; to questions of ownership rights and decision-making powers in genetic governance; to traditional bioethical concerns regarding what counts as harm in research. For Widdows, whether and how effectively these practical concerns of governance can be addressed depends on the prior ethical framework that one adopts. Thus whether and how groups feature in ethical frameworks profoundly impacts upon what is good governance.

Widdows argues that any effective ethical framework must include groups as ethical loci as well as individuals. Moreover, in her examination of groups she argues that in the context of genetic governance, group models which rely only on collectives of individuals are not always sufficient to prevent harm and protect interests in all instances. To illustrate this she uses examples of research on indigenous groups and argues that in these cases the group interests do not equate directly to the interests of existing group members; thus robust conceptions of groups and their rights are necessary. Despite advocating the inclusion of robust group models in any ethical framework, Widdows is well aware of the criticisms of such corporate models (in particular the need to protect individuals); thus she advocates the use of collective models where possible and suggests that for many groups, such as participants of biobanks, this model is sufficient to provide protection and ensure that rights and entitlements are adequately recognised. She concludes that any effective framework for ethical governance must accommodate the individual and groups of varying constructions in order that all the ethical pertinent features of any situation can be clearly recognised and addressed.

In the next chapter of this section, 'Rights, responsibility and stewardship: beyond consent', Brownsword, like Widdows, addresses this key fault-line of genetic governance; that of the balance between the community and the individual, between private rights and the public good. He is dissatisfied with the current over-individualised practice of consent, however; his alternative approach is based on a reassessment of the ethic of individual rights. He argues that if implemented properly, such an ethic is capable of recognising both communal and state obligations as well as the rights of the individual. Brownsword begins with the current focus on the individual and the criticism of this 'sovereign individual' from a public good perspective. Brownsword is wary of advocates of both positions and suggests that, rather than dismissing the individual, we should temper the narrative of consent by considering the ethic of individual rights which lies behind it. He argues that if implemented correctly this ethic is capable of supporting the healthcare interests of the community as well as the individual. In order to do this, Brownsword first interrogates the notion of consent; what it is intended to protect and the way it functions. He examines its function in data protection law: as procedural justification, as agent relative and as authorising the negation of a right. Brownsword clearly shows the attraction of consent as a simple governance mechanism which does not require justificatory reasons. Yet he warns against the 'tick box', 'sign here' 'routinisation' of consent which reduces it to a mechanical or perfunctory procedure. Conversely, he rejects views which over-emphasise consent and denies both that robust consent is always necessary and that it is capable of justifying prima facie wrongs. He argues that it is absurd to suggest that for an action to be legitimate the consent of all who are affected is required. Indeed, he suggests that to assert this is to commit the 'Fallacy of Necessity' in relation to consent and he illustrates his argument with cases throughout.

Brownsword then proceeds to examine the responsibilities and obligations that an ethic of rights lays on individuals in a community of rights. In his picture an ethics of rights is not simply a matter of consent but of positive obligation to others in the community, balanced by stewardship responsibilities of the state. Brownsword argues that there are positive responsibilities or, in other words, duties of assistance, in a community of rights. Brownsword outlines the conditions of positive rights and applies this framework to UK Biobank. He argues that in a community of rights there are positive obligations to participate and these are matched by obligations on UK Biobank, for example, for feedback in certain instances: an obligation which cannot be rescinded by UK Biobank's denial of responsibility and participants' consent. In addition, Brownsword argues that a community of rights also requires rights-holders to accommodate the state's stewardship duties, including those pertaining to legitimate public health interventions. In sum, for Brownsword larger healthcare goals and the public good are justified not by the abandonment of an ethic of rights but by its full application which includes obligations and responsibilities to others.

In the final chapter of this section, 'Who decides what? Relational ethics, genetics and well-being', Wilson introduces a relational approach, drawing on the ethics of care as a supplement to the current individualist model. Wilson shares concerns about the individual model of current governance with Widdows and Brownsword, and is particularly keen to establish a framework which prioritises issues of social justice (like Widdows she is concerned with the issues of commodification, biopiracy and profiteering which are not adequately addressed in the liberal model). Wilson begins from the same starting point as Widdows, noting the emerging (or converging) rhetoric of community and social solidarity in governance of genetic information; for example, as found in rhetorics of the genome as the common heritage of mankind, of public goods and of benefit sharing. Wilson explores this communal turn using one philosophical framework, that of 'relational ethics' which draws on feminist ethics and particularly the 'ethics of care'.

The care perspective regards individuals as embedded, interconnected and interdependent selves, in contrast to the separate, individually autonomous individual of traditional political and moral theory and bioethics. Wilson argues that a perspective of care is useful in offering an alternative to individualist accounts and in providing a more comprehensive ethical framework which allows a greater number of significant ethical issues to be addressed. For example, if one applies a traditional liberal (and bioethical) model to genetic enhancement, the ethical issues are those of individual choice, recreational autonomy, parental rights and the rights of the child. From a relational perspective this liberal reading ignores key ethical issues such as those of social justice, access and inequality, as well as concerns about the social constructions of persons (particularly women) and their relationships. Accordingly the individualistic model is judged to be ethically reductionist, competitive, overly abstract (ignoring the relational and emotional context) and over-simplistic (rejecting complex frameworks for binary ones). A care approach to genetic enhancement raises ethical issues which are simply not visible on liberal individual models such as the inherent values of the technological mechanisms, the underlying objectives of genetic enhancement, possibilities of exploitation and issues of commercialisation. Wilson argues that the ethics of care's ability to address issues of injustice and inequality is particularly important in the global context and in differentiating the burdens placed on the vulnerable (for example, women and children).

Having discussed the benefits of the ethics of care as an alternative ethical framework of governance in the context of genetic enhancement, Wilson returns to the issue of genetic information and the communal turn. Wilson explores the key features of this communal turn, particularly reciprocity, mutuality and solidarity. She interprets and expands on such concepts from an ethics of care perspective, providing examples of how such an ethical framework might be brought to bear on key issues of genetic governance. In the final section Wilson introduces principles of gender equity to flesh out her alternative approach to governance and develop an account which relates social justice and institutional justice. She concludes that principles drawn from such an account, namely those of antipoverty, antiexploitation, antimarginalisation and antiandrocentrism, could be used to develop this perspective and develop more comprehensive governance mechanisms.

Section Three: Redesigning governance

Having considered the key issues of the governance of genetic information in the first section of the volume and possible constructions of comprehensive ethical frameworks in the second section, the third section of this volume will make suggestions about how such frameworks should be redesigned. The three chapters in this section by Kathryn Hunter and Graeme Laurie, by Andrew Edgar and by Ruth Chadwick and Heather Strange, are all concerned with the design of governance mechanisms and the ways in which they should be constructed in order for comprehensive and good practices of governance to be implemented. These authors address differing aspects that should be considered in designing governance: Hunter and Laurie focusing on participation in UK Biobank; Edgar on the role of public debate in determining the governance of biobanks; and Chadwick and Strange on the need for different voices in a harmonisation of governance mechanisms. Taken together, and in conjunction with the second section of the volume, a number of robust models are offered for the redesign of current practices of genetic governance.

In the first chapter of this section, 'Involving publics in biobank governance: moving beyond existing approaches', Hunter and Laurie ask what constitutes effective public involvement in biobanks deemed so necessary for good governance? They address this issue in the context of UK Biobank and the calls for greater participant involvement in its governance mechanisms. Hunter and Laurie outline UK Biobank's status, purpose and governance mechanisms and recount its attempts at public engagement and the criticisms thereof. They proceed to explore how such criticisms can be met and more effective forms of public participation in governance established. Hunter and Laurie first explore and assess Winickoff's claims that public engagement must move from consultation to representation and his 'shareholder' model.[1] The shareholder model is intended to address the lack of agency of donor collectives in biobank governance. Donors would have the option to become members of a Donor Association which would have membership on the UK Biobank Board of Directors and the Ethics and Governance Council. Despite praising Winickoff's model, Hunter and Laurie are not convinced either that it does meet the agency gap or that it addresses the problems of maintaining trust. They suggest that the model faces both practical and conceptual problems, including: lack of fit with a public body such as UK Biobank; issues of effective representation; and contradictions between notions of shareholding and partnership.

---

[1] D. E. Winickoff, 'Partnership in U.K. Biobank: a third way for genomic property?', *Journal of Law, Medicine & Ethics*, 35, 3 (2007), 440–56; and 'Governing population genomics: law, bioethics, and biopolitics in three case studies', *Jurimetrics*, 43 (2003), 187–228.

In the light of such debates and drawing particularly on the discourse of deliberative democracy, Hunter and Laurie suggest an alternative 'stakeholder approach'. The stakeholder model intends to go beyond representation to participation with emphasis on inclusion, accountability and ongoing engagement. The stakeholder model then (like UK Biobank) is committed to participants, users and society, with this wider commitment to society being fundamentally important. Hunter and Laurie go on to address aspects of the practical functioning of such a model, such as identifying stakeholders and considering the nature of stakeholder involvement. In conclusion, they endorse the stakeholder model on the grounds that it meets deliberative democratic goals of participation, involvement and inclusion and thus is in fit with the aims of UK Biobank and moreover has the added advantage of being able to develop and adapt over time.

The second chapter of this section, 'Genetic information and public opinion' by Edgar, is concerned with the role of public debate in the development of biobanks, and introduces the importance of taking seriously public understanding and knowledge, and in particular cultural factors, if good ethical governance is to be achieved. Edgar explores the process of public debate regarding the collection and use of genetic information, focusing on the development of DNA biobanks. Edgar maintains that while public consultation and involvement are crucial to legitimate such projects, achieving any effective participation is problematic.

Edgar begins by describing the rise in biobanks and the ethical issues which are widely understood to arise in such developments (such as informed consent, privacy and data misuse) and the further complexities arising from the communal nature of genetic information. He argues that these issues create a need for public acceptance if genetic research and technologies are to be legitimately sustained, and suggests that recognition of the need for public acceptance has motivated the use of public consultations over the development of biobanks. However, Edgar argues that the conduct of these consultations has been problematic, and he suggests this stems in part from unwarranted assumptions about public understanding of science. In turning his attention to public debate on genetic science, he challenges the view that the sole potential for difficulty in gaining public acceptance stems from limitations in public understanding of scientific processes and knowledge. He considers how public policy on genetic science may rely either on 'golem science' (that is, science about which we cannot yet have confidence) or on 'reflexive historical science' in which the effects of science will be influenced by human decisions. Edgar suggests that in either case, public debate can go beyond expression of subjective opinions and holds the potential to contribute to the development of knowledge.

To elaborate on this claim, he draws on Habermas's notion of the public sphere and his model of decision-making under ideal conditions. Edgar argues that Habermas provides a positive account of decision-making and offers a critical tool that can be developed for application to debates about the exploitation of genetic information and thus serve as a tool for governance. He applies this model to genetic information, highlighting the difficulty of public debate in this context. In so doing he argues that there is a tension in the debate on genetic science between the Habermasian validity claims of 'truth' and 'rightness'. Analysing the emergence of the public engagement on science, he suggests that the Habermasian approach is useful in highlighting the necessity of real public dialogue on values, while nonetheless recognising that some positions are more defensible than others. Moreover he argues that the Habermasian model takes account of ideological distortions, thus permitting the inclusion of cultural understandings and popular perceptions of genetics. It is this aspect of genetics that Edgar concludes with – that of the cultural power of genetic discourse which makes it such a complex issue for public deliberation. He concludes by arguing that the task of the expert is less of a knowledge conduit and more of a facilitator and interpreter of dialogue as the complexity of the debate is negotiated.

In the final chapter of this section, 'Harmonisation and standardisation in ethics and governance: conceptual and practical challenges', Ruth Chadwick and Heather Strange remind us of the need to take account of wider jurisdictions and the global context in issues of genetic governance. Chadwick and Strange address the calls to harmonisation at both scientific and ethical levels which have increasingly beset the governance of genetic information and particularly the governance of biobanks. Chadwick and Strange problematise the notion of harmonisation and question the assumptions that lie behind it. Chadwick and Strange consider what harmonisation of ethical frameworks might mean in the global sphere and what benefits it might bring. They consider different models of the harmonisation of ethics and ethical agreement – those of the human rights model, the ethical agreement model and the cultural dialogue model – and argue that harmonisation must be an ongoing process and more than an end-point for scientific progress.

Chadwick and Strange suggest that what has been achieved in places of apparent harmonisation is not actually harmonisation but is instead standardisation. This has occurred, for example, in the HUGO Ethics Committee's statement on Benefit Sharing. Chadwick and Strange argue that in the case of biobanks, and the pan-European Biobanking and Biomolecular Resources Research Infrastructure in particular, such standardisation is not sufficient and harmonisation (which requires more than one voice and collective performance) is necessary. This focus on the necessity of a plurality of voices is key and, they assert, should be maintained in any pressure for harmonisation. Having argued for a nuanced understanding of harmonisation in the context of the governance of genetic information, they suggest that there are areas where standardisation might be appropriate: namely, with regard to consent to participate, access, feedback and privacy. However, even here they are sceptical of the need for pan-European and global standards and they suggest that different approaches may be necessary: for example, consent may need to be standardised but feedback may not; and procedures to protect privacy may require that multiple voices are maintained.

Taken together, the chapters in this volume signal the need for ethical attention to the development and design of ethical frameworks and mechanisms of genetic governance. Unlike many issues in ethics, in which so often ethical commentators enter the debate somewhat after the fact to congratulate or condemn, in these debates on genetic governance, questions of what will become standard practice (or harmonised practice if we take seriously the claims of Chadwick and Strange) are still very much open to question. As Hunter and Laurie forcibly remind us, the governance practice of UK Biobank is new and designed to evolve, and thus can be influenced and shaped as we attempt to overcome the ethical issues of genetic governance, which were problematised at the beginning of this volume by Manson, Holm and Mullen. Whatever else is concluded, the current state of play with its over-individual focus is no longer adequate, as is borne out by the new models being adopted by UK Biobank and elsewhere (described throughout this volume). Given this need for new approaches, it is hoped that insights from this volume, regarding the need to balance the rights and needs of the community and the individual so strongly asserted by Brownsword, Widdows and Wilson, and the fundamental importance of effective public participation and engagement championed by both Hunter and Laurie, and by Edgar, will be a useful contribution to rethinking governance and more importantly to redesigning and actually implementing more ethical forms of genetic governance.

SECTION I

Problematising governance of genetic information

The medium and the message: tissue samples, genetic information and data protection legislation

NEIL C. MANSON

There are many ethical, legal and regulatory issues surrounding the acquisition, possession and use of genetic information. But what is genetic information, and why and when do such issues arise? Here the aim is to provide something by way of an answer to these questions, and I will do so by focusing on whether certain regulatory instruments that apply to the use of personal information ought to apply to archives or collections of human tissues, in so far as such samples – including blocks, slides and other artefacts – contain genetic information.

Human tissue samples are acquired and stored for a variety of good reasons: for example, as part of a process of individual diagnosis, or as part of a forensic investigation or autopsy. Samples may also be taken and stored for teaching and training purposes, or as part of clinical audit and performance assessment, and so on. In the UK – which is to be our focus – actions involving human tissue fall under the regulatory scope of the Human Tissue Act 2004 (HTA04).[1] But most human tissue samples contain genetic material and genetic material is standardly assumed to contain genetic information, including personal information about the source of the tissue: information about their current or future state of health, for example.[2] In the UK the legal instrument that pertains to the storage and use of personal information is the Data Protection Act 1998 (DPA98).[3] DPA98 specifies a range of obligations upon those responsible – typically in institutions – for the acquisition, storage or use of certain types of information.

---

[1] HTA04 is the implementation in UK law of European Parliament and Council Directive 2004/23/EC on setting standards of quality and safety for the donation, procurement, testing, processing, preservation, storage and distribution of human tissues and cells (31 March 2004). Scotland has its own implementation in the Human Tissue (Scotland) Act 2006.

[2] We shall see that this way of speaking about genetic information and personal information is not as straightforward as it may seem.

[3] Available online at: www.hmso.gov.uk/acts/acts1998/19980029.htm.

This raises two questions: first, whether, and to what extent, DPA98 applies to the possession and use of human tissue in so far as it contains genetic information; second, whether data protection legislation *ought* to be used to control and regulate the acquisition, storage and use of genetic information.

But the purpose of this chapter is not simply to determine whether or not human tissue samples, or tissue collections and archives, fall under – or ought to fall under – DPA98. By focusing on questions about what genetic information is, and about what it is for an object to *contain* genetic information, we gain some useful resources for engaging with other questions about the regulation of genetic information. Both HTA04 and DPA98 are regulatory instruments which give a central and substantive role to *individual consent*: they are what we might call *consent-centred* forms of regulation.[4] Part of the task here is to expose some important, but initially non-obvious, connections between, on the one hand, standard ways of thinking about genetic information and, on the other, standard ways of thinking about consent. These standard ways of thinking are misleading, at least in some respects, and may contribute to a distorted regulatory landscape – especially for consent-centred regulatory instruments – which, in turn, may place unnecessary burdens upon those who seek to use human tissue for a variety of legitimate purposes.

Human tissue and data protection

First we should note that many actions involving human tissue simply fall outside the scope of DPA98, and rightly so. For example, suppose Tom has a finger severed in a DIY accident. Tom keeps the severed finger in a jar of formalin in his bedroom. He possesses human tissue, and the tissue contains genetic information, including, in principle, personal information about Tom. Simply possessing tissue is not enough to bring in the duties and responsibilities specified in DPA98. The tissue sample must either be subject to automated processing, or – and this is more relevant for our purposes – must be part of a 'relevant filing system'. Vast numbers of tissue samples are stored, filed and archived

---

[4] Indeed, in the guidance notes to HTA04 we are told: 'The purpose of the Act is to provide a consistent legislative framework for issues relating to whole body donation and the taking, storage and use of human organs and tissue. It will make consent the fundamental principle underpinning the lawful storage and use of human bodies, body parts, organs and tissue and the removal of material from the bodies of deceased persons.' www.opsi. gov.uk/acts/acts2004/en/ukpgaen_20040030_En_1.

in a way that makes them part of a relevant filing system in hospitals, laboratories, tissue banks, universities, and so on. So, do these samples fall under DPA98? Let us be clear about what DPA98 applies to. DPA98 pertains to the acquisition, storage and use of 'personal data'. First, 'data' are defined as:

> information which (a) is being processed by means of equipment operating automatically in response to instructions given for that purpose; [or] (b) is recorded with the intention that it should be processed by means of such equipment; [or] (c) is recorded as part of a relevant filing system or with the intention that it should form part of a relevant filing system, or (d) does not fall within paragraph (a), (b) or (c) but forms part of an accessible record as defined by section 68.[5]

And *personal* data are:

> data which relate to a living individual who can be identified (a) from those data, or (b) from those data and other information which is in the possession of, or is likely to come into the possession of, the data controller.[6]

Do tissue samples contain information? There is a simple line of argument here. Tissue samples can be informative about a source subject's medical traits, about her present or future health, in just the same way that an entry in a medical record can be. Both tissue samples and medical records contain personal information. Given this similarity, then of course tissue samples should fall under DPA98.

But this simple line of argument is unsatisfactory. In particular, it fails to pinpoint important disanalogies between human tissue samples on the one hand and standard medical records on the other. There is a sense in which *any* object can be viewed as containing information about other things. For example, consider a firm that stores furniture

---

[5] DPA98, Part 1, section 1. In section 68 an 'accessible record' is defined as a health record, an educational record, or an accessible public record. The latter two are, in turn, clarified at Schedules 11 and 12 to DPA98, whilst 'health record' is defined as 'any record which (a) consists of information relating to the physical or mental health or condition of an individual, and (b) has been made by or on behalf of a health professional in connection with the care of that individual'.

[6] DPA98, Part I, section 1. This formulation of personal data is closely based upon that found in Directive 95/46/EC where ' "personal data" shall mean any information relating to an identified or identifiable natural person ("data subject")'. European Parliament and Council Directive 95/46/EC on the protection of individuals with regard to the processing of personal data and on the free movement of such data (24 October 1995) Chapter 1, Article 2 (a).

and other personal possessions in a warehouse. A person's furniture may be informative about their financial status (only someone rich could afford furniture like *this*). But it would be absurd to view a furniture storage warehouse as constituting a relevant filing system by virtue of the furniture that it stores. Why should we think of tissue samples as containing information at all? There are two broad reasons why this is so, but in order to understand properly what these reasons are, we will first need to be clear about what information is, and what genetic information is.

What is information?

'Information' is an ambiguous concept. In everyday English 'information' is an epistemic term, to do with knowledge, especially in the context of communication. We talk of seeking information; giving information; going to the information desk, and so on. Information in this sense is always information *about* something. We talk of people possessing, having, getting, acquiring, sharing, disclosing and passing on information. These are agentive terms, identifying people as entities that are in a position to do something with information. When we convey information we must do so by modifying our material environment. Our material environment becomes a *medium* of the conveyance of knowledge, or information. Some communication involves local, transient, modifications of the material environment (e.g., in speech we modify the air around us). But we can also make durable marks on, for example, rock, slate or paper. These long-lasting modifications can be used to 'store' knowledge or, as we typically say, the books, records, and other texts *contain* information. This is by way of deference to the role such material objects play in the communication of information (identified as something abstract and immaterial). Books and records act as material *containers*, *stores*, *repositories*, or *vehicles* of information, information that is *about* things other than the book and the marks on it. Such information depends upon mutually accepted conventions and norms which allow us – as speakers and authors – to produce appropriate marks and – as audience or readers – to understand them.

So, whilst people possess, acquire and convey information, the media of communication are said to *contain* information. A book may *contain* or *be full of* information about something, but it does not acquire, share, or do anything with it. But in each case – when we talk about people communicating, or the media of communication – our talk is framed in terms of, and shaped by, a specific set of metaphors: *conduit* and *container* metaphors.[7]

With this initial clarification in place, let us return to the analogy between human tissue (stored as part of a relevant filing system) and other kinds of records, data, files, texts. Medical records and human tissue samples may both seem to contain personal information. But this claim fails to highlight some important differences, for different kinds of inanimate objects can be viewed as 'containing' information in different ways.

First there are objects that have been created by human agents to play a communicative role: paper texts, books, CD-roms. But tissue samples are – standardly at least – not texts.[8] Although tissue slides and blocks may be artefacts, and though they may be produced with their informativeness in mind, they are still unlike texts and textual records. Texts, medical records and other data that DPA98 applies to are *linguistic* communicative artefacts. Linguistic communication draws upon a finite set of modifications (various 'alphabets' of phonemes, letters, symbols) which can be combined into complex groups (lexemes, words, symbol-strings), which, in turn, can be combined in various ways to convey an indefinitely large range of information.[9] Successful communication requires speakers/authors and audiences to have a grasp of the rules and conventions which govern the systematic arrangement of sounds, marks, and so on. You know what 'STOP!' means but not what '-%@=' means, even though both involve relatively arbitrary modifications of the perceptible environment. So, even though tissue samples are artefacts, and even though they are created and stored by way of allowing others to gain knowledge, there are important disanalogies between texts and tissue samples. The informativeness of a tissue sample is not a result of its parts being arranged in line with a set of linguistic communicative norms and conventions.

So in what sense do tissue samples contain information at all? An analogy may help. Consider a tree's rings. A tree's rings are informative about the age of the tree. There is a causal correlation between the tree's age and the number of rings. A person who knows of this correlation can

---

[7] M. Reddy, 'The conduit metaphor: a case of frame conflict in our language about language', in A. Ortony (ed.), *Metaphor and Thought* (Cambridge University Press, 1979), 284–324.

[8] Of course, given that human tissue can be manipulated in systematic ways, such samples *could* be modified and used as communicative tools.

[9] There are other ways of communicating that may not involve such 'alphabets' or symbolic systems of representation: e.g., non-verbal communication, or acts of communicating by pointing, waving, and so on.

infer something about the tree's age from viewing the rings (or can infer something about the tree's rings from its age, if known).[10] The conduit and container metaphors allow us to talk of accessing information, getting information, or acquiring information *from* the natural world. Here we have two options for thinking about information in a sense other than the communicative one: we can view the tree rings as containing information in a derivative, metaphorical, sense. What we really mean is that the tree rings are good *evidence* for making judgments about the tree's age. They are informative *for* human agents. Alternatively, we might view information as something natural, something that is 'out there' in the tree rings, something that we detect, but that was there all along, independent of human agency. Natural information would then be something that is constituted by the causal and logical relations between things.

So, this initial clarification suggests that we can view objects as 'containing' information in three ways. For our purposes it will simplify things if we refer to three different senses of information.

(i) Communicative information.
(ii) Information as evidence.
(iii) Natural information.

We can view these three senses of information in terms of their distance from the core notion: that of information as knowledge that is communicated amongst agents. Information as evidence picks up on the fact that we can gain communicable knowledge from the natural world, whilst the 'natural' information notion removes agency and communication from the picture and locates information 'out there' in the world.

What is genetic information?

We are a little clearer about what information is, but what is *genetic* information? Mendel's notebooks might be viewed as containing genetic information (even though Mendel did not use the term 'gene'), in so far as they are texts which inform us about the nature of heredity. An undergraduate textbook of molecular biology might also contain genetic

[10] As Dretske puts it 'A state of affairs contains information about X to just that extent to which a suitably placed observer could learn something about X by consulting it.' F. Dretske, *Knowledge and the Flow of Information* (Cambridge, MA: MIT Press, 1981), 45. Dretske builds upon Grice's notion of 'natural meaning' (e.g., dark clouds *mean* rain in so far as the darkness of the clouds reliably co-varies with the (impending) occurrence of rain). H. P. Grice, 'Meaning', *Philosophical Review*, 66 (1957), 377–88.

information: information *about* genes and their causal and chemical features. But human tissue does not contain genetic information in either of these senses. Contemporary ethical, legal and regulatory concerns about genetic information – of which there are many – are not concerns to do with information *about* genes or genetics. Rather, the concern is with *personal* information – information about identifiable subjects – that is 'contained' within genes, information that might be acquired or accessed via genetic testing upon an individual or upon other family members. Here, the adjective 'genetic' signifies something about the *source*, or *location* of the information.

There are many familiar ethical and legal issues to do with information derived from – or contained within – DNA.[11] Should employers ever be permitted to require a job applicant, or an employee, to provide a DNA sample which would then be used to test for various 'predispositions' to certain traits?[12] Should insurers have a right to seek genetic information about potential policy holders?[13] Is it ever permissible to override patient confidentiality in order to disclose useful, relevant but perhaps disturbing genetic information to family members who may be, unwittingly, at risk of developing some debilitating condition in later life?[14] Given such concerns, if it is the case that human tissue contains genetic information, then surely the storage of human tissue in archives and other filing systems should be subject to regulation *by virtue of* the information contained within such samples.

But in what sense do tissue samples contain genetic information? The answer here is complicated, and the reason why is that talk of genetic information weaves in further notions of information, in addition to the three noted so far. First there is a mathematical, quantitative notion of information, measured in 'bits' and 'bytes' and 'megabytes' and so on.

---

[11] Two useful collections are A. K. Thompson and R. F. Chadwick (eds.), *Genetic Information: Acquisition, Access, and Control* (New York: Kluwer, 1999); D. Chadwick, G. Bock and J. Whelan (eds.), *Human Genetic Information: Science, Law and Ethics* (Chichester: John Wiley, 1990). See also the report by the UK Human Genetics Commission, *Inside information: balancing interests in the use of personal genetic data* (May 2002) www.hgc.gov. uk/Client/Content.asp?ContentId=557

[12] E.g., B. M. Knoppers, 'Who should have access to genetic information?' in J. Burley (ed.), *The Genetic Revolution and Human Rights* (Oxford University Press, 1999), 39–53.

[13] E.g., see essays 3–7 in Thompson and Chadwick, *Genetic Information*; J. Burley, 'Bad genetic luck and health insurance' in J. Burley (ed.), *The Genetic Revolution and Human Rights* (Oxford University Press, 1999), 54–61.

[14] M. Parker and A. Lucassen, 'Genetic information: a joint account?', *British Medical Journal*, 329 (2004), 165–7.

This mathematical notion of information is a measure of 'reduction of uncertainty'.[15] Molecular biology adopted this quantitative notion of information from the early 1950s onwards.[16] Before this time, biologists had talked of how (as yet unidentified) genetic material must 'specify' the particular proteins and protein constituents which are the building blocks of biological entities. Rather than talking of 'information', molecular biologists talked of 'specificity' and the transmission of 'specificity' from one intracellular entity to another.[17] DNA and genes are viewed as containing *quantities* of information in the mathematical sense. But this information – measured in bits, bytes, gigabytes, etc., – is not viewed as information *about* other phenomena.[18] Genetic information, in this sense, is not genetic information *about* anything at all (and so cannot count as personal information for data protection purposes).

Although the mathematical notion of genetic information has a place in biology, there are other notions of genetic information in play. For example, linguistic and communicative metaphors are extremely common in talk of the intracellular molecular activity of DNA. This is because the *causal* significance of DNA depends upon the form, or arrangement of a small set of components. There is talk of cells, or intracellular structures, *expressing, reading, communicating* and *deciphering* and *translating*. Molecules are viewed as *communicating* with one another; molecular systems can make *translation errors*. Indeed, the central dogma of molecular biology is cast in terms of information flow: 'genetic information' flows from DNA to RNA to proteins.

These metaphors draw upon the functional similarities between a person reading a text and giving appropriate outputs. That is, the 'outputs' systematically depend upon which determinate arrangement out of a number of possibilities is 'written' in the 'text'. Here we have a double layer of metaphor and simile. By treating molecular entities *as if* they

---

[15] For a fuller discussion of this notion see N. C. Manson, 'What is genetic information and why is it significant?', *Journal of Applied Philosophy*, 23, 1 (2006), 1–16.

[16] L. E. Kay, *Who Wrote the Book of Life? A History of the Genetic Code* (Stanford University Press, 2000).

[17] Sarkar argues that 'there is no clear, technical notion of "information" in molecular biology. It is little more than a metaphor that masquerades as a theoretical concept.' S. Sarkar, 'Biological information: a sceptical look at some central dogmas of molecular biology' in S. Sarkar (ed.), *The Philosophy and History of Molecular Biology: New Perspectives* (Dordrecht: Kluwer, 1996), 187–232.

[18] As Dretske puts it: 'Communication theory does not tell us what information is. It ignores questions having to do with the content of signals, what specific information they carry, in order to describe how much information they carry.' Dretske, *Flow of Information*, 41.

were conscious subjects communicating with one another, the tropes appropriate to characterising human communication are then deployed to characterise certain of the causal relations that obtain amongst these entities. It may then seem that what molecules *do* depends upon what is 'communicated' to them by other molecules and this returns us – via a metaphorical path – to the more familiar kind of communication and information: communication between agents that is *about* things.

Whilst this seems to be nothing but a metaphorical use of communication and information terms, there are stronger claims that can be made about genetic information. Just as a tree's rings 'contain' information about its age in so far as age and rings co-vary with one another, genomic sequences co-vary with, and thus bear information about, other molecular events. Or, if we draw upon a looser sense of natural information, where something bears information about something else in so far as we can make inferences about the latter on the basis of the former, then DNA might even be viewed as containing information about phenotypic traits.[19] On this view there is nothing especially distinctive about DNA as a bearer or container of natural information: it only bears information in so far as knowledgeable observers can draw upon *their* knowledge of the causal significance of DNA to make inferences about other phenomena.

But some philosophers and biologists argue that genetic material contains information in a way that tree rings do not.[20] At the heart of their argument is an idea drawn from philosophy of mind and language. Philosophers have long puzzled over the fact that thoughts, desires, words, emotions and so on, are about other things and, more strangely, they can be about things that do not exist, or that have not yet happened. Thoughts and statements can also be wrong. How can one bit of the natural world be about another bit? How can a bit of the natural world wrongly represent another? How can something be about something that does not exist?

Teleosemantics is one attempt to answer these problems, in a naturalistically acceptable way, in terms of the evolutionary function that certain

---

[19] This line of thought is problematic, and is contested by developmental systems theorists; see S. Oyama, *The Ontogeny of Information. Developmental Systems and Evolution*, 2nd edn (Durham, NC: Duke University Press, 2000); S. Oyama, P. E. Griffiths and R. D. Gray, *Cycles of Contingency. Developmental Systems and Evolution* (Cambridge, MA: MIT Press, 2001).

[20] J. M. Smith, 'The concept of information in biology', *Philosophy of Science*, 67 (2000), 177–94; N. Shea, 'Representation in the genome, and other inheritance systems', *Biology and Philosophy*, 22 (2007), 313–31; E. Jablonka, 'Information: its interpretation, its inheritance and its sharing', *Philosophy of Science*, 69 (2002), 578–605.

entities or traits are *supposed* to play.[21] In the case of genetic information, the argument – simplified a great deal – is that genomic sequences are the way that they are because evolutionary pressures have favoured sequences which produce certain effects, perhaps even including adaptive phenotypic traits. This line of argument is coupled with another: one which picks up on the functional analogy between molecular 'communication' within the cell and communication proper.[22] Central to this line of argument is the idea that the intrinsic properties, or the precise chemical properties, of DNA are *arbitrary*. Other chemicals could perform the job. So, the relationship between DNA and amino acid production, or even between DNA and phenotypic traits, is like the relationship between a written instruction and an action performed on the basis of interpreting that instruction.[23]

The aim is to clarify what it is for an inanimate object to 'contain' information and, to recall, three senses of 'information' have initially been identified:

(i)   Communicative information.
(ii) Information as evidence.
(iii) Natural information.

Some senses of *genetic information* fall under these. Mendel's notebooks contain *communicative* genetic information. DNA can be viewed as *evidence* for traits, paternity and so on, or we can view the causal relations – knowledge of which provided the basis for drawing inferences on the basis of evidence – as somehow constituting a 'natural' information that is in the DNA. We can also add:

(iv) Quantitative information (a measure of information in bits, bytes, etc).
(v)   *Metaphorical* communicative information (e.g., where molecules are viewed as communicating, translating, decoding).

---

[21] R. Millikan, *Language, Thought and other Biological Categories* (Cambridge, MA: MIT Press, 1984); D. Papineau, 'The status of teleosemantics, or how to stop worrying about swampman', *Australasian Journal of Philosophy*, 79, 2 (2001) 279–89; F. Dretske, *Naturalizing the Mind* (Cambridge, MA: MIT Press, 1995).

[22] U. Stegmann, 'The arbitrariness of the genetic code', *Biology and Philosophy*, 19 (2004), 205–22.

[23] Of course, those who object to the idea that genes contain information about phenotypic traits – in the 'natural information' sense noted above – object even more strongly to the claims that DNA *really does* contain information, in some special biological sense, about development and phenotypic traits.

(vi) Biological information (where biological information is viewed as something *sui generis*, and not merely as a species of natural information).

So what kind of genetic information is it that is contained in human tissues? Human tissues are not a medium of communication, so we rule out (i) above. We can also rule out (v) as merely metaphorical, whilst (iv) is not going to be of relevance to this discussion which is concerned with information *about* identifiable individuals (and not with a measure of *amounts* of information). This leaves (ii), (iii) and (vi). Does DPA98 (and other data protection legislation) apply – and *ought* it to apply – to information, if information is construed in these ways?

Data subjects' rights and objective genetic information

One thing that senses (ii), (iii) and (vi) have in common is that genetic information is viewed as something that is 'out there' and 'inside' biological material. Let us ignore the differences between these three senses and introduce a label – *objective genetic information* – for genetic information that is about other things independently of human communicative activity. If some of this objective genetic information is about personal traits, then it would seem that some objective genetic information is personal information. But objective genetic information is not something that is put there by human beings in their communicative activity, and there are vast amounts of objective genetic information that nobody knows. These facts have implications for our question about whether tissue samples fall under DPA98.

DPA98 specifies different types of obligation. For example, there are general obligations upon data controllers to comply with certain specified standards in acquiring, processing, using and disclosing personal data. These obligations are stated in eight 'Data Protection Principles' and in further 'schedules' which specify the conditions under which personal information, and 'sensitive' personal information, may legitimately be acquired, stored, processed or used. In addition to these obligations, there are obligations that are the correlates of subjects' rights with regard to information held about them. These rights include rights of access to stored personal information, and the right to revise or correct personal information held by institutions.

But it is not at all clear that all these obligations are coherent if they are taken to apply to objective genetic information. For example, consider the third data protection principle: 'Personal data shall be adequate, relevant and not excessive in relation to the purpose or purposes for which they are processed.' If DNA contains genetic information it contains an awful lot of information: if objective genetic information counts as personal data then any tissue sample may be viewed as an excessive repository of information. But how on earth is a data controller meant to ensure that the information is 'adequate' and 'relevant' to their purposes? They may have no idea just what objective genetic information a tissue sample contains.

Or, consider the fourth data protection principle: 'Personal data shall be accurate and, where necessary, kept up to date.' Supposing we view objective genetic information as biological information, as some philosophers do, we might talk of 'errors' in a particular genotype (indeed, biologists talk of 'translation' errors in replication). But these are errors in a very unusual sense. In particular, the notion of accuracy that is relevant to DPA98 is accuracy that a human agent can identify and, if necessary, rectify (e.g., a factual error in one's textual medical record). This kind of accuracy features in the list of data subjects' rights as part of 'The right of rectification, blocking, erasure and destruction'.

> The Data Protection Act allows individuals to apply to the Court to order a data controller to rectify, block, erase or destroy personal details if they are inaccurate or contain expressions of opinion which are based on inaccurate data.[24]

Suppose, for the sake of argument, that there is a sense in which objective genetic information can be wrong, in terms of there being 'errors' in DNA sequences. But a tissue sample will contain many millions of cells all with the same genetic material. How are such errors to be corrected? In some cells? All of them?

A further worry arises when we consider the 'right of subject access' where individuals are entitled to find out what information is held about themselves on computer and some paper records.[25] This seems coherent for communicative information. Communicative information is meant to be accessible, at least to certain parties (its audience). There is no point in keeping a record, or writing a text, whose content is, in principle, inaccessible to anyone – indeed, it is not clear that this would be communication at all. But a person who possesses, or uses, an object that contains

---

[24] Legal Guidance to DPA98, section 4.6, www.ico.gov.uk.   [25] DPA98 Part II, section 7.

objective genetic information may have no inkling what that information is. So how can a data controller give access to genetic information that is contained within stored human tissue: other than, for instance, to give a sample of the tissue itself?

The reason why these rights and obligations seem incoherent when applied to objective genetic information is that the data subject's rights are framed, primarily, in terms of communicative information. There is good reason why this is so. It is a matter of historical fact that data protection legislation came into being as a way of regulating communicative information (especially after the development of automated ways of processing and communicating financial information).

But communicative information is different from objective genetic information in certain important ways. First, for communicative information the specific material medium is, to a certain extent, irrelevant. I can communicate one and the same information in a wide variety of ways: by modifying sound waves; modifying electrical or magnetic properties; by making marks on a page; by waving flags, flashing lights, or using my hands. It is not that communicative information is entirely independent of the material world. Communicative information is, rather, what we might call *medium indifferent*. What matters for communicative information is that various parties (e.g., speaker and audience; author and reader) have a practical grasp of specific conventions or rules that apply to any of a range of systematic modifications of the material environment.

There is a second, distinctive, feature of communicative information. Although it is commonplace to use spatial and material metaphors to talk about information – as something that can be acquired, stored, transmitted, passed on, conveyed and so on – these metaphors fail to register a key difference between material objects and information. If I give you the contents of my pockets, my pockets will be empty. In contrast, I can share the contents of my thoughts, or my books, with countless others without any reduction in the material objects that I possess. This feature of communicative information is unsurprising. When I communicate my knowledge to you I do not thereby lose it.[26] Communicative information is *non-destructively replicable*.

These features of communicative information underpin the demand for, and need for, certain kinds of regulation. There are many important practical and social concerns which require communication and 'storage'

---

[26] Now this creates vast problems for the protection of 'intellectual property' but that is not our concern here.

of knowledge. Banking depends upon reliable record keeping of deposits, transfers, interest and so on. The treatment of patients is made more effective if clinicians have a record of a person's medical history. Schools, employers and the state all have a legitimate need to use personal information of various kinds. But other parties have an interest – perhaps illegitimate – in such information: thieves, fraudsters, blackmailers and other tormentors. When records were kept on paper, information security was a matter of simple, and obvious, measures: social and professional measures like ensuring the honesty of financial and medical staff; and practical measures such as keeping records in locked cabinets in secure buildings.

But modern information and communication technologies allow personal information to be communicated and distributed across vast distances, and to vast numbers of people, in different countries (with different legal systems, forms of government, and different attitudes to information security) – all in a fraction of a second, and without anyone having to leave their desk! Because communicative information is medium indifferent and replicable it can be *very hard to keep track of*. Data protection legislation came into being by way of trying to secure legitimate and permissible communication of personal information whilst discouraging – and sanctioning and punishing – improper communication.

These distinctive features of communicative information underpin the way that the data subject's rights are framed. Copies of information are readily obtainable – albeit at some cost – without destroying one's own record or data. So, we might conclude that DPA98 is simply not meant to apply to anything other than communicative information (where access, duplication and rectification are all coherent demands).

Images, x-rays and data protection

But there is a problem with this line of response, For DPA98 applies to artefacts other than purely communicative entities like texts, records, databases. It also applies to *images* – including photographs and x-rays (and, we might add, photographs of tissue samples!). In what sense does a photograph contain information, or data, about a data subject? Photographs contain information about what they are photographs of because they allow us reliably to form beliefs about objects perceived in this way. Just as books and texts act as a kind of 'frozen' and displaced communication (allowing communication with audiences at other times, and distant places), images can act as a kind of 'frozen' perception, allowing others, at other times and places, to 'see' something that it is not physically present to them. But photographs and x-rays differ from communication via speech or writing. The arrangement of the pigment, or pixels, or chemicals, on a photograph, image or slide, does not come to be in place solely as a way of communicating someone's knowledge. Rather, pigments, pixels and so on, *correlate* with certain properties of material objects (just which properties they are will depend upon the apparatus used to take, record, store, edit and display the image in question). Photographs and images might be better construed as *evidence* for the properties or situations that they are informative about. But this aligns them with tissue blocks and slides which are created as an epistemic resource for other parties, at a later date. Rather than being a 'representation' of the perceptible surface of a material object, the tissue sample simply *is* a material object. But both can act as evidence for making reliable inferences about personal traits.

What about the problems with *access* rights and *rectification* rights? Would it not also be that similar problems arise in the case of images? Not necessarily, because photographs, x-rays and other images share some of the features of communicative informational entities (such as texts or records). Images can be digitised, stored, duplicated and copied without destroying the original (or, in the case of digital imaging, without any 'original' being created at all). Images – like texts – are a readily replicable form of epistemic artefact. One can pass on a 'copy' or duplicate of an image. So, it is possible to give subjects access to a copy of the information without destroying the original, and without 'disproportionate effort'.[27]

What would the analogous act be for tissue samples and objective genetic information? One could, in principle, give a sample of the genetic material (a sample of the sample, as it were). Depending on how we read the subject's access right, this might be viewed as giving the data subject *uninterpreted* genetic information (after all, there is no obligation specified in DPA98 to provide data subjects with expert interpretation of stored information!). Or, perhaps the data subject could be given a sample of 'relevant' genetic material amplified by polymerase chain reaction (though at disproportionate cost!). Images that are stored in an archive or record may be uninterpreted, or it may be unclear exactly what can be inferred from them (as with the tissue samples, what inferences one can

[27] 'The individual is also entitled to have communicated to him in an intelligible form, all the information which forms any such personal data. This information must be supplied in permanent form by way of a copy.' Legal Guidance to DPA98, section 4.1.

make depends upon what else one knows). So, images and tissue samples do seem to be akin, at least in some respects, with regard to the subject's access rights.

What about the right of rectification and the duty to keep accurate records? Earlier, the accuracy of a textual record was contrasted with tissue samples. It seemed that neither the samples themselves, nor the objective genetic information within them, could be accurate (or inaccurate) in any sense relevant to DPA98. But, if we compare *images* and tissue samples, it seems that notions of accuracy and inaccuracy may be applicable in a certain way. An image may be inaccurate if it was, say, taken with faulty equipment or processed incorrectly (e.g., an x-ray may show a shadow that is the result of a processing error, not evidence of a tumour). But the same point might be made for tissue samples: samples may be misprocessed, or acquired in ways which are misleading such that an informed party examining the sample would be likely to draw false conclusions (not through any defect in their own knowledge or reasoning, but because of defects in the provenance or storage of the sample). So, there is a sense in which particular samples might be misleading, but this is not because they contain *false objective genetic information* (as if there were such a thing), it is because their causal history has rendered the sample misleading. If the right of rectification could be interpreted as a right to have misleading data removed, rather than that of having inaccurate data corrected, then this would seem to apply to tissue samples too: i.e., the error would be rectified by getting rid of the faulty sample, not by correcting it.

Let us take stock: data protection primarily applies to linguistic *communication* (including various deferred forms of communication in archives, records and so on). The communication that is relevant here is *epistemic* communication: it involves the conveyance of knowledge (or information). Images and x-rays are not linguistic communicative artefacts in the way that, say, textual records are, but they can and do play an important epistemic role. So, data protection legislation pertains more broadly to include artefacts which play certain kinds of epistemic roles. Some artefacts (like images) are stored and archived because they provide evidence about the traits or properties of an identifiable individual. Tissue samples – if non-anonymised – can and do play a similar kind of role. But, unlike images, they are not so readily communicable or replicable (though an image can be taken of, say, a relevant part of a tissue slide). They are not artefacts which are produced as a representation of how things are (and thus can be more or less accurate) in the way that

THE MEDIUM AND THE MESSAGE

texts are (though they can be misleading). But what is clear is that it is not the *objective genetic information* in samples that makes human tissue samples akin to standard records. It is not the fact that human tissue contains objective genetic information that makes them similar to images: it is the fact that both images and tissue samples are – at least in part – artefacts which are produced and stored for epistemic purposes (to provide evidence, to be consulted, to be the basis for inferences).

Privacy, information and consent-centred regulation

We are now in a position to return to the questions raised at the outset of this chapter. What is genetic information and why is it of ethical, legal and regulatory significance? Here our clarification is of assistance. *Objective* genetic information is not directly of ethical significance any more than, say, tree rings and the tides are. This kind of information is radically impersonal, in that it is information that is not possessed by, understood by, or directly used by, agents. The genetic information that *is* of relevance is *knowledge* that is acquired, communicated and used by human agents. The conduit and container metaphors underpin a blurring between different senses of 'information'. Because human agents can acquire genetic information via various epistemic interventions on biological material, it may seem that one and the same 'stuff' – genetic information – is 'out there' in the world and then gets to be 'in' our minds or in our communicative activity. But 'information' really means very different things when we talk of genetic information contained *within* biological material in contrast to the genetic information that people possess and communicate.

To highlight this contrast, I will briefly expand upon one of the purposes of data protection regulation. It was noted earlier that one reason for regulating the acquisition, storage and use of personal information was that developments in information and communication technology render information less secure, and harder to keep track of. Whilst this is true, it does not exhaust the rationale for introducing data protection legislation. Viewed more broadly, data protection regulation is typically viewed as being an instrument for the protection of certain kinds of *privacy* rights.[28]

Now consider an example. Suppose a person 'passes on' a late onset, high-penetrance, single-gene dominant Mendelian disorder to their

---

[28] For a fuller discussion of this see Neil C. Manson and Onora O'Neill, *Rethinking Informed Consent in Bioethics* (Cambridge University Press, 2007), chapter 5.

child. Their child's tissue contains genetic information that could be
construed as information about, not just the late onset trait of the child,
but also about the parent's traits. But it would be absurd to claim that the
tissue, or the cells, or the child, in any way breach the parent's information privacy. The same point would apply, surely, in the case of a tissue
archive where tissue is being stored and used as part of a longitudinal
cancer study. The *archive* may contain personal genetic information
about late onset traits *but no person* possesses this information, so no
breach of privacy can have taken place.

This kind of example, though fanciful, points towards a more fundamental problem with data protection legislation. Data protection legislation essentially involves the classification of information. For some types
of information – personal information – any kind of 'processing' is subject to regulatory constraint. But the notion of processing is defined very
broadly, and includes acquiring, organising, altering, retrieving, consulting or using, blocking (and even 'erasure or destruction') of the data.[29]

This is not just broad, but is, surely, very odd. The *purpose* of data
protection legislation is to protect people against a range of actions
which breach important rights, including privacy rights. But not all
actions involving personal information breach individual rights. For
example, suppose that legitimately acquired medical data are reused as
part of an epidemiological study. Here personal information is being
used for *impersonal* ends. The epidemiologist may have no interest at
all in individual subjects, or their traits: the concern is with statistical
features of populations. The same point applies, of course, to many
uses of human tissue. Although human tissue may *contain* personal
information – in one of the senses discussed earlier – it does not follow
that the possession or use of such samples thereby breaches informational privacy rights.

The discussion above allows us to offer an explanation of why DPA98 –
and other data protection legislation – is framed in this way. The conduit
and container metaphors make it seem entirely 'natural' to view information as a kind of 'contentful stuff'. With this in the background it is all too
easy to infer

(i) *Some* actions involving personal information about, say, an
individual's health, or financial status, breach important rights (e.g.,
intrusive ones).

---

[29] Legal Guidance to DPA98, section 2.3.

(ii) Such actions would be impossible, or harder, without personal information.

(iii) So *personal* information must be of special ethical significance.

(iv) So *all* systematic uses of personal information by institutions should be regulated and constrained in various ways.

Laid out in this way, of course, the line of argument is poor. But the conduit and container metaphors, arguably, help to render it plausible.

But there is another way in which the conduit and container metaphors shape the regulatory landscape. It was noted earlier that both HTA04 and DPA98 are *consent-centred* regulatory instruments. Individual consent is, in most cases, assumed to be necessary and, in even more cases, taken to be sufficient to permit the use of personal information.[30] Consent is a communicative act that plays a distinctive role in adjusting sets of rights and obligations.[31] Consent typically acts as a *waiver* and renders permissible actions that would otherwise breach certain rights. Consent involves two different kinds of rights. There are first-order rights (e.g., property rights; rights over one's body; privacy rights, and so on). Then there is a derivative 'liberty' right, whereby an individual can waive their first-order rights should they wish. But it is easy to blur different kinds of rights, and to get confused about the role and importance of consent.

Suppose a clinic possesses genetic information about an identifiable individual. Let us assume that it has acquired this information in a consensual way. In the current regulatory climate if the clinic wishes to reuse this information for, say, genetic epidemiology, consent will have to be sought for this new use (unless such uses were specified in the original process of securing consent). The epidemiological study is not intrusive, and does not concern the individual *as an individual*. So why should consent be required at all? Here we seem to have a second kind of inferential 'slippage'. Because consent is required for *some* uses of (or for the acquisition of) personal and genetic information, it then may seem that consent is required for *any* use. But if consent is a waiver of first-order rights this simply does not follow: consent should *only* be required if the further action were to breach certain first-order rights. Because consent involves a derivative liberty right, it is easy to slip into thinking that people have

---

[30] There are exceptions. Consent is not necessary where personal information is being used, for example, in pursuit of a criminal investigation.

[31] See Neil C. Manson, 'Consent and informed consent' in R. Ashcroft, A. Dawson, H. Draper and J. McMillan (eds.), *Principles of Health Care Ethics*, 2nd edn (London: John Wiley, 2007), 297–304.

some kind of special right *over* personal information *per se* rather than a
right to waive their first-order rights against certain kinds of actions that
involve personal information. In bioethics in particular, consent has been
construed in a particular way: consent is typically justified by appeals to
respect for individual autonomy and lurking in the background of any
discussion of informed consent is a concern with the limits of paternalism. Such lines of thought pick up on important aspects of consent, but
do risk downplaying the framework of first-order rights and obligations
against which communicative acts of consent play their procedural role of
adjusting (and tracking adjustments in) various rights and obligations.

A related distortion appears in claims about information privacy which
frame the putative privacy right as a right to *control* personal information.
Alan Westin, for example, defines the *right* of information privacy as 'the
claim of individuals, groups, or institutions to determine for themselves,
when, how, and to what extent information about them is communicated
to others'.[32] This makes it seem as if there is some kind of quasi-proprie-
tary right over personal information. Once again, the conduit and container metaphors may mislead us here. Information is not *really* a kind of
stuff that one can own. For example, if Tom views Sue regularly smoking
in a public place, he can infer that she is at increased risk of cancer. This
is personal, medical information. But Sue has no right to stop Tom from
viewing her in a public place, and no right to stop him from inferring
(and thus 'acquiring personal information'). Sue does have rights against
Tom finding out about her medical status in certain ways (e.g., by examining her when she sleeps; or by breaking into her house), but she does not
have a right over the information itself.

In DPA98 the conduit and container metaphors have an influence in a
number of ways. Information is classified into types, as if types of information were themselves significant. This downplays or ignores the fact
that personal information can be acquired, possessed or used in ways
which breach no fundamental rights. The centrality of consent in such
legislation, when conjoined with a classification of information into significant types, makes matters worse, with the result that many actions
that breach no rights (such as secondary *impersonal* uses of legitimately
acquired personal information) are identified as requiring individual
consent.

[32] A. Westin, *Privacy and Freedom* (New York: Atheneum, 1967), 7. For a critical discussion
of this conception of informational privacy see G. Laurie, *Genetic Privacy: A Challenge to
Medico-Legal Norms* (Cambridge University Press, 2002).

Conclusion

This chapter began with two questions: first, about whether DPA98 applies, and about whether it *ought* to apply, to the possession and use of human tissue in so far as it contains genetic information. Perhaps unsurprisingly – given the many senses of information, the different roles played by data protection legislation, and the different kinds of artefact that fall under it – there is no simple answer here. Part of the underlying problem is that data protection legislation is concerned with knowledge – or information – in the context of human communication and record keeping. The primary purpose of such regulatory instruments is to constrain and direct communication. But there are artefacts *other* than linguistic communicative ones that can be viewed as containing information. At this point the conduit and container metaphors serve to blur various distinctions amongst different senses of information. Images and x-rays are not linguistic artefacts but they do play an important epistemic role, and they share some of the distinctive features of linguistic communicative artefacts – they are medium indifferent and non-destructively replicable.

Human tissue samples are artefacts that can be viewed as containing information in a variety of ways, but they are not linguistic communicative artefacts, they are not medium indifferent or non-destructively replicable, and as such they do differ considerably from the paradigm artefacts which DPA98 applies to. Objective genetic information might be viewed as non-destructively replicable, but objective genetic information is not information that human beings possess. When agents acquire genetic information – including personal information – from DNA, then DPA98 pertains to their communication in the standard way. Objective genetic information is too divorced from human agency, knowledge and communication to make DPA98 applicable, especially in so far as the obligations correlative to the various data subject's rights cannot readily or feasibly be met.

Given that tissue samples are artefacts that play an epistemic role akin to x-rays and images, *should* their acquisition, storage and use be regulated *because* they too play this type of role? Here the discussion of the ways that the conduit and container metaphor shape the regulatory landscape come into play. Debates about information privacy are framed in terms of significant classes of information. Data protection regulation seeks to classify and to constrain a very wide class of actions that pertain to information of certain significant kinds. Ethically speaking, this way of thinking about information is unfortunate: at the very least it risks rendering illegal acts which breach no important first-order rights. Matters are made worse by the fact that data protection regulation is *consent-centred* and much thinking about consent is distorted – laying stress on a second-order liberty right, rather than other more fundamental first-order rights and obligations. Actions that breach no important first-order rights do not require consent, and a proper regulatory framework would, surely, be sensitive to this. Ideally, regulatory instruments would be sensitive to, and would pertain to, certain *uses* of tissue – e.g., uses that breach important first-order rights – and to the *mere* storage or use of tissue *because* it (supposedly) contains personal information.

But perhaps this is too abstract. Regulatory instruments must operate in the real world and cannot be sensitive to every nuanced distinction that philosophers may identify. Perhaps a bit of 'regulatory overkill' is necessary. That is, if we are to ensure that many wrongs are to be avoided we may have to risk sanctioning or penalising actions that could bene-fit many, which harm no one and that breach no important first-order rights – or, at the very least, we risk imposing undue burdens upon those who perform such actions. In other words, regulatory pragmatism might trump philosophical argument.

Even if this is right, there is no reason why we should refrain from trying to be as clear as possible about the ethics of communication and information, even if our findings are at odds with the current regula-tory framework. For, although regulatory instruments exhibit consider-able inertia (UK regulation is heavily constrained in a variety of ways by European Union law and regulation), they can be changed, amended, clarified and revised. Being clear about various distorting influences on the way that we think about communication, information and consent, may help contribute to a clearer and more robustly justified regulatory framework, albeit in the longer term. It is hoped that the discussion here might help to clarify these complex issues a little.

2

Me, myself, I – against narcissism in the governance of genetic information

SØREN HOLM

> In John Smith's family there is a history of sudden cardiac death and he has recently read in the newspapers that there is now a test for a genetic mutation that predisposes people to sudden cardiac death. After reading the newspaper article and 'Googling' the test on the internet, John decides that he would like to have the test and goes to his doctor. His doctor refers him to the genetic services and after appropriate counselling he has the test and is given the result with post-test counselling and information about what it means and what his options are. The result is also, like many other pieces of health information generated as part of medical practice, recorded in John's medical notes for future reference.

This brief story is prima facie completely unexceptional and similar genetic testing takes place many times every day in countries across the world. What is exceptional, however, is that there is still ethical discussion concerning whether John Smith should be allowed to control the use of the test result after it has been produced. In this chapter I want to consider two areas of ethical contention related to the control of the test result:

(i) Whether John Smith's family have a legitimate claim to control the use of the test result?

(ii) Whether the state or society[1] has a legitimate claim to the use of existing (i.e., already produced) genetic information in gene-epidemiological research or for other purposes?

These are not the only issues of control that arise in this situation. There are, for instance, important questions about the extent to which commercial actors should be allowed to control genetic information, but I have

---

[1] In the present chapter 'state' and 'society' are used interchangeably, because if we allocate control to society this will, in all modern societies, involve giving control to the executive branch of government, i.e., the state.

chosen to focus on questions where economic or intellectual property questions are not central. The two questions that are in focus are, as will become evident, complicated enough in themselves.

Two unhelpful approaches

There are many frames within which one can discuss the questions of control of genetic information. This chapter is purely philosophical and not legal or sociological, but even within moral philosophy there are many approaches to choose from. Before moving on to a discussion of the questions themselves I therefore want to dispose of two approaches that are sometimes used, but which are unhelpful in the current context.

The first unhelpful approach frames the questions as questions of ownership of genetic information. But if the individuals from whom the genetic information derives, or others, have legitimate claims to control genetic (and other) health information, such claims do not primarily emanate from the information being some kind of quasi-property. It would, for instance, be fairly absurd for John Smith to claim property rights in the memories of the genetic counsellor who counselled him and who still remembers his test result.[2] But absence of property rights does not preclude claims to control the information legitimately.[3] John Smith may, for instance, have a perfectly justifiable right to control who his genetic counsellor shares the knowledge with and the counsellor may have an obligation of confidentiality, whether or not she or her place of work technically owns the information or the hard disk on which it is stored. Such legitimate claims to control may be based on a wide range of considerations other than property and these will be discussed in more detail below.

The second unhelpful approach is to try to decide the issue of control based on whom the information in question is about. A genetic test result is clearly about the person who is tested, but it is also about his ancestors and descendants, about the human species and about any of the broader species classifications that have *Homo sapiens* as a member. This is the case whatever the test result is. A 'normal' test result and an 'abnormal' one are equally about a whole range of individuals and entities. Even

---

[2] And importantly it would be equally absurd for his family to claim such ownership.

[3] Since all property rights can be analysed into a bundle of rights (e.g., right to alienate, right to exclude, right to destroy etc.) it is possible to reconceptualise the discussion of control in this chapter to a discussion about elements relating to control in the property rights bundle, but I personally do not find this very helpful.

if a mutation detected is new, the test result is still about others as well because the remaining unmutated background is still informative about others. But this means that claims to control the information simply 'because it is about me' become vacuous.[4] The number of possible claimants becomes much too large for any definite claim to be made on the part of an individual or specifiable group.

Three idealised positions

Before moving on to the analysis, it may also be helpful briefly to state the possible positions that one might take concerning the control of genetic information. As will become apparent, I will argue that none of the main positions in the literature is sustainable, but it is nevertheless important to state them clearly. In the literature three main positions have been put forward with regard to who should control genetic information.[5] In ideal typical form they are:

(i) John Smith is the only person (or other type of agent) who has a legitimate claim to control the information.
(ii) John Smith's family (with him included) jointly have the primary legitimate claim to control the information.
(iii) Society has the primary legitimate claim to control the information.[6]

The first of these positions is what we could call the modern position with regard to all types of medical information. The information which is passed from patient to health care professional, or which is generated from investigations of the patient and his body, has to be held in confidence by the health care professional. The health care professional can

---

[4] It is important to distinguish this from a claim based on (genetic) privacy where the claim is that I want to control who knows, because that control is important to me.

[5] None of the positions should be read as absolute, i.e., as stating that the primary decision maker has an absolute and non-overridable right to control the information. All positions admit the possibility of overriding the decisions of the primary decision maker in some (rare) instances, as is discussed further in the remainder of this chapter. Arguing against an absolute, non-overridable allocation of control will in most instances be arguing against a straw man.

[6] In what follows the analysis of this option will be ethical and not legal and will thus not consider whether a state might legally claim 'eminent domain' over genetic or any other type of personal information. In modern societies it will almost always be the case that it is the state that issues regulations codifying who has rights to control genetic information and in this sense the state is 'the primary decision maker', but this still leaves open the question concerning what the regulations ought to say and who ought to be the actual decision maker.

only share this information with others if those others have a need to know because they are involved in the treatment of the patient. Further disclosure of the information requires the consent of the patient. The second position is the traditional position in many (perhaps most) countries where it was previously common to share information with the whole family, and sometimes to share more information with the family than with the patient.[7] It has recently been advocated specifically for genetic information. The third position is rarely advocated in the stark form presented here, but it underlies many discussions about the justification for using information in patient records for research and for allowing the research use of 'clinical waste', e.g., what remains of blood or tissue samples after diagnostic use or therapeutic excision.

In the justifications for each of the positions it is possible to discern a number of different arguments that may broadly be classified as:

(i)   Arguments based on the origin of the material being tested, the context of testing or the 'nature' of the result being generated. This is a fairly mixed bag that inter alia contains arguments based on control of the original biological sample, on whether testing is medical or non-medical, on whether the process has involved familial information etc.

(ii) Arguments based on general moral obligations (e.g., autonomy, privacy, non-maleficence, beneficence, general reciprocity).

(iii) Arguments based on more specific moral obligations (e.g., familial obligations, specific reciprocity).

(iv) Secondary arguments, e.g., counterarguments against the opposing position or arguments aimed at protecting one's own position against obvious objections.

The arguments for the patient/client as primary controller

Let us first briefly look at arguments for giving John Smith primary control over the test result. If we discount ownership, John Smith's claim to control can be based in well-rehearsed moral categories such as autonomy, privacy,[8] avoidance of harm, or any combination of these. These are

[7] O. O. Thomsen, H. R. Wulff, A. Martin, P. A. Singer, 'What do gastroenterologists in Europe tell cancer patients?', *Lancet*, 341, 8843 (1993), 473–6.
[8] For present purposes it does not matter whether privacy can be reduced to autonomy or not; for this discussion see J. Rachels, 'Why privacy is important', *Philosophy and Public Affairs*, 4, 4 (1975), 323–33; J. J. Thompson, 'The right to privacy', *Philosophy and*

all forward looking justifications, that is, they are based in features John Smith possesses now and that ought to govern our dealings with him and the information in the future. But there is also a possible backward looking justification, in the consideration that John Smith was the primary agent involved in the generation of the information. Unless he had taken the initiative to have the information generated and performed the necessary actions to make generation possible, the information would not exist.

It is important to note initially that nothing in this position, even in its strongest form, precludes us from pointing out to John Smith that there are situations where it is morally right proactively to inform family members of his test result, or let his test result be available to inform future genetic counselling of others. We may, to use Millian terms, remonstrate with, reason with, persuade or entreat him in order to get him to fulfil what we take to be his moral obligations.[9] Nothing commits us to being non-directive in our interaction with him.

What are the problems with the individual control position that make it unsustainable in its strong form, i.e., the form where the claim is that John Smith's control of the information should never be overridden? The first problem is a very general problem for any position claiming that some right or consideration is absolute and non-overridable. It is almost

---

Public Affairs, 4, 4 (1975), 295–314; J. H. Reiman, 'Privacy, intimacy, and personhood', *Philosophy and Public Affairs*, 6, 1 (1976), 26–44.

[9] Mill allows these interventions in a rarely quoted part of the *locus classicus* from 'On Liberty' explicating his famous so-called 'Harm principle' (my emphasis):

> 'The object of this Essay is to assert one very simple principle, as entitled to govern absolutely the dealings of society with the individual in the way of compulsion and control, whether the means used be physical force in the form of legal penalties, or the moral coercion of public opinion. That principle is that the sole end for which mankind are warranted, individually or collectively, in interfering with the liberty of action of any of their number, is self-protection. That the only purpose for which power can be rightfully exercised over any member of a civilized community, against his will, is to prevent harm to others. His own good, either physical or moral, is not a sufficient warrant. *He cannot rightfully be compelled to do or forbear because it will be better for him to do so, because it will make him happier, because, in the opinions of others, to do so would be wise, or even right. These are good reasons for remonstrating with him, or reasoning with him, or persuading him, or entreating him, but not for compelling him, or visiting him with any evil, in case he do otherwise.* To justify that, the conduct from which it is desired to deter him must be calculated to produce evil to some one else. The only part of the conduct of any one, for which he is amenable to society, is that which concerns others. In the part which merely concerns himself, his independence is, of right, absolute. Over himself, over his own body and mind, the individual is sovereign.'

J. S. Mill, *On Liberty*, E. Rapaport (ed.) (Indianapolis, IN: Hackett, 1978), 9.

always possible to find a real life example where upholding the absolute consideration will lead to strongly counterintuitive results, and for this (and other) reasons our regulations almost never include absolute rights, or if they do we usually officially or unofficially condone breaches of the supposedly absolute consideration.

The second and perhaps more interesting problem is that the moral categories that give John Smith the primary legitimacy to control the information do not map the complete moral terrain. Without adopting an impersonal view from nowhere, we can recognise that John Smith himself has moral obligations towards a range of other entities in the world; and furthermore that his own commitment to these obligations may in itself give specific others sufficient reason to override some of his decisions regarding genetic information. If John Smith has, for instance, strongly committed himself to his children and their welfare, there may be good reason to override a refusal to share genetic information with these children. But considerations of this kind are by their very nature localised and specific. They illustrate that there are situations where overriding the decisions of an individual decision maker is justified, even within that person's own justificatory scheme. But they do not tell us who should do this overriding in general, or whether we could formulate general rules for when, for instance, a genetic counsellor can legitimately usurp decision making from a person.

The arguments for the family

The arguments for giving the family primary control usually focus on the 'nature' of genetic information as familial, the role of family information in genetic practice and the specific obligations of family members toward each other. Parker and Lucassen, for instance, enumerate the arguments in favour of a 'joint account' model of genetic information in the following way[10] (with my footnotes added):

> Perhaps the strongest ethical principle in favour of the joint account model is that of justice, or perhaps reciprocity. Genetic information is, spontaneous mutations aside, essentially and unavoidably familial in nature. It is this feature of genetics that allows individuals to benefit from genetic testing and diagnosis. When a patient attends a genetic clinic, or discusses genetics with his or her general practitioner, a family history

[10] I have chosen this version of the argument for familial control because it is clearly expressed and more cogent than most.

will be constructed, drawing on familial information about diseases and illness supplied by the patient about other family members, often without their consent. In many cases an extensive family history is needed to assess the usefulness of genetic testing. Given this, there is no obvious reason why one family member should be able to benefit and yet, at the same time, be allowed to exclude others from access to such benefits.[11]

A further justification for the joint account model arises out of the benefits to be gained and harms to be avoided by routinely sharing genetic information. The current application of the personal account model, and of strict confidentiality, means that many potential benefits of genetic testing are untapped. Family members who might otherwise have benefited from testing, surveillance, or reassurance do not come forward because they are unaware of their family history. In addition, when relatives who were not informed about their risk develop symptoms or become aware of their family history, and that this was withheld from them, they may lose trust in their doctors. More generally, if it becomes widely known that information of this kind is being routinely withheld, at the request of affected family members,[12] it may lead to a more widespread crisis of trust in the clinical genetics service and possibly legal action.[13]

One additional advantage of the joint account model is that it is consistent with the nature of practice in clinical genetics. Geneticists work with families. This means that geneticists often come to know and to feel a sense of responsibility for several members of the same family. The joint account model takes seriously the familial nature of genetic information and clinical genetics and offers the possibility of broad access to the benefits of testing, where this does not cause serious harm to the index patient.[14]

How can we parse this extended argument? There is a reference to justice and/or reciprocity, a reference to genetic information being 'essentially and unavoidably familial in nature', a reference to the use of family histories, a reference to benefits that could be generated for family members, a reference to trust in the profession, a reference to the fact that

[11] It is unclear in what way someone who benefits from the information generated by the drawing and interpretation of a family history and does not allow that information to be used by others is actually excluding anyone, unless the person possesses knowledge about the family that other family members do not have. If this is not the case, any other family member could have precisely the same family history constructed and interpreted and nobody seems to be excluded from anything.
[12] It might of course also be withheld by non-affected family members.
[13] I submit that it seems equally plausible that widespread distrust and legal action could be generated if a policy of sharing of genetic information was instituted.
[14] M. Parker and A. Lucassen, 'Genetic information: a joint account?', *British Medical Journal*, 329 (2004), 166.

geneticists work with families and finally the caveat or rider 'where this does not cause serious harm to the index patient'.

Let us briefly look at the caveat first. At the same time as families are one of the primary environments in which we can experience love and affirmation, they are also one of the environments where we can be hurt and harmed most profoundly. It is in many cases rather unlikely that the genetic counsellor will be in a better position than the index patient to predict whether other family members will use any information they get to benefit or to hurt the index patient. To claim otherwise is bordering on counselling hubris. We are rightly sceptical of any therapeutic privilege to withhold information and should be equally sceptical of a therapeutic privilege to share it.

But let us return to the positive arguments presented by Parker and Lucassen. The claim that genetic information is 'essentially and unavoidably familial in nature' is only even approximately true if we are talking about families defined by genetics, and in that case it is no longer an interesting synthetic statement but purely analytic. But the family reported in the family tree is not exclusively the index patient's genetic family, it often includes many people who are simply married to or in relationship with people who are genetically related to the patient. And the hypothesised lack of trust that may occur also extends to the whole of the index patient's family (and possibly circle of friends) and not only or even primarily to his or her genetic relations. We can thus see that some of the arguments for family control rely on a genetic understanding of the family,[15] others on an anthropological or social understanding[16] and others again on an affiliative understanding.[17] But these different ways of understanding families do not match up with each other.[18] This is perhaps most obvious in terms of those adopted children who have no interest in their biological parents and identify completely with their adoptive family. Their genetic family is completely separated from their affiliative family and almost completely from their anthropological.[19] This is not the place to resolve whether adopted children have

---

[15] Roughly, those people to whom I am genetically related.

[16] Roughly, those people who would be recognised as my family members by other members of my society.

[17] Roughly, those people to whom I feel special obligations because they are 'my family'.

[18] There is a very large anthropological literature on kinship illustrating this in very fine detail. See, for instance, M. Strathern, *After Nature: English Kinship in the Late Twentieth Century* (Cambridge University Press, 1992).

[19] Other even more modern kinds of familial disjunction are created by assisted reproductive technologies which have created new and separate roles for genetics,

any obligations in justice or reciprocity towards their biological/genetic relatives, but it should be obvious that, if they have such obligations, they are in most cases much weaker than their obligations towards their adoptive family.

The same disjunction can be found to some extent in most families. The strength of the affiliative ties rarely matches the precise genetic or social degree of connection. Many people have stronger ties with some family members to whom they are not related 'by blood' than to some with whom they share some genes, and widely varying affiliative ties to family members within the same category of genetic relationship. In most exogamous societies people still feel a responsibility to some members of their family to whom they are only related 'in law'. Furthermore, our society is characterised by great fluidity in family configurations due to high rates of divorce or other types of partnership dissolution. This means that membership of a person's anthropological and affiliative family is also a fluid concept. The people who were drawn in John Smith's family history today may not all be considered members of his family in ten years' time.

It is worth noting that the proposition 'Geneticists work with families. This means that geneticists often come to know and to feel a sense of responsibility for several members of the same family' would still be factually true if we exchanged 'geneticist' with 'paediatrician', but the reference to 'family' would have changed its extension. 'Family' is not a rigid signifier, and the extension of 'my family' even less rigid! It is furthermore worth considering whether there could be any justification for a geneticist only feeling a sense of responsibility towards those who are members of the family, *as defined by genetics*. Clinical geneticists hopefully also feel a sense of responsibility towards the fathers of boys with X-linked disorders inherited from their mothers, or towards the partners of adults with Huntington's disease, whether the couple has children or not.

A separate problem with the familial control position is that if the justifications that are put forward are accepted, the scope of familial control must extend to a significantly wider range of health information than just genetic information. Knowledge about the social circumstances and non-genetic illnesses of other members of a patient's family often

gestational and social mothers and genetic and social fathers, as well as increased possibilities for two parent families with both parents of the same sex and gender. I will omit a discussion of the problems this raises for familial decision making.

plays a significant role in determining the diagnosis and prognosis of the patient, and this information is often gathered from the patient without consent or permission being sought from family members. If we accept the line of argument put forward for familial control of genetic information, we also have to accept that there will be many circumstances where information about a patient's non-genetic illness should be made available to the family. Justice and reciprocity require it as strongly as in the genetic case and the information is inherently familial, although not genetic.

And if we take the arguments for familial control really seriously – as we should since they are presumably put forward as serious and important arguments – we will see that their reach extends even beyond the family. The arguments for instance seem to imply that if a student who lives in digs with four other students, two of whom are smokers, goes to the GP with a respiratory complaint and gets a diagnosis of bronchitis and advice that the prognosis will be much better if he or she moves to a smoke-free environment, then that student's health information should enter the 'joint account' and be available to the other four who live in the house. The student has given the GP information about them, it is important to them to know the diagnosis and it may even form the basis for some anti-smoking intervention specifically targeting the two smokers, thereby leading to considerable harm reduction.

A final problem is that in reality we are not talking about familial control, but about individual control exercised by family members. Most families have no mechanism for reaching 'a family decision' or a fortiori for reaching such a decision in a way that takes account of the interests and views of all family members. In the small, nuclear family there may conceivably be a way to reach a common view, but in a larger extended family that will, in most circumstances, be impossible. Many adults do not see their uncles, aunts, cousins, nephews and nieces that frequently, not to mention the cousins twice removed who may still be viewed as part of the genetic family by a genetic counsellor, although they have receded beyond the fuzzy border of the anthropological and affiliative family long ago.

It might of course be suggested that in cases where family decision making is a fiction (i.e., in most if not all cases) it should be the geneticist who should decide. But in that case we are no longer talking about a joint account held by the family members and controlled by the family, but of a trust controlled by the geneticist as the self-appointed trustee or gatekeeper. We can note that nothing in this argument against family control of genetic information negates the idea that *specific members* of John Smith's family may have a legitimate moral claim against him in regard to the disclosure of his test result. But the justification for such a claim does not arise merely from the genetic family connection.

The argument for the state

What then about the state or society? Should society have the primary claim to control the use of genetic information? Given that we have seen above that both the individual and the familial claim to control are problematic in some situations, giving society primary control might seem to be the only remaining position that should then be adopted as a default. However, this would be to rely on a false trichotomy. We have no a priori reason to believe that any of these three options should be adopted in all cases and therefore the fact that an option is problematic in some cases does nothing to show that it may not be the best option in other cases. It only shows that it cannot be applied across the board. That it is a false trichotomy is further reinforced by the observation that there is no moral theory, except ethical egoism, which allocates absolute moral protection to the decisions of only one class of decision maker. Even the strictest form of libertarian theory does, for instance, admit that the decision of a person can be overridden if the action the person wants to perform is directly harmful to others and breaches their rights.

Can a general claim be made for societal control of genetic information? If such a claim can be made, it is difficult to see how it can be made in a way which includes genetic information but excludes other health information. Rightly or wrongly (wrongly in my view),[20] genetic information is seen as more sensitive than other health information, so a justification giving the state primary control over this information but not over less sensitive information will be difficult to construct. A consequence of the state having primary control would be that it should be entitled to preclude John Smith from having access to his own test result. It is difficult to see how a justification can be constructed for such a strong conception of state control. But is there a good argument for making the state (or its agents) the primary decision maker in relation to access by other people to John Smith's test result?

---

[20] See S. Holm, 'There is nothing special about genetic information', in A. K. Thompson and R. F. Chadwick (eds.), *Genetic Information – Acquisition, Access, and Control* (New York: Plenum Press, 1999), 97–103.

   Such an argument must proceed along broadly consequentialist lines, because it is highly implausible that society has any deontologically based right(s) to control genetic information about its members/citizens. Even if we bracket any rights-based claims that John Smith or his family have, the argument would have to show that great benefit can be produced, or great harm averted, if control is allocated to society. More than this, it would have to show that generalised state control of genetic information dominates alternative allocations of control in terms of the net benefit produced. This is a burden of proof that society is unlikely ever to be able to lift. Our current allocation of decision making control does not create massive harms, so an argument for wholesale change would have to show that overall societal control could generate very substantial benefits. Under the current allocation of control, most people share important genetic information with their relatives in circumstances where such sharing is relevant because the information is important for their relatives, so although overriding the decisions of any recaltritrant persons may produce some benefit, it is unlikely to produce very large benefits.

   Let us instead look at more circumscribed reallocations of decision making authority from the person and his family to society or the state. Where is the case for societal control of person identifiable genetic information strongest?[21] There are several discrete areas where a strong claim for society can be made: some of these areas are simple extensions of other supposedly legitimate state usage of health information, some are more specifically genetic (this is probably only an indicative and not an exhaustive list):[22]

- When the information indicates that the index person has a condition that is likely to put others at risk (e.g., in relation to driving or operating machinery).
- When the information is important in relation to the detection, investigation or prosecution of (significant) crimes.[23]

---

[21] As in the other sections of this chapter, the focus here is on person identifiable, non-anonymised genetic information. The ethical issues raised by the use of information that is not and cannot be linked to any specific person are beyond the scope of the discussion (but see papers in J. H. Solbakk, S. Holm and B. Hofmann (eds.), *The Ethics of Research Biobanking* (Springer, 2009, forthcoming)).

[22] In the present context I am not going to argue independently for each of these but just take it as read that strong arguments for state control have been provided in the articles and reports that are referenced.

[23] Nuffield Council on Bioethics, *The Forensic Use of Bioinformation: Ethical Issues* (London: Nuffield Council on Bioethics, 2007).

- When the state can use the information to generate important (scientific) knowledge that cannot be generated if control of the information is left dispersed to individuals or families.

One important feature of this list is that all the areas where a strong societal claim can be made are related to a specific purpose, something of significant moral importance that can only be done if control of the information is given to the state. But this specificity limits what the state can legitimately do with the information it controls. It only has justification for pursuing the specific goals and not for using the information for other purposes. General disclosure of the results clearly falls outside of these purposes and this generates an obligation of confidentiality on those agents of the state that have access to the information.

Deciding whether research is sufficiently important to generate a legitimate state claim is not simple. It is not enough that the research question is valid and the research likely to give an answer to the research question. It must also be shown that the research question is worth answering and that it cannot be answered unless the state allocates decision making power over the information to itself. Both the value of the research and whether it can be done in other ways involve complex value judgements. How these should be made is beyond the scope of this chapter, but it is evident that they have to be made by someone who does not have a stake in the outcome of the decision.

Conclusion

In this chapter I have argued for the following fairly moderate conclusions:

(i) That it does in general make sense to allocate primary decision making power over the use of genetic (and other health) information to the person who has the test that generates the information.

(ii) That the idea that we should instead give families control over such information is incoherent because the argument justifying the position elides different notions of 'family' and is so fraught with practical difficulty that it could not be implemented.

(iii) That society does have a legitimate claim to control genetic (and other health) information but that this claim is circumscribed to areas where something of significant moral importance can only be done effectively if society assumes the decision making power.

(iv) That despite individuals being the primary decision makers, there are circumstances where it is perfectly legitimate to override their decisions to avoid significant harm to other persons, but that genetic counsellors have no special prerogative to decide when that is the case.

Why are these conclusions important? Because they show that any fetish-istic focus on only one person or one group of people as the legitimate deci-sion maker in relation to genetic information is unjustified and misguided. There is sometimes in bioethics a tendency to reduce complex questions to simple questions in order to produce simple and exception-less answers. This is in general a tendency that should be resisted. Many ethical ques-tions are truly complex and their answers really context dependent and these characteristics should not be analysed away. In regard to control of genetic information there are many circumstances where we need to analyse the specific situation where the question about control arises and where we need to recognise that any 'rules' about allocation of control we apply are only rules of thumb that will give us a starting point for further deliberation, not a final answer.

Acknowledgements

I gratefully acknowledge the support of the ESRC Centre for economic and social aspects of genomics (Cesagen) and the patience and construct-ive comments of the Editors.

3

Decisions, consent and expectations of the individual

CAROLINE MULLEN

Recognising the potential contribution of genetic research in treating illness, improving health and saving lives, arbiters of ethical standards such as UNESCO have supported the collection of donated tissue samples and related genetic information for use in medical research. This support is tightly bound with the condition that human tissue samples and associated genetic information should be used only with the informed consent of the persons from whom they came.[1] Its role in research which might improve health and lives means that donation can be considered commendable or generous, especially in circumstances where the donors can expect no direct or immediate personal benefit from their participation in research (as is the case for donations made to biobanks).[2] However, with few exceptions,[3] these ethical standards are silent on questions of whether people have any moral duty to participate in research or whether there are moral considerations that people can be expected to consider in deciding whether to participate in research. Consequently, beyond possible commendation for those who decide to

---

[1] United Nations Educational, Scientific and Cultural Organisation (UNESCO), *International declaration on human genetic data* (2003). This position also appears in statements and opinions from bodies such as the Nuffield Council on Bioethics; see *Human tissue: legal and ethical issues. Response from the Nuffield Council on Bioethics to the Human Tissue Bill* (London: Nuffield Council on Bioethics, 2004). www.nuffieldbioethics.org and UK Biobank Ethics and Governance Council; see *UK Biobank Ethics and Governance Framework* Version 3.0 (October 2007), www.ukbiobank.ac.uk.

[2] See F. Dekkers, G. Laurie and C. Kent Shalev, *Genetic Databases. Assessing the Benefits and the Impact on Human and Patient Rights* (European Partnership on Patients' Rights and Citizens' Empowerment, A Network of the World Health Organisation Regional Office for Europe, 2003), 7.

[3] See J. Harris, 'Scientific research is a moral duty', *Journal of Medical Ethics*, 31 (2005), 247. Harris suggests that an exception which appears to imply a moral duty to facilitate research is the Human Genome Organisation's Ethics Committee, *Statement on Human Genomic Databases* (2002) www.hugo-international.org/Statement_on_Human_Genomic_Databases.htm.

51

undertake a generous act of donation, the ethical standards do not imply that there is room for any further moral judgement of people's decisions.[4] The situation is different in wider ethical debate where the case has been made for moral assessment of people's decisions about allowing tissue samples and related information to be used in research. Knoppers and Chadwick point to trends of understanding donation for research in the contexts of reciprocity, mutuality, solidarity, citizenry or universality,[5] and Harris has made the case for an obligation to participate in medical research.[6] In different ways, these arguments maintain that we can have moral expectations of people who are deciding whether to participate in research, even where they cannot expect direct benefit from their donation.

This chapter takes up the question of whether there are moral considerations that individuals should be expected to take account of in deciding whether to donate tissue samples and related genetic information. If we find that there are such considerations, then it might be defensible to make moral judgements about individuals' decisions which go beyond praise for what are held to be generous actions above the call of duty. This would have implications for our understanding of the way in which consent should be sought from potential donors. To claim that we can make moral judgements on people's decisions is not necessarily to suggest that the requirement of gaining consent should be removed, or even that it should be limited, since there may still be strong reasons to maintain that ultimately the individual should decide whether to take part in research. However, such a claim would imply that it is acceptable for people to be asked for consent in a context that includes certain moral expectations and pressures.

The first part of this chapter examines arguments which might support claims that the question of donation should be at the discretion of the donor, who should be free to give or withhold their consent in a context in which they are not subject to moral expectations. These arguments are then assessed through an account which draws on Harris's claim that people can have an obligation to participate in medical research, so long

---

[4] Points made by Harris, 'Scientific research', 242; and B. M. Knoppers, 'Of genomics and public health: Building public "goods"?', *Canadian Medical Association Journal* 173, 10 (8 Nov 2005), 1185.
[5] B. M. Knoppers and R. Chadwick, 'Human genetic research: emerging trends in ethics', *Nature Reviews Genetics* 6 (2005), 75–9.
[6] Harris, 'Scientific research', 242–8.

as that research meets certain conditions.[7] As a result of this assessment it is suggested that there is the possibility of an obligation. However, it is also argued that in order to understand whether, or in what conditions, this obligation would apply, we will need to think about what concern we should show for the interests of others, and how we should compare our interests with those of others. These questions are tackled in the second part of the chapter which develops an account of the way in which we should treat each other. On the basis of this account it is argued that there is only a clear obligation to donate tissue samples and genetic information in specific and rather ideal conditions. Where these conditions are not met, the question of whether a person should participate in genetic research turns on moral assessments of the circumstances of the donor and the relative value of that research. The question is not just one of assessing potential harms associated with the research and judging whether the research offers the possibility of beneficial results. Instead it involves the question of whether the specific research is part of an overall approach to medical research and provision of healthcare which meets standards of fairness reflecting the moral value of every person's life. It also involves questions of any burdens which the potential donor faces in participation, and of any other contributions which they are making for the benefit of others. There may be good reasons to participate in the research, but the circumstances for a particular donor may mean that the obligation is removed. In other circumstances this moral assessment could lead to the conclusion that not only is there no obligation to participate in the research, but further that it would be wrong to do so. In other words, the possibility of an obligation to allow our tissue samples and genetic information to be used in research exists within the context of a wider responsibility to think about the concern that we should show for other people, and to consider how we can act to bring this about. The final part of this chapter suggests that the responsibility of assessing the value of research is something that should normally be left to democratically accountable institutions capable of influencing and shaping research priorities, rather than falling to the individuals who are asked for donations. Nevertheless, individuals retain a responsibility to check the decisions of such institutions. If there are strong reasons to hold that institutions are not working as they should, then individuals have a responsibility to challenge the decisions of institutions, and one way in which individuals might do this

---

[7] *Ibid.*

is to use their genetic information as a resource which has power to press for change.

Justifying absence of expectation

There are numerous arguments which can be used to justify the claim that genetic information should be used for medical research only with the informed consent of the person from whom it came. At least some of these arguments might lead to the further claim that the donor should be free from moral expectations in making their decision. One approach would be to begin with moral arguments which include the idea that it is primarily the individual who should make decisions where their own interests stand to be affected. This approach has the promise of clearly supplying a reason to require consent from participants, since people's interests can be affected in several ways if they decide to allow their tissue samples and genetic information to be used for research. This type of argument could also be relevant in deciding whether it is acceptable to impose moral expectations on people to participate in research, if it can be shown that expecting a person to take part would indefensibly interfere with their entitlement to control their own interests. A second approach is to look at the need to avoid coercion and deception of potential donors when seeking consent.[8] Again, these are considerations which might lead to a requirement for informed donor consent in a context without moral expectation. The following section examines these two approaches to arriving at the requirement that a person's tissue sample and genetic information should be used only with their consent, and seeks to clarify whether they also require that consent is given in a context without expectation. The section begins by outlining how a donor's interests can be affected by giving tissue samples and genetic information for use in research. It then considers arguments which maintain that it is primarily for the individual to make decisions where their interests are affected, before moving on to consider requirements necessary for avoiding coercion and deception.

Donor interests

To some extent, a person's interests will be affected by the time and effort taken in actually participating in research. More significantly, there are

---

[8] Considerations raised by O. O'Neill, 'Some limits of informed consent', *Journal of Medical Ethics* 29 (2003), 4–7.

substantial senses in which a person's interests can be affected if their genetic information is used in medical research. For instance, UNESCO notes that genetic information 'can be predictive of genetic predispositions concerning individuals' and that such predictions can be relevant not only to the individual but also to their biological relations and even to wider society.[9] Assessment of how people's interests will be affected by the predictive nature of genetic information is complicated by the fact that this genetic information 'may contain information the significance of which is not necessarily known at the time of the collection of the biological samples'.[10] The sense and extent to which the predictive feature of genetic information might affect the interests of the individual donor is not necessarily straightforward: it can depend on factors such as whether the donor is informed of any predispositions identified at the time of donation, and whether the information is anonymised, or irreversibly anonymised after donation. As Harris and Keywood note, a person's interests can be affected simply by the prospect of knowing about genetic predispositions (or rather evidence of predispositions) since such information can impact on a person's outlook.[11] Nevertheless it may be that any harmful effects can be minimised if the person concerned can choose whether they are informed of any predisposition, or can choose the circumstances in which they would be informed.[12]

Beyond this, the Advisory Committee on World Health[13] points to risks that genetic information could be used by insurers or employers in discriminatory practices, and to further possibilities that it could be of use to the police. It is possible that donating genetic information for research could lead directly to discrimination if that genetic information is not irreversibly anonymised, and if adequate protection is not in place.[14] Donation might also contribute indirectly to genetic discrimination if used for research that in turn facilitated the development of genetic tests used by employers or insurers. As with the revelation of genetic predispositions, the prospect that donation might contribute to discrimination

---

[9] UNESCO, *Genetic data*, Article 4.   [10] *Ibid.*

[11] J. Harris and K. Keywood, 'Ignorance, information and autonomy', *Theoretical Medicine*, 22 (2001), 415–36.

[12] This also raises the question of whether genetic relatives should be informed of any predispositions revealed by the donation.

[13] WHO Advisory Committee on World Health, *Genomics and World Health* (World Health Organisation, 2002), 157–60.

[14] For discussion of issues associated with anonymisation of genetic information in research, see Parliamentary Office of Science and Technology, 'The UK Biobank', *Postnote 2* (2002), 3; www.parliament.uk/documents/upload/POSTpn235.pdf.

raises complex issues. Assuming that genetic discrimination is recognised to be morally unacceptable, it may be hoped that there will be sufficient measures implemented to prevent its use. Moreover it can be suggested that the risk from discrimination does not stem from donation of tissue, and associated genetic information, nor from the medical research for which it was donated. Rather the risk is a consequence of wider societal failure to protect against that genetic information later becoming used for discriminatory practices. However, if donated tissue were used in a way that later provided information for discriminatory practices, then those affected may not be convinced that their interests were unharmed by donation. UNESCO raises the further consideration that genetic information may have 'cultural significance for persons or groups'.[15] If people vest an account of identity in their genetic information, then they may judge that their sense of identity, and hence their interest, is affected by a decision to allow their genetic information to be used in research.

Against these concerns for the consequences of donation we should keep in mind that a donor might benefit as a result of medical knowledge or treatment resulting from research facilitated by their participation. However, there is no certainty of a direct link between contribution to a research project or study and receiving the medical benefits of that contribution. This is particularly the case where the invitation to participate in research involves donation of genetic information to a biobank (or database) which becomes a resource for further research studies, since '[t]he value of databases derives from the collective nature of their data. Often, the prospect of direct individual benefit is minimal.'[16]

Control of interests

With this outline of the possible impact of donation on a person's interests, let us consider whether we can get to the claim that donors should be free from moral expectations, from either of two distinct forms of argument involving the idea that it is primarily the individual who should make decisions affecting their own interests. First, there are forms of argument which give weight to each of two ideas about a person's interests. These arguments accept that the individual should have priority in making decisions which can affect their own interests, and in deciding what it means for their interests to be met. However, these arguments also

---

[15] UNESCO, *Genetic data*, Article 4.   [16] Dekkers et al., *Genetic Databases*, 7.

maintain that there is a moral requirement on all of us to show concern for other people and for their interests.[17] This idea that concern should be shown for other people's interests implies that there is some positive obligation on all of us (and so on society) to protect and secure the interests of one another. Protecting the interests of others can come at the cost of one's own interests, and so the obligation to show concern for others can mean that an individual has an obligation to give up some of their own interests for the sake of others.[18] Yet this obligation need not require an individual to give up all of their own interests.[19] Indeed it would not make sense for a person to give up all of their own interests: if a person should show concern for the interests of others, then surely they should also have concern for their own interests? To the extent that a person is entitled to look to their own interests, they are entitled to make their own decisions when these interests stand to be affected.[20] It is quite straightforward to see how, with this sort of argument, there could be the possibility of claiming both that potential donors of genetic information should give informed consent, and that they should not be subject to any expectations in making that decision. If the interests affected by donation were among those that the donor is entitled to control, then it would be plausible to argue that any expectations imposed would detract from their entitlement to exercise this control. If this were the case, then other people would have an obligation to show concern for the interests of the donor, and this would involve ensuring both that the donor's interests are not affected without their informed consent, and that their consent was not influenced by moral pressure.

As Harris has argued, the difficulty is that this form of argument commits us not only to having concern for the interests of potential donors, but also to having concern for the interests of potential beneficiaries of research (whether or not they have themselves contributed to the

[17] These two ideas would be held by some utilitarian or egalitarian arguments.
[18] Justification for this claim will be given in the next section of this chapter.
[19] There are questions about whether the obligation to show concern for the interests of others should apply to each individual action, or to actions over a lifetime or part of a lifetime. Shapshay and Pimple's discussion of the rule of beneficence raises this question, and we shall return to it later in this chapter. S. Shapshay and K. D. Pimple, 'Participation in biomedical research is an imperfect moral duty: a response to John Harris', *Journal of Medical Ethics*, 33 (2007), 414–17.
[20] Wilson discusses the notion of a '*sphere of decisional privacy*' which is the range of interests that the person would not be expected to give up and which they are entitled to control. J. Wilson, 'Is respect for autonomy defensible?', *Journal of Medical Ethics*, 33 (2007), 353.

research).[21] Since medical genetic research offers prospects of sustaining life and health, there is at least the chance that its potential beneficiaries have substantial interests in its conduct. If it can be shown that there are conditions in which the interests of potential beneficiaries should take priority, then there may be obligations on others, including potential donors, to contribute to protecting those interests even at a cost to themselves. In other words the interests that stand to be affected by donation may not be among those that the individual is entitled to control, given the substantial interests of others that could be affected by the results of research. In this case it may be defensible to impose expectations on potential donors. The question is, what concern should we show to one another and how should the interests of potential donors be compared with those of potential recipients of the benefits of research: is there something about those interests affected by donation which means that the interests should be protected even at the potential cost of benefits of research? This question will be discussed in the next part of this chapter, in which we will develop an account of how these differing interests can be compared. At present we can simply note that accepting the idea that we should have concern for the interests of others opens the possibility that we may have obligations to participate in research which would benefit others.

The second form of argument follows Nozick[22] in claiming that individuals have a right of self-ownership which involves the right to determine what happens to their person. On this argument there is no obligation to show concern for interests of others,[23] and moral responsibility is limited to ensuring that one does not violate the rights of others to determine what happens to their own person. Donating genetic information impacts on the person of the donor because it requires physical interaction with the person, and removal of physical material, and so full consent would be required from the donor in order to avoid a rights violation.[24] Moreover, because it is for the individual to decide what happens to their own person, and there is no obligation to act to protect the interests of others, this argument leaves no room for imposing any

[21] Harris, 'Scientific research', 243–4.
[22] R. Nozick, *Anarchy, State and Utopia* (Oxford: Blackwell, 1974).
[23] Nozick, *Anarchy, State and Utopia*, 30–4 argues that an obligation to show concern for others would amount to violation of an individual's right to determine what becomes of him or herself.
[24] It could also be maintained that the genetic information itself is part of the person it came from and that therefore the person is entitled to decide what becomes of it. However, for present purposes we do not need to consider this point as the physical aspect of donation is sufficient to give the potential donor control.

expectation on potential donors (although a decision to participate in research might be applauded as an act above duty). Obligations to participate in research might exist if people have voluntarily entered into contracts involving participation; however, on this argument, a person could not justly be criticised if they decide not to enter into a contract. The argument that will be developed in this chapter does not directly challenge the position of a right of self-ownership and its consequent denial of an obligation to participate in research. However, this chapter does present and defend an account which is incompatible with the right of self-ownership and therefore to the extent that the chapter is successful in making its case, it will count against the claims that follow from that right of self-ownership.

Protection from bad practice

There is a second type of argument which might lead to defence of a requirement for consent to be given in a context without moral expectation. This type of argument does not rely (at least directly) on claims about an individual's entitlement to control their interests. O'Neill has argued that '[t]he ethical importance of informed consent in and beyond medical practice is, I think, more elementary. It provides reasonable assurance that a patient (research subject, tissue donor) has not been deceived or coerced.'[25] As O'Neill goes on to note, it is plausible to maintain that deception or coercion of donors are wrongs which should be protected against. O'Neill further argues that to achieve these goals, consent must involve the donor having an adequate understanding of what the donation involves, although it can be counterproductive to interpret this as a requirement to provide donors with very specific and detailed information.

The suggestion that people could be expected to participate in research provides no apparent reason to deceive potential participants (or anyone else) about what is involved in that research. Moreover, any obligation to participate in research would seem dubious if it were not coupled with a requirement that the participants are not deceived, since deception would, at minimum, create conditions in which it might be feared that participants would be exploited, and would possibly increase the risk of exploitation actually occurring. However, the aim of avoiding coercion does appear to create tension for the permissibility of imposing moral expectations on potential donors. Of course, there is clear tension between

---

[25] O'Neill, 'Informed consent', 5.

avoiding coercion and any claim that an obligation to participate in research could be enforceable in some way.[26] Even without enforcement, the idea of seeking consent in a context where there is moral expectation is open to the claim that it puts a pressure on donors which amounts to a form of coercion. It is reasonable to suppose that a person making decisions on donation in the context of wider social expectation will be influenced (and perhaps feel pressure) from those expectations. However the question is exactly whether we should have these expectations – with their impact on the decision making of individuals – and so we cannot reject them in advance on the grounds that they have moral force. If these expectations are acceptable, then the sense in which they impose pressure on individuals would not amount to unacceptable coercion. It can be added that if there is a case for allowing these expectations, it clearly does not follow that there is a case for indefensible expectations or judgements about people's decisions (that is, expecting too much of people), and if the expectations were indefensible, then it might be claimed that they had the effect of unacceptable coercion. If people are to be subject to moral expectations, then those expectations need to be based on defensible criteria. However, seeking consent in a context where people face defensible expectations need not be at odds with aims of preventing either deception or coercion.

Individual responsibilities and important people

The previous section of this chapter has suggested that we might be able to provide a moral basis for maintaining that people should not face moral expectations in making decisions about donating tissue samples and genetic information for use in research. The justification would be that although each person has some obligation to show concern for the interests of others, this obligation is limited, and where it does not apply then the person is entitled to protect and control their own interests. If the interests affected by donation are among those that the individual is entitled to control, then they should not face moral expectations over decisions on participation. However, as was also suggested, the question of whether this view can be sustained, or whether it is justified to have moral expectations of people who are deciding whether to donate, depends on what concern we should show for one another, and what priority should

---

[26] Harris, 'Scientific research', discusses the possibility of an enforceable obligation to participate in research.

be given to differing interests. The following section begins to address this question by seeking a basis for the argument that we should have concern for one another, and using this basis to provide a means of comparing differing interests. This argument is used to suggest that there can be a general obligation to support genetic research. However, the discussion shows that when this argument is applied in a way that takes account of the circumstances of different people, and the different distributions of risks and benefits associated with research, the obligation to support research becomes less obvious, although we may still have expectations of potential donors.

Significant interest in life

One way of constructing the argument that we should show concern for one another's interests is to base it on recognition of the moral significance of people's consciousness and capacity to care about their own lives.[27] In other words, we can appeal to the recognition that people matter because they are aware of, and can care about, what happens in their life – people matter because things can matter to them. If each of us matters, then we have a reason to show concern for each other. Recognition of this moral significance of people leads to the further claim that each person matters equally, since possession of consciousness and the capacity to care about life is all or nothing: it is not something that is possessed to a greater or lesser extent. Further, if we accept that each person matters, then it is at least plausible to maintain that the interests of each person can also matter (although this is not to suggest that we should attach moral significance to all the interests that a person could have).[28]

As long as we accept that there are any interests that should be given significance on the basis that people matter, then it will be difficult to maintain that improved health or delayed death should not be among them, since both act as a basic condition allowing people to achieve other goals that they may have.[29] So we have reasons to act to protect the lives and

[27] The capacity to care about one's life would arguably involve self-consciousness.
[28] This account of the moral significance of the person is a summary of an argument presented in C. Mullen, 'Sustaining life, enabling activity and inflicting death: What risk and physical harm caused by transport is morally defensible?', unpublished PhD thesis, University of Manchester (2004), chs. 2 and 4.
[29] A similar point is made by J. Harris, 'The rationing debate: maximising the health of the whole community. The case against: what the principal objective of the NHS should really be', *British Medical Journal*, 314 (1997), 669–72.

health of one another. But, even if we assume that genetic research is likely to achieve the aim of sustaining life and health, does this provide a sufficient reason to convince us of the potential for an obligation to participate in genetic research? The justification for maintaining that we should have concern for the interests of one another also – of course – implies that we should have concern for the interests that can be affected by donation. As we have discussed in the previous section, the interests that can be affected by donation are not trivial. Donating tissue samples which yield genetic information may lead to a revelation of information about a person's genetic predispositions, and contains the risk of contributing to certain forms of discrimination. Genetic information may also have a cultural significance, meaning that its use in research impacts on people's sense of identity. These possible impacts on donors may be difficult to assess; however, it is plausible to maintain that there is the prospect of donors' interests being significantly harmed or limited by donation. This prospect may persist even against attempts to minimise harm.[30]

If we are to claim that each person and their interests matter equally, then we need to compare the possible harms caused by donation with the potential benefits of research. For research which has the possibility of maintaining or securing basic health, the comparison is between the possibility of donors' interests being damaged or limited, and potential research beneficiaries failing to secure their health and thus maintain minimal conditions in which to realise their interests. In this circumstance we may accept that we have an obligation to conduct the research despite its potential costs. An exception to this might be cases where donation contributes to genetic discrimination relating to health insurance. In countries where private health insurance is a substantial means of providing health care, then such discrimination could have the effect of denying the means of securing basic health.[31] We may also note that where the potential research benefits do not include aims of securing basic health, then the comparison is liable to change.

Individual responsibility

While this general argument may convince people that there can be a general obligation to support genetic research (assuming it does have the

[30] For instance, by asking donors whether they wish to be informed of any information about genetic predispositions.
[31] This is a concern raised by WHO Advisory Committee on World Health, *Genomics and World Health*, 158.

prospect of helping to improve basic health), individuals might question whether it compels them in particular, rather than other people (or society) in general, to bring this research about. Harris offers two approaches to answering individuals who question the possibility that there is a specific obligation on them to contribute to medical research. First he draws on the broad acceptance of the 'obligation not to harm others'.[32] As he maintains, we accept that we have a responsibility to avoid causing harm to others even when this creates some burden to ourselves (and limits the scope of our freedom to control our own interests). If we accept the view that people matter (that they have moral significance), then we can make the further claim that the reason for the obligation not to harm others is based on the understanding that those others matter. However, if it is plausible to maintain that we should accept some burden in order not to cause harm to people in virtue of their moral significance, then there is also a reason to claim that we should accept some burden in order to assist those people for exactly the same reason.[33]

Harris describes his second argument as 'an appeal to basic fairness. This is sometimes expressed as an appeal to the unfairness of being a "free rider".'[34] Harris argues that since we live in a society where we have each benefited, and continue to benefit, from the results of medical research which has been made possible by the involvement of research participants, we each have an obligation to offer a similar contribution to the pursuit of further benefits of research. This line of argument might also be framed with reference to the view that as each person matters, we should show concern for one another. The claim will be that we are living in a society which shows concern for significant health interests of each of us, and that showing this concern requires that some people contribute through participation in research. In other words, showing concern for health interests requires that at least some people accept the impact on their interests entailed by research participation. If we accept that each person has equal moral significance, and so the (equal) interests of each person have equal significance, then (all other things being equal) there is as much reason for the burden of research participation to fall on one person as another. For some people to rule themselves out of research participation opens them to the claim that they are setting their own interests above those of others who agree to participate.

[32] Harris, 'Scientific research', 242.
[33] A detailed discussion of this argument is given in J. Glover, *Causing Death and Saving Lives* (London: Penguin, 1977), ch. 7.
[34] Harris, 'Scientific research', 242–3.

Participant objections, medical demands and the force of equality

The arguments offered by Harris make the case that as individuals we should accept the possibility that we have an obligation to participate in medical research, on the basis of the significance of providing means of improving health, and the argument that we are all responsible for accepting a role in making this provision. Nevertheless, Harris adds the caveat that people should be expected to participate in research only if that research has rigour and potential value,[35] takes account of the relative risks to participants considered against benefits from the research, and also takes account of the distribution of the benefits of the research.[36] In the following discussion we shall see that this caveat is crucial. Drawing further on the account of the (equal) moral significance of people shows that questions of the relative value of the research and the situation of the donor affect the way in which we can understand any individual obligation to participate in research. That is, these questions affect the expectations that can be made of potential donors to genetic research.

We can begin by noting that there are two ways of interpreting both of the arguments Harris presents; that is, the argument that as individuals we have a responsibility to accept some personal burden in order to assist others (for brevity let us call this the 'assistance' argument), and the argument that we each have a responsibility to contribute to a practice within society that brings benefits to each of us (let us call this the 'contribution' argument). One interpretation of either argument is primarily concerned with the question of whether benefits realised are greater than the burdens involved in achieving them. The second interpretation places emphasis on people's relative situations, and on the distribution of the benefits and burdens. On the first interpretation, the question of whether the 'assistance' argument applies will depend primarily on whether the importance of that other person's need is substantially greater than the burden which the person will face in assisting. Also on this first interpretation, the question of whether the 'contribution' argument applies will depend primarily on whether the contributor is better off given the existence of that practice than they would be otherwise. If the possible obligation to participate in research is interpreted in this first sense, then there will be circumstances in which it is faced with objections from those who are expected to accept the obligation to participate. There will be other cases

---

[35] *Ibid.,* 242.   [36] *Ibid.,* 246.

when it is criticised by those who have health needs which could be met by the results of research. Finally, it could be subject to complaints from those who have significant needs which could be met if resources were not directed to expensive research. By considering each of these objections to this first interpretation, the following discussion makes the case for the second interpretation with its emphasis on distributive issues and the relative situation of different people.

Potential participants might object to the responsibility to assist others at the cost of some burden to themselves, if that burden puts them in a worse situation relative to other people. This objection can be backed up with reference to the argument that since each person has equal moral significance, the imposition of this relative burden is not justified. One response to this objection would be that the person in need of assistance has a greater claim since, if they do not receive the health benefits of the research, the worsening of their relative situation would be greater than it would be for the participant. However, while this response might amount to an argument that *someone* should participate in the research (as the possible benefits are likely to be greater than the costs to participants), it does not show that one person rather than another should be the participant. Nevertheless, this response does emphasise that a potential participant will need to do more than simply point to the fact of their suffering some burden, if they are to claim reasonably that their interests would be treated less seriously than those of others if they, rather than another, participated in the research. A participant's objection could have force if they begin from a position in which they already suffer relative disadvantage as compared with others, and the burden that research participation would involve would serve to compound that disadvantage (for instance if research participants were recruited from relatively disadvantaged communities). In this case they could plausibly claim that they, and their interests, are treated as of less importance than the interests of other potential participants who begin from a position of less relative disadvantage. Where this objection applies, it might be mitigated by some forms of benefit sharing if this had the effect of reducing the relative disadvantage faced by the potential participants. Both the possibility of this objection, and the suggestion of benefit sharing as a means of resolution, point to the difficulties for the first interpretation of the responsibility of assisting others. Further, both the objection and its potential resolution increase the plausibility of the second interpretation which takes account of distributive issues and the relative situation of those who are asked to participate in research.

Potential participants will also have scope for raising objections if the obligation to contribute to the practice of research from which we all benefit (the 'contribution' argument) is interpreted as simply requiring that the contributor is better off given the existence of the social practice than they would be otherwise. Clearly this interpretation imposes an obligation only when the burden of participating in research is less than the benefits that the participant can expect from the wider practice of research. Nevertheless, the interpretation would justify the obligation even where expected benefits only marginally made up for the burden (or expected burden) of participation. This may not present much difficulty if the only options are research offering marginal benefit, or no research. However, the objection could have force if the options also include other systems of organising and prioritising research which could be expected to provide less marginal benefits for research participants. In this case a participant might claim that their interests are not being treated with the importance that they could be. Nevertheless, for this objection to have moral relevance, the claim would need to be not only that their interests are not treated as they could be, but further that they are not treated as they *should* be. This is because the interests of research participants have equal, but not greater, moral significance compared with the interests of others,[37] and those others will include people with health needs which may also be better met by some research programmes and priorities than by others. So in addition to considering whether potential donors receive as many benefits as they could, we need also to consider the entitlements of others. What this suggests is that in this case, as in the last, it is not sufficient to consider only whether participants benefit from the system to which they are asked to contribute, and we also need to think about the distribution of those benefits.

Assessing whether research participants receive sufficient benefit from a given system of organising research – given the alternative possible systems – will depend on understanding the effects that each system will have on the interests of both participants and potential beneficiaries of research. It should be noted that this assessment will be complicated by a number of issues, including further questions of how different types of interest can be compared. Reasons have been given above for prioritising basic health, but we also need to think about how other comparisons can be made: for instance how we compare genetic discrimination faced by one person with a health gain leading to enhanced quality of

---

[37] Again, a point emphasised by Harris, 'Scientific research', 245.

life, provided to another; or how different risks and probabilities can be compared (for instance the comparison between the possibility of genetic discrimination, and the prospect of a health gain from research).[38] We can note that it is possible that an interpretation of the obligation to contribute to research, which does not involve this sort of assessment of distribution of benefits under different systems, could operate without causing any problems. This would be the case if the system of research which happened to be in place was the one that defensibly realised different people's interests. However, in the absence of any assessment, we simply would not know if the system we had was this sort of defensible system.

The systems and priorities used to determine what research is undertaken may be subject to objections not only by potential research participants, but also by others who have health needs that could be better met by some other system. This in turn could add to objections from potential research participants if the research to which they are being asked to contribute is not meeting the needs that it should. It might be suggested that this is misplaced concern for the demands of those whose needs would not be met by research, since they themselves are not participating in the research and so have less reason to complain if they receive fewer benefits than they could under another system (unless, of course they contribute in some other way to research, or provision of healthcare, or more generally to providing the conditions needed for sustaining health). However, if we accept that beneficiaries matter, and that therefore their interests matter, then it is not obvious that any lack of direct contribution on their part serves to diminish their objections. The issue of whether they should expect to receive benefits from systems of research and healthcare does not directly depend on whether they have contributed to that system. Instead, they can expect benefits on the grounds that these benefits amount to fundamental interests of health, and these interests matter because the people they belong to themselves matter. This is not to deny that (for the reasons discussed above) people may have an obligation to contribute to research and to healthcare more generally, it only maintains that claims to receive benefits of research should not be determined by contribution. Again the question of whether people's interests are treated

---

[38] It is beyond the scope of this chapter to consider how these further, and complex, comparisons can be made. For discussion on approaches and difficulties in measuring prospects of health gains from research, see Mullen, *Sustaining life*, ch. 5; S. Holm and T. Takala, 'High hopes and automatic escalators: a critique of some new arguments in bioethics', *Journal of Medical Ethics*, 33 (2007), 1–4.

as they should be, by the systems of research in operation, will depend on distributive questions of how their interests are met in comparison with the interests of others, and how their interests could be met under a different system.

Is there an obligation not to donate?

Objections by research participants can stem from judgements that participation will make worse someone's already relatively difficult situation, or that the participant receives fewer benefits than they are entitled to expect from research, or that other beneficiaries do not receive the benefits that they should. In each case it has been suggested that, under certain conditions, these objections would be well founded. What is not clear is whether these objections can justifiably remove any obligations to contribute to research. With respect to objections that those being asked to participate are in a relatively poor position already, there is a case for maintaining that the obligation should fall first on others. If others do not take up this obligation then the situation is more difficult. However, it is plausible to maintain that there would be no obligation if participation would put the participant in a worse position than the beneficiary would be in if they did not gain the health benefits of research (for genetic research this would be a difficult judgement as the burdens and risks of donation are of a different kind from the health benefits of research).

For objections which are based on the inadequacy of research benefits, it may be that there is a system of organising and prioritising research which would better meet people's defensible claims to benefits. Nevertheless, it may also be that there is little prospect of a better system coming about or, at least, little prospect in the near future. In other words it can seem that the options are between inadequate research and no research. On this basis, as long as the inadequate research is at least marginally more beneficial than no research, then, despite valid objections, there are reasons and obligations to participate. However, this perception of a choice between inadequate research and no research treats the whole system of research as a single entity and may well be misleadingly simplistic. There are numerous different research programmes and studies, and these are organised in many different ways (such as public, private, charity and combinations of the three). Further, genetic research is only a part of wider health provision which includes healthcare, and also factors such as access to food and water, safety measures and laws, and environmental protection. With this in mind we can consider whether it is reasonable to hold that there may be aspects of research which are open to the sorts of objections discussed above, and for which there is a feasible alternative that will more defensibly meet people's interests. For instance, Holm and Takala suggest that focusing effort on alleviating the scarcity in resources for basic healthcare across the world could have a greater impact on meeting health needs than would some forms of medical research.[39] Alternatively there may be concerns that a research programme is controlled in a way that will limit its potential for meeting health needs; for instance there are questions on whether practices of patenting research findings can have a detrimental impact on other beneficial research, and further questions about the impact patents have on the availability and affordability of treatments.[40]

If alternatives to a proposed research programme or study offer better prospects of defensibly meeting health needs, then we need to question again whether people should be expected to participate in that proposed research. We might hope that both the alternatives and the proposed research (assuming that it brought some benefit) could be supported by society. If so, this may place individuals in a dilemma of deciding what to give support to if they cannot support everything. This dilemma has led Shapshay and Pimple to argue that:

> we must make others' happiness our end, and act in good faith to help some others some of the time, but we may justifiably use our own discretion as to whom, how and how much to help.[41]

However, if decisions are made with reference to considerations of the equal significance of each person, then arguably the individual need not resort to discretionary choice. Although it will not be a neat or precise calculation, it may still be possible to expect people to make decisions which take account of factors including the prospect that an action will be effective, the likelihood of some needs being met by others, and consideration of where the needs of some are currently not being met. While individuals may not be expected to decide actually to participate

---

[39] Holm and Takala, 'High hopes', 2.

[40] For instance, see D. Dickson, *SciDev.Net*, 2006; www.scidev.net/en/news; and the Intergovernmental Working Group on Public Health, Innovation and Intellectual Property, *Elements of a global strategy and plan of action* (2006) www.who.int/gb/phi/.

[41] Shapshay and Pimple, 'Imperfect moral duty', 416.

in research, they may still be expected to consider whether they should participate.

The further question arises when society cannot support both research and its alternatives, or when research actually acts as an obstacle to the alternatives. This might occur when the conduct of research prevents other more valuable research from taking place, or the resources devoted to the research detract from resources that could support the alternatives. In this case, supporting that research effectively harms the interests of those who could have benefited from the alternatives, and who moreover have interests which they are entitled to have met by that alternative. It is in this circumstance that it can be claimed that not only is there no obligation to participate in research, but that participation would be wrong.

Working out how your genetic resources should be used

The conclusion that there are circumstances in which people can be expected to consider allowing their genetic information to be used in research, but that there are other circumstances in which it would be wrong for them to do so, creates a difficult situation for any potential donor. In addition to the expectation that they will accept the risks and burdens of donation, people also face the problem that if they donate to the wrong research then their sacrifice may be harmful, and working out whether a given research programme is one that they should support is not straightforward. As has already been noted, an assessment of how a given research project will meet the interests of different people involves an account of how concerns such as genetic discrimination, or impact on conceptions of identity (associated with genetic information), can be compared with health gains. Further, it will involve consideration of how different risks and prospects of benefits should be compared: for instance how can the risk of developments leading to genetic discrimination by employers or insurers be quantified, and then compared with the quantified prospect of people's health being enhanced by research? Finally we need to assess whether a research project can be held to be an obstacle to more beneficial health provision.

There is reason to argue that the decision on whether to participate in given research projects should not be left solely to each potential donor to make. Where there are grounds for maintaining that research should be supported, there remain reasons to hold that the individual will need to make the final decision about whether they participate, if only because, as Shapshay and Pimple argue, one person cannot do everything.[42] So, as is argued above, individuals will need to consider whether participation is the most effective use of their time and effort (and one consideration might be whether others have agreed to participate). However, it is in the assessment of whether a research project is one that should be supported that we may look beyond the individual. The reason is less concerned with the difficulty of the assessment,[43] but instead suggests that this would be to place a disproportionate weight on the moral assessment by those individuals who are in a position of deciding whether to participate in research. Donation of genetic information is an act which has an impact on the interests of many people beyond the donor. While we might accept that each person should have a say in the debate on moral decisions which inform public policies, this is not the same as attempting to claim that each person's moral judgements should directly determine their activities in relation to public policy. Still less does it imply that policies should be determined by the judgements of a minority who are potential donors. Therefore, there are reasons to maintain that assessment of the value of different research projects, and hence support and expectation of donation, should be settled through democratic debate and institutions which are accountable through democratic processes. Nevertheless, as was mentioned at the beginning of this chapter, this assessment can only be left to institutions in so far as they make accountable and defensible decisions. If the decisions are starkly indefensible – if, for instance, research is clearly failing to address health needs – then the responsibility of individuals to contribute to a society that meets people's needs may justify using their control over the use of their genetic information as a means of creating pressure for change.

Conclusion

This chapter has given an answer to questions of whether there are moral considerations that we can expect people to make when deciding whether to participate in research. The answer has developed through an account of how people matter and what concern we should show for one another. This basic idea allows us to begin to think about how we can compare the interests of different people. If we accept this account, then

---

[42] We may also argue that although people might be expected to participate in some research, they should not be forced to do so.

[43] Although of course this is a difficult assessment to make, and it would clearly be unreasonable to expect some people (for instance, children) to take it on.

unfortunately we will be faced with fairly complex questions of whether there is an obligation to allow tissue samples and genetic information to be used in specific research projects. The discussion has suggested that there can be such an obligation, despite potentially significant risks and burdens that donors may face. The sense in which the obligation can arise is within the context of the wider expectation that people consider how they can and should act to help to show concern for each person's life and interests. Donating tissue and genetic information for research may be a way to show this concern for one another. However, this is not necessarily the case. Even where the research being undertaken holds the prospect of beneficial results, and the risks of participation are minimal, there can still be reasons to direct efforts to other activities. It is ultimately the individual who should decide whether to participate in a given research project. Nevertheless, we can expect them to base their decision on an assessment of the potential value of that research which is informed by democratic debate and accountable institutions.

SECTION II

Ethical frameworks of governance

SECTION I

Ethical issues in biotechnology

4

Constructing communal models of governance: collectives of individuals or distinct ethical loci?

HEATHER WIDDOWS

This chapter explores the recent move from individual models towards communal models of ethical governance. It draws on thinking about group rights to explore what conception of groups is necessary for an effective ethical framework. In particular it asks whether it is sufficient to regard groups as collectives of individuals – with their moral status and attendant rights dependent on the rights of individuals – or whether a more robust conception is necessary to establish the ethical protections required. Examining the nature of groups and group rights is crucial to issues of genetic governance, as whether or not one includes groups and the types of groups one includes fundamentally affects the framework of ethical decision making. It changes the key actors involved and the issues of ethical priority, thus in a very real sense it affects which ethical issues are recognised and frames how they will be addressed. For example, if groups do not feature in the ethical framework, then certain types of injustice are at worst invisible and at best parasitical (and secondary) to individual concerns. Accordingly, such conceptual concerns regarding groups and their rights speak directly to the practice and policy concerns of genetic governance addressed in this volume: from the structure of benefit-sharing and stakeholder models to political concerns regarding what counts as participation; to questions of ownership rights and decision making powers in genetic governance; to traditional bioethical concerns regarding what counts as harm in research. For in addressing all these issues, the ethical framework we use determines what we recognise as an ethical issue and what mechanisms are appropriate to address such issues. Thus how we conceive of groups determines what counts in our ethical framework and what we deem to be ethically good governance.

In order to address the issue of what is the appropriate unit of concern in issues of genetic governance and the ethical framework which

should be adopted, this chapter will first explain why traditional medical
ethics – with its emphasis on individual autonomy upheld by the practices of confidentiality and informed consent – is no longer adequate in
the genetic era. Second, it will outline the move to communal models and
list examples of such emerging models. Third, it will examine the structure of groups: considering groups constructed as collections of individuals (where the needs, interests and rights of the individuals converge
into group needs, interests and rights) and more substantial conceptions
where the group has needs, interests and rights which do not directly
equate to the collective needs of the individuals within the group. To
examine these issues, arguments from the human rights debate will be
introduced and Jones's distinction of 'collective' and 'corporate' group
models will be employed.[1] Finally, arguments for and against group rights
will be assessed in relation to the group models of bioethics. Throughout,
indigenous groups and biobank participants will be focused on, as both
are important in the genetic governance debate and representative of very
different types of groups.

The problems of individualism in bioethics

First then, the individualism of bioethics and its inadequacy in the genetic era. It is nothing new to suggest that bioethics is an individualistic
discipline which 'has reified the individual and individual autonomy'.[2]
Bioethics has traditionally seen the individual as its focus and has
excluded – to the point of invisibility – the group or groups which the individual is from, including family units and ethnic, cultural and religious
groups. This focus on the individual has resulted in an ethical framework
which is incapable of seeing (and thus rectifying) injustices which are
not purely individualistic. Accordingly injustices which are connected to
group identities or practices – for example, those derived from race, gender and class or, as is our concern here, genetic relatedness – are only ethical concerns in a secondary way as they impact on the individual. In an
individualistic framework they can only be addressed using individual
methods of protection (for example, the protection of autonomy), rather

---

[1] P. Jones, 'Human rights, group rights and peoples' rights', *Human Rights Quarterly*, 21,
1 (1999), 80–107; and P. Jones, 'Group rights and group oppression', *Journal of Political
Philosophy*, 7, 4 (1999), 353–77.
[2] B. A. Koenig, 'Why not grant primacy to the family?', *American Journal of Bioethics*, 1, 3
(2001), 33.

than by using group orientated methods such as anti-discrimination legislation and practices.

There are a number of reasons for the individualist focus of bioethics (something that I have discussed in more detail elsewhere).[3] Perhaps most importantly, bioethics emerged from a professional ethic of doctor and patient which necessitated that the individual was the only ethical locus: indeed for the doctor to take into consideration others' needs and rights would have been profoundly unethical. Thus bioethics 'was developed for and takes as its paradigm a binary, non-organisational relationship between a single physician and a patient'.[4] The professional ethics of the doctor and patient developed into bioethics' primary methodology of principlism.[5] This methodology expanded the individual values of the doctor-patient relationship into the established ethical framework of all health care professionals. In addition, bioethics has an Anglo-American heritage which has tended to focus on autonomy as the primary and, at times, the only moral value.[6] Pivotal to the individualist framework are the key practices of confidentiality and consent, both of which are challenged by genetic advances.

Confidentiality is owed by the practitioner to the individual patient (irrespective of the impact upon others). Thus, confidentiality is concerned only with the individual and is strongly dependent upon the principle of autonomy: 'if we look with a strictly "autonomous eye", the other family members are irrelevant'.[7] However, confidentiality cannot now be guaranteed, as genetic information is identifying and the possibility of identifying the individual from whom the information was derived, or their genetically related family members, at any time in the future is a real possibility, and one that becomes increasingly likely as the number of people who have their information stored (particularly on large-scale databases) continues to grow and the use of genetics in clinical practice becomes more common.

[3] H. Widdows, 'Conceptualising the self in the genetic era', *Health Care Analysis*, 15 (2007), 5–12; H. Widdows, 'Reconceptualising genetics: challenges to traditional medical ethics' in C. Lenk, N. Hoppe and R. Andorno (eds.), *Ethics and Law of Intellectual Property: Current Problems in Politics, Science and Technology* (Farnham: Ashgate, 2007), 159–73.

[4] A. Buchanan, 'Trust in managed care organisations', *Kennedy Institute of Ethics Journal*, 10, 3 (2000), 189–212.

[5] For a discussion of the primary methodology of principlism and its critics, including those from the developing world, see Widdows, 'Reconceptualising genetics'; and H. Widdows, 'Moral neocolonialism and global ethics', *Bioethics*, 21, 6 (2007), 305–15.

[6] Widdows, 'Conceptualising the self'; Widdows, 'Reconceptualising genetics'.

[7] D. J. Doukas and J. W. Berg, 'The family covenant and genetic testing', *American Journal of Bioethics*, 1, 3 (2001), 4.

Thus practically ensuring confidentiality is problematic, but more importantly it is ethically questionable whether confidentiality should be a priority. The assumption that 'underlies and supports the general practice of medical confidentiality is that medical information is first and foremost about the patient, and so the patient has the greatest interest in that information and in controlling who has access to it'.[8] However, this long held assumption may no longer be true in the genetic era (and even in pre-genetics health status was relevant to family members and procreative partners). For example, if an individual tests positive for a genetic condition, such as Huntington's disease, or as a carrier of the BRCA1 or BRCA2 genes (indicators for breast cancer), this information has relevance for family members (consanguineous relations may wish to be tested themselves, and sexual partners may desire the information when making reproductive decisions). Accordingly, it is not clear that confidentiality should continue to be regarded as ethically fundamental.

Likewise the effectiveness of informed consent, the second guarantor of ethical practice, is also brought into question in the genetic context. The ascendancy of informed consent as an ethical priority is related to the horrors of Nazi research practices and the wish to prevent such atrocities occurring again. To prevent the recurrence of such practices 'ethically the post-war consensus – from Nuremberg to Helsinki to the Common Rule – is that, to the greatest extent possible, people should not be exposed to the risks of human subjects research without their informed consent'.[9] This key lesson regarding the need to safeguard the individual has made informed consent the most important tool in ethical practice, particularly when concerned with research on human subjects.[10] Thus, informed consent is regarded as the final ethical guarantee for the individual and this is the 'tool that is intended to safeguard autonomy and promote the freedom to choose'.[11] Understandably, given this historical context, informed consent is concerned by definition exclusively with the individual and consequently the practice is fundamentally individualistic.

[8] D. W. Brock, 'Genetics and confidentiality', *American Journal of Bioethics*, 1, 3 (2001), 34.

[9] H. T. Greely, 'Human genomics research: New challenges for research ethics', *Perspectives in Biology and Medicine*, 44, 2 (2001), 223.

[10] A. Goldworth, 'Informed consent revisited', *Cambridge Quarterly of Health Care Ethics*, 5 (1996), 214–20.

[11] Fatima Alvarez-Castillo, 'Limiting factors impacting on voluntary first person informed consent in the Philippines', *Developing World Bioethics*, 2, 1 (2002), 22.

Both informed consent and confidentiality assume that only the individual is vulnerable to harm and thus the ethical practices are designed to protect the individual. However, it is precisely this premise that is no longer true and 'the fact that genetic information about one person can be of value to others poses an important challenge to the primacy of respect for the principle of autonomy in medicine'.[12] No longer do health decisions only or even fundamentally concern the individual, as 'disclosure of genetic information by individual DNA donors also exposes information about others with similar genetic profiles'.[13] Thus we move necessarily from the individual to the group as the 'key feature about genetic information is that it is typically information about a family, or even ... about a larger community not just about an individual patient'.[14] Therefore the question is whether the individual should continue to be the ethical focus as 'one-to-one models of informed consent give ... genetic bystanders no say in decisions about whether to proceed with potentially harmful research, since such normative frameworks invest individual research subjects with the sole power as agents of consent'.[15] Arguably, individuals should not be able to make independent decisions or consent to use of their genetic material, as the material reveals information not only about themselves, but also about those genetically related to them. Thus it has

---

[12] M. Parker, 'Confidentiality in genetic testing', *American Journal of Bioethics*, 1, 3 (2001), 21.

[13] G. R. Mitchell and K. Happe, 'Informed consent after the human genome project', *Rhetoric and Public Affairs*, 4, 3 (2001), 376.

[14] Brock, 'Genetics and confidentiality', 34. Possible family models suggested in the literature are the 'joint account' (M. Parker and A. Lucassen, 'Genetic information: a joint account?', *British Medical Journal*, 329 (2004), 165–7) and the 'family covenant' (Doukas and Berg, 'The family covenant'). The joint account model sees genetic information as belonging to, and available to, all family members. While there may be cases where information could be withheld (for example in situations where such disclosure would seriously harm the individual), the 'default' position would be that genetic information is familial and not individual (Parker, 'Confidentiality in genetic testing'). The 'family covenant' is perhaps the most discussed model of family consent, where the family and not the individual is the 'unit of care'. The family covenant is suggested as a model which dictates the manner in which results from genetic tests are to be shared with family members; as such it 'offers the individual, family and physician a mechanism to help resolve competing claims for confidentiality and disclosure' (Doukas and Berg, 'The family covenant', 3). It was intended to pre-empt questions of when and how to disclose potentially distressing information about the genetic status of individuals within families. The thinking behind this approach is that the 'bonds that hold families together may not survive such dynamic tension unless there is some framework constructed to allow for balancing of individual and family interests' (*ibid.*). I have discussed these in more detail elsewhere (Widdows, 'Reconceptualising genetics').

[15] Mitchell and Happe, 'Human genome project', 376.

been claimed that genetic information does not belong to the individual and therefore the individual should not be able to consent to its use. As a result the traditional mainstays of medical ethics (informed consent and confidentiality), supported by the assumptions of individualism, are brought into question as adequate guarantors of good ethical practice.[16]

The global failure of individual models

This issue becomes increasingly problematic when we expand our focus and consider the ways in which these practices have been expanded in the global context. In such wider contexts the ineffectiveness of these individual practices of informed consent and confidentiality to protect vulnerable individuals and groups is clearly manifest. In the global sphere ethical concerns are exacerbated as 'new genetic technologies have greatly enhanced the *informational* power of human tissue, transforming it into a commodity and an object of privacy',[17] thus making the rewards of unethical behaviour more attractive. Concerns have been raised particularly with regard to the behaviour of Western researchers in the developing world, as the new genetics, stem cell technologies, and other advances lend commercial importance and value to the tissues and genomes of populations in developing countries.[18] In such contexts profits can be made from 'bioinformatics', that is to say 'a biological information processing system – comprising computers, databases, on-line networking, and specialised software – that has given birth to a new research paradigm in which genotypic and phenotypic information is "mined" to identify genes, to model protein structure and to discover drug targets'.[19]

Given what is at stake here, for example, international research collaborations, healthcare inventions and new drug developments (not to

---

[16] J. Husted, 'Autonomy and a right not to know', in R. Chadwick et al. (eds.), *The Right to Know and the Right not to Know* (Aldershot: Ashgate, 1997); B. M. Knoppers (ed.), *Human DNA: Law and Policy* (The Hague: Kluwer Law International, 1997); B. M. Knoppers, 'Who should have access to genetic information?' in J. Burley (ed.), *The Genetic Revolution and Human Rights* (Oxford University Press, 1999), 39–53.

[17] D. E. Winickoff, 'Governing population genomics: law, bioethics, and biopolitics in three case studies', *Jurimetrics*, 43 (2003), 189.

[18] L. S. Cahill, 'Genetics, commodification and social justice in the globalization era', *Kennedy Institute of Ethics Journal*, 11 (2001), 221–38; D. Dickenson, 'Commodification of human tissue: implications for feminist and development ethics', *Developing World Bioethics*, 2 (2002), 55–63; B. Tedlock, 'Indigenous heritage and biopiracy in the age of intellectual property rights', *Explore*, 2, 3 (2006), 256–9.

[19] Winickoff, 'Governing population genomics', 189.

mention the profits and market share of pharmaceutical companies), it is not surprising that the individual-orientated practices of bioethics – such as informed consent and confidentiality – are not equipped to address the ethical needs of those involved. This is clearly illustrated in the worst examples of bad practice of research on indigenous populations. The identifying nature of genetic material means that genetic research on one member of the group 'has implications for all members of those groups, whether or not they decided – or even were asked – to take part in the research'.[20] Accordingly, in such instances, even if standards of fully informed consent are met – the traditional method of protecting research subjects – it is not enough to ensure that practices are ethical. For, in an argument parallel to that regarding family members, informed consent is only sought from those subjects who participate in research, not from those who do not but are related, even though the research will have implications for these individuals too.

Perhaps the most famous example of this type of controversial practice is that of the patenting of unmodified DNA taken from the Hagahai people of Papua New Guinea (a group who had had no contact with outsiders until 1984). In 1994 a patent was granted on a cell line containing unmodified Hagahai DNA and several methods for its use in detecting HTLV-1-related retroviruses, the intention being to develop a diagnostic tool or vaccine for certain types of leukaemia. This patent was criticised for a number of reasons: first, for the now familiar use of 'invention' in the genetic context to describe not 'invention' but rather recording or decoding;[21] second, for the assumption that unmodified DNA can be owned;[22] and third and most importantly (and less controversially), for the lack of control that the Hagahai had regarding both the ownership of their (unmodified) DNA and the possible profits which would accrue from any subsequent developments. In this instance the

---

[20] Greely, 'Human genomics research', 222.

[21] There are three conditions to patents: that they must be new, involve an inventive step and have applicability for industry; moreover they must exclude 'phenomena of nature' (J. Philips and A. Firth, *Introduction to Intellectual Property*, 4th edn (London: Butterworths, 2001)). Thus there is much controversy over whether genetic patents pass these criteria.

[22] Connected to the issue of 'invention' there has been much discussion of 'patents of life' and the morality as well as the legality of such genetic patents is a point of heated debate (V. Shiva, *Biopiracy: The Plunder of Nature and Knowledge* (Cambridge: South End Press, 1997); V. Shiva, *Protect or Plunder? Understanding Intellectual Property* (London: Zed Books Ltd, 2001); V. Shiva, *Earth Democracy: Justice Sustainability and Peace* (London: Zed Books Ltd, 2005)).

'US government had shared invention on the patent with Carol Jenkins, principal research fellow at the Institute of Medical Research in Papua New Guinea'.[23] Although a 'benefit-sharing' agreement was widely claimed stating that the Hagahai were entitled to 50 per cent of any royalties accrued, in fact this amounted to an informal agreement with the researcher, who promised to hand over her share to the Hagahai. Thus there was no formal benefit-sharing agreement according to which the Hagahai could claim rights or entitlements to a share of the profits. Moreover, their DNA was effectively the property of the US government.[24] This patent was 'disclaimed' in 1996 both because it turned out to be of little commercial value and also in response to mass protest. However, the Hagahai cell line remains in the public domain and is still available to the public at the American Type Culture Collection as ATCC Number: CRL-10528 Organism: Homo Sapiens (human), at a cost of $290 per sample.

The Hagahai example was not a lone instance of such practices and similar patent applications were filed by 'US federal health agencies on genetic samples derived from indigenous peoples in the Solomon Islands and Panama'.[25] Again the cell lines were taken from consenting individuals – one from a 40-year-old woman and one from a 50-year-old man.[26] However, in the Panama case (of research on the Guaymi tribe) the consent was already dubious as the woman 'who was illiterate and unschooled was said to have given "informed oral consent" to the research, even though neither the tribe nor the woman knew anything about the development of the cell line or the patent application'.[27] Again, under pressure, the patent claims were withdrawn. However, as with the Hagahai, the cell lines remain on deposit at the American Type Culture Collection.

These incidents raised awareness regarding genetic governance and the inadequacy of current ethical practices to safeguard group interests. Such patenting of 'group DNA' outraged the Rural Advancement Foundation International (RAFI) and other campaigners for the rights of indigenous groups who regarded the Hagahai case as 'an example of

[23] S. Lehrman, 'US drops patent claim to Hagahai cell line', *Nature* 384, 6609 (1996), 500.
[24] Another group model which may have been appropriate here would have been Group Patenting as used in the PXE (pseudoxanthoma elasticum) case in which a member of the patient advocate group was listed on the patent. Perhaps in this case representative members of the Hagahai could have been listed and thus become patent holders.
[25] J. Barker, 'The human genome diversity project: "peoples", "populations" and the cultural politics of identification', *Cultural Studies*, 18, 4 (2004), 595.
[26] *Ibid.*
[27] Winickoff, 'Governing population genomics', 200

"biopiracy" and human "bioprospecting" '.[28] Such campaigners assert that 'the cultural heritage of indigenous peoples is a collective right, and, as such, the responsibility for its use and management in accordance with indigenous laws and traditions, is borne by the community as a whole'.[29] Given this, it is not surprising that:

> In several early writings about the [Human Genome Diversity Project] HGDP by indigenous peoples and advocacy groups, the HGDP and its participants were characterized as blood sucking vampires swooping down into remote villages, sucking the blood of unsuspecting victims and callously leaving them to die while flying off to far away labs and patent offices where monsters and biological weapons were being designed in the dark and under-the-table financial deals were being made in secret.[30]

As a consequence of these experiences 'indigenous groups opposed this "vampire project" '[31] and group orientated ethical protocols have been, and are in the continued process of being, rethought.

The move towards communal models

Such discussion shows that, across the board in the genetic context, more communal models are being sought as the individual models of bioethics, characterised by the practices of informed consent and confidentiality, prove inadequate to protect individuals and groups in the genetic era. This is true of families in instances of individual diagnosis which impact on family members and at international levels where the genomes of indigenous populations are valuable sources for research.

   In response, different types of communal models have been sought in different instances and to protect different kinds of groups and the individuals within them. For the most part, implementations of such alternatives have been done in an ad hoc manner and with more or less systematic implementation depending on the needs involved. For example, in the family context the failure of the individual model has been widely acknowledged and new models such as the 'family covenant' and the 'joint account' model suggested.[32] Yet despite the awareness

[28] *Ibid.*
[29] G. Cajete, *Native Science: Natural Laws of Interdependence* (Santa Fe, NM: Clear Light Books, 2000), 275.
[30] Barker, 'Human genome diversity project', 583.
[31] Winickoff, 'Governing population genomics', 196.
[32] See Widdows, 'Reconceptualising genetics' for further detail of these models and their critics.

of the need for such rethinking, such models have not integrated into standard practice – perhaps because of the ingrained individualism of clinical practice. However, in the area of population genetics new models are arising and being implemented. Not only in instances where there is an easily identifiable group – such as is the case with indigenous groups – but in other instances where individual models fail, either because they are not practical given the numbers involved, or because of the uncertainty regarding the nature of future research, as is the case with biobanks. This seeking of more communal models represents a general trend towards communal ethical frameworks which Knoppers and Chadwick describe as a trend towards reciprocity, mutuality, solidarity, citizenry and universality.[33] Models which are being considered and to some extent implemented include versions of group consent, benefit sharing, group patenting and trust, and the example of trust in UK Biobank will be expanded to serve as a second case study along with the Hagahai.[34] It is important to note that these models are not exclusive and can work alone or together. For example, benefit sharing can work alongside the model of charitable trust and/or group consent and there is still a place for individual consent as an additional requirement to such group models. Before moving to consider our core question regarding the nature of groups, the emergence of such models will be briefly outlined.

Group consent has emerged as an attempt to respond to the criticisms of the HGDP and the examples of bad practice of patenting of indigenous DNA which we have discussed. Research councils have 'proposed the adoption of "group consent" as a normative rule governing genomic research to alleviate this ethical blind spot in traditional informed consent doctrines'.[35] Such attempts are becoming standard practice and group consent in the form of 'prior consultation and communication with these specific communities and populations' is gradually becoming an 'ethical prerequisite'.[36] For example, following the initial bad practice connected to the HGDP, the National American Research Council put together a

[33] B. M. Knoppers and R. Chadwick, 'Human genetic research: emerging trends in ethics', *Nature Reviews Genetics*, 6 (2005), 75–9.

[34] A recently concluded EU-funded project led by Widdows and Mullen examined these models of governance and their ethical status. For further information see the Property Regulation in European Science, Ethics and Law Project (PropEur) project website (www.propeur.bham.ac.uk).

[35] Mitchell and Happe, 'Human genome project', 377; for example, see the Nuffield Council on Bioethics, *The Ethics of Research Related to Healthcare in Developing Countries* (London: Nuffield Council on Bioethics, 2002).

[36] Knoppers and Chadwick, 'Emerging trends', 76.

'Proposed Model Ethical Protocol' which explicitly recognises the communal nature of genetic information. Thus it states that, 'the Project intends to study populations, not individuals. As a result, we believe that the populations, as well as the individuals, must give their free consent to participate.'[37] Such a starting principle represents a fundamental shift away from the individual model and the document continues, 'we believe … that the population-based nature of this research requires population-based consent and we will insist on it'.[38]

Benefit sharing derives from exactly the same impetus and intends to ensure that populations are justly treated when their tissue or knowledge is used for profitable research. Benefit sharing does exactly what the name states and shares the benefits of any profit from research with the community from which the samples, knowledge or other materials or information were derived. Benefits which have been suggested include 'medical care, technology transfer, or contribution to the local community infrastructure (e.g., schools, libraries, sports, clean water …)'.[39] Moreover, such benefits, as suggested by the HUGO Ethics Committee, should be determined with the community and before research begins. Accordingly, on this model 'consultation with individuals and communities and their involvement and participation in the research design is a preliminary basis for the future distribution of benefit and may be considered a benefit in itself'.[40]

With the trust model the impetus to find new more communal models has been slightly different, although again it is very much driven by practical concerns. The trust model has been adopted in large scale population research, particularly biobanks, where quite simply to insist on the 'gold standard' of fully informed consent would be both impracticable and unrealistic. Such a requirement would require a return to the donors for every new study – and potentially for every subsequent study which drew on previous data. To do this would not only be administratively cumbersome but, more importantly, overly burdensome on the donors to the point of impossibility. Thus if standard notions of informed consent were insisted upon, then broad based population studies would be unworkable.

[37] NARC (National American Research Council) (1999) *Model Ethical Protocol for Collecting DNA Samples*; www.stanford.edu/group/morrinst/hgdp/protocol.html.
[38] *Ibid.*
[39] Human Genome Organisation (HUGO) Ethics Committee, *Statement on Benefit Sharing* (2000), Section G; www.hugo-international.org.
[40] *Ibid.*

UK Biobank has adopted the trust model and provides a good example of this model in practice, as it has explicitly rejected fully informed consent as the appropriate ethical tool for a resource of this kind, both because of the scale of the project and because of the uncertainty regarding the nature of future research. UK Biobank will recruit 500,000 people aged 40–69. It will take physical samples, ask lifestyle questions, and link this information to health-relevant records. Consent is sought 'for research in general that is consistent with UK Biobank's stated purpose (rather than for specific research)'.[41] Thus consent is given for research on 'trust'. In other words the participants trust UK Biobank to use their material and information only in ways which fit the stated purpose of UK Biobank; that is, to 'build a major resource that can support a diverse range of research intended to improve the prevention, diagnosis, and treatment of illness and the promotion of health throughout society'.[42] Broad consent is supported in the trust model by the establishment of an Ethics and Governance Council (EGC) and the right to withdraw.[43]

For UK Biobank to succeed it must maintain participation levels and thus it must maintain the trust of the participants and the trust of the public more broadly as the resource is developed and utilised. Accordingly, 'the Ethics and Governance Council … will keep use of the resource under review … to assure itself, and others, that the resource is being used in the public interest'.[44] Public interest is therefore central to this model: participants give their data to the biobank to serve the public interest and the biobank conducts research in the public interest. The concern is not for individuals and the individual participants are made aware that they themselves will not directly benefit. Moreover, given the nature of the study it is not likely to be current participants that benefit but younger persons and future generations. Thus, while consent and confidentiality remain a part of the picture – and it is hoped that real individuals will ultimately benefit – it is the trust model and the language of public interest and public good which are the foundation of UK Biobank's ethical approach.

[41] UK Biobank Ethics and Governance Framework, Version 3.0 (October 2007), 5; www. ukbiobank.ac.uk/docs/EGF20082.pdf.

[42] *Ibid.*, 3.

[43] The EGC is independent of UK Biobank, and its remit includes 'acting as an independent guardian of the *Ethics and Governance Framework* and advising the Board on its revision; monitoring and reporting publicly on the conformity of the UK Biobank project within this Framework; and advising more generally on the interests of participants and the general public in relation to UK Biobank' (*ibid.*, 15).

[44] *Ibid.*, 13.

In all of these group models – group consent, benefit sharing and trust – similar issues arise, most notably questions of 'What is a group?' and 'Who is capable of granting group consent?' The NARC suggests that consent should be sought from the 'culturally appropriate authority', but 'who would be the relevant authority for groups like Ashkenazi Jews, Irish Americans, "Blacks", or people who speak Cree?'[45] In the case of UK Biobank, after the initial, individual broad consent to participate, decisions become group decisions safeguarded by the EGC. Thus in this instance the EGC is deemed the 'appropriate voice' of the participants and, to some extent, of the wider public, given the remit to safeguard the public good. However, in most instances determining the 'appropriate authority' is problematic, yet this is not sufficient reason not to seek such consent, as any recognition of the interests of groups helps to address the current ethical imbalance. For example, in the Panama case discussed above, if any kind of group consent had been sought from any possible authority it is far less likely that such bad practice could have occurred. Given these myriad injustices, it is clear that some ethical mechanism is needed to protect group concerns.

Constructing groups and their rights

Having considered the emergence of group models and noted the current candidates of family models, group consent, benefit sharing and trust, we will now turn to the core question of the chapter and ask how groups and their rights should be understood if we are to ensure that all the pressing ethical issues are to be recognised and addressed. Most crucially we are concerned with whether it is sufficient to have collective models which view groups as collections of individuals (where the needs, interests and rights of the individuals converge into group needs, interests and rights), or whether the group as an entity should be regarded as having interests and rights which do not equate directly to the collective interests of individuals within the group. Distinguishing between the rights and interests of groups in this way is not an unimportant or merely semantic endeavour, for the way we conceive of groups and their claims has implications for the rights of individuals. 'Group rights' conceived as belonging not to a collective of individuals but to the group as a moral entity are (at least potentially) in conflict with individual rights. However, despite this concern, group rights of some kind seem increasingly important, as, for

---

[45] Winickoff, 'Governing population genomics', 198.

example, in the case of the Hagahai it is unlikely that a group right as merely conceived as a collection of individual rights will be enough to protect the genetic material or information in question. If we do conclude that substantial group rights are necessary to rectify the current neglect of communal concerns, then thought must be given as to how to safeguard simultaneously the claims of individuals. For nothing would be gained if, in rectifying the current imbalance, a similarly imbalanced framework was created which failed to recognise the ethical issues of individuals.

In the last five to ten years (in a discussion which parallels the bioethics discussion) thinking on group rights has modified, as it has become increasingly recognised that an ethical framework which only recognises the rights of individuals is unable to protect all key rights and interests. Given this, the previous rejection of all group rights – based on a justified fear of individuals being oppressed by, or even sacrificed for, the group – is being reassessed as it seems 'merely arbitrary to insist that people can have rights only to goods that they can enjoy individually and never to goods that they can enjoy collectively'.[46] In order to explore further the construction of groups in the bioethics debate we will draw on the parallel human rights debate. We will consider alternative constructions of groups and their rights (namely, Jones's 'collective' and 'corporate' constructions) and their advantages and disadvantages as well as their applicability to bioethics.

The collective conception constructs group rights from the collective rights and interests of individuals. According to this framework 'group rights arise when the joint interest of a number of individuals provides sufficient justification for imposing duties upon others even though, if we were to consider the interest of only one of those individuals, that single interest would not provide the necessary justification'.[47] In this collective understanding of group rights the group right is held jointly by the individuals who make up the group. No separate group right exists that has moral standing or status which is different from the rights of the individuals considered collectively. Thus 'the right is held only by the group, but the interests that make the case for the right are separate, yet identical, interests of the group's members ... the group qua group has no standing that is not reducible to the moral standing of its members'.[48] Accordingly, the collective conception is applicable to different types of groups, merely on the basis of common interests. For example, those who live in the vicinity of a polluting factory all have an interest in their environment

[46] Jones, 'Group rights', 353.   [47] Jones, 'Human rights', 84.   [48] *Ibid.*, 85.

not being polluted which taken together becomes sufficient for a right.[49] Thus a group is created only because of shared interests, irrespective of nation, culture, religion or other issues which might usually be used to define groups. According to this construction of group rights the individuals may share nothing other than the common interest of not being polluted and, on this model, this is 'enough to make them a group for right-holding purposes'.[50]

In contrast to the collective model is the corporate model of group rights which ascribes moral standing to the group as such (rather than merely to the individuals who make up the group). Thus, rather than the group right being held by a collection of individuals, the right is held 'by the group as a unitary entity: the right is "its" right rather than "their" right'.[51] Such an understanding derives from very different premises and returns us to key questions such as 'What is a group?' and more particularly 'What constitutes a group capable of bearing rights?' (questions avoided on the collective model). On the corporate model a group 'must possess a morally significant identity as a group independently, and in advance of whatever interests and rights it may possess'.[52] In sum then, the starting point for corporate group rights is the opposite of that of collective group rights. On the corporate model it must be established that the group in question has moral standing and then its interests and rights assessed; on the collective model the group emerges from individuals' collective rights and interests. The corporate model is the one normally applied to religious, national and cultural groups which assert rights by virtue of the status of the group *qua* group and in the light of the harm that can be done to the group, not just to individuals within the group, if such rights are not respected. Rights in this category include land rights, rights to self determination and rights to cultural practices and religious freedoms, in short rights that are deemed necessary for group identity and the flourishing of individuals within the group. These two, very different, alternative models for constructing group rights offer different protections for groups and those within groups and each model has benefits and drawbacks.

Assessing the corporate model

The first difficulty with substantive models of group rights – here termed the corporate model – is what constitutes a group and whether such an

---

[49] Jones, 'Human rights'; Jones, 'Group rights'.
[50] Jones, 'Group rights', 358.   [51] Jones, 'Human rights', 85.   [52] *Ibid.*, 86–7.

entity can be a rights bearer. These theoretical questions directly parallel the bioethical concerns regarding who can speak for the group and grant group consent. Prior to this question for the corporate model is the question of whether a group is the kind of entity that can bear rights. Traditionally, only persons are regarded as having moral standing and therefore only persons are capable of being rights bearers, as 'moral standing is a precondition of right-holding'.[53] Following this line of reasoning, persons are moral agents capable of being wronged and harmed and thus deemed worthy of protection and consequently the bearers of rights and entitlements. So, the question is do groups have the necessary moral standing to be rights holders in a way which is significantly similar to that of persons? In the human rights debate a primary candidate for holding group rights has been nations, 'where nationhood is understood to mean something more than, or other than mere, statehood'.[54] In this construction then, nationhood and the associated elements of shared history, self-identification, religion, ethnicity and culture all play a part in defining what a group is and it is argued that this group can be harmed, discriminated against or damaged. Thus we have reasons to protect a group and allot moral status to it and to deem it a rights bearer.

This view that groups can be identified and suffer harm and thus be rights bearers is becoming standard and it is recognised that culture and heritage can fail to be adequately respected and consequently the group can suffer. Moreover, the group can be harmed even if all individuals within the group are not. This is especially the case with indigenous group concerns for heritage and traditional knowledge and the 'value of indigenous knowledge (IK) is becoming recognised by scientists, managers, and policy makers, and is an evolving subject of national and international law'.[55] The least controversial groups in this category, in terms of law and rights theory, are indigenous groups which are differentiated easily on ethnic and cultural lines and which have valuable material or practices. In order to protect these groups and their interests a substantive model, such as the corporate model, is necessary (at least at times). However, this again raises the familiar problem of group rights, of how to protect vulnerable

---

[53] Jones, 'Group rights', 362. This question often enters the debate when there is a lack of clarity regarding what counts as a person, for example the foetus in abortion or future generations in environmental debates.

[54] Jones, 'Human rights', 97.

[55] F. Mauro and P. Hardison, 'Traditional knowledge of indigenous and local communities: international debate and policy initiatives', *Ecological Applications* (2000), 1263.

individuals and minorities within groups and the 'fear that individuals and their claims of right will be crushed beneath the greater weight of groups and their claims of right'.[56] For example, in the case of indigenous groups should we protect the group and cultural diversity and tradition even at the expense of individuals within the group? The issue of women has been at the heart of this debate about group rights and the protection of individuals and minorities within such groups and it is to this debate we shall now turn.

Protecting individuals and corporate groups

The usual solution to conflict between group rights and individual rights has been to insist on a 'right of exit'. The assumption is that if it is always possible for the individual to leave the group, then they will be protected from any undue suppression or oppression. This solution has been widely criticised, most famously by Susan Moller Okin from a feminist perspective.[57] She argues that 'any liberal defender of the rights of groups should recognise that individuals must not only be formally free but substantively and more or less equally free to leave their religions or cultures of origin; they must have realistic rights of exit'.[58] Okin argues that although liberal theories profess to protect such rights, they do not in fact do so as they fail to recognise the real constraints which render such a right irrelevant to young women who, 'by the time they reach young adulthood in many cultures and religions ... are effectively far less able to exit their respective groups of origin than are men'.[59]

Because of the tendency to disempower women within such groups, the expectation that women are able to access a right of exit is somewhat naive. For 'because of the tendency of most cultures to control the lives of girls and women more than those of boys and men, women's capacities to exit their cultures of origin are usually considerably more restricted than men's'.[60] Thus, while a formal right of exit may exist, actually to make this choice would be unthinkable, for while girls 'chafe against and are sometimes severely distressed by the restrictions placed on their lives' they are 'very far from considering the option of leaving their cultural or

---

[56] Jones, 'Human rights', 92.

[57] S. M. Okin, *Is Multiculturalism Bad for Women?* (Princeton University Press, 1999); S. M. Okin, ' "Mistresses of their own destiny": group rights, gender and realistic rights of exit', *Ethics*, 112 (2002), 205–30.

[58] Okin, ' "Mistresses of their own destiny" ', 206.   [59] *Ibid.*   [60] *Ibid.*, 216.

92 HEATHER WIDDOWS

religious group'.[61] Thus, despite the existence of such rights Okin considers the rights meaningless, as although:

> a young woman ... has a formal right of exit ... she could legally change her religion. So also could she appeal to the law against her parents in order to prevent the unwanted marriage. But clearly neither of these options is thinkable for her, for, given the manner in which she has been raised, by doing either, she would lose much of what she most values in life.[62]

The right of exit then is no right, as 'what kind of a choice is one between total submission and total alienation from the person she understands herself to be?'.[63] Thus, Okin concludes that a right of exit is inadequate protection and moreover that 'women may well be harmed rather than benefited by special group rights'.[64]

If Okin is correct and vulnerable individuals (in this instance women) are not protected by the right of exit and therefore harmed by the establishment of group rights, we should consider carefully whether what we hope to protect in group rights really is valuable enough to justify such norms. Thus criticism of substantive group rights suggests that any model – such as the corporate model – which threatens the primacy of individual rights or runs the risk of subordinating group members to the wishes of the group should be eschewed. This would seem to support a conclusion that we should adopt a collective model of groups and their rights as it is derived from, and ultimately reduces to, individual rights and interests. Thus we will now consider the collective model of groups and their rights and in particular ask whether they can protect the group rights and interests we have discussed, namely those of the Hagahai and those of UK Biobank participants.

Assessing the collective model

The collective understanding of rights presents group rights as following seamlessly from respecting the rights of individuals, as 'the respect and concern that generate a claim of individual right can generate a cognate claim of collective right'.[65] Because of this progression from individual interests to group rights, there is less potential for conflict between individual rights and group rights as ultimately the claims reduce to contests between individual rights. As a result, group rights

---

[61] *Ibid.*, 222.　[62] *Ibid.*, 222.　[63] *Ibid.*, 229.　[64] *Ibid.*, 207.
[65] Jones, 'Human rights', 90.

that are unduly burdensome would be rejected as unjustifiable over and against the rights of others, which would automatically ensure that individuals are not sacrificed to the collective. Thus criticisms such as Okin's regarding group rights do not apply (or at least apply less strongly) to the collective model.

A further advantage of the collective model is the simplicity with which it defines groups. Straightforwardly, what constitutes a group is merely their shared interest and thus there is no need for any prior definition of what constitutes a group or discussion about whether this group is the kind of group which is capable of being a rights bearer. For, on the collective model, 'groups may be ragged at the edges, they may overlap, some may be contained within others, some may have less than uniform memberships. None of that complexity and untidiness is fundamentally problematic for the collective conception. All we need to ask is whether, somewhere in all this sociological confusion, there is a set of individuals with a common interest that grounds a right.'[66] Therefore the problematic debate of what constitutes a group and whether this or that group is an appropriate right holder is neatly bypassed. No additional structure is needed for the establishment of right holding other than the recognition that individuals have interests and these can be pooled. On the collective model, whether a group is formed from strictly contingent interests, such as happening to live in the vicinity of a polluting factory or less contingently from shared interests in ethnicity, culture or religion, is irrelevant in this regard as 'the moral structure of the group right, understood as a collective right, is the same in both cases. The right is grounded in the interests of those who jointly hold the right.'[67] Thus it is always reducible to individuals' interests.

Given these advantages of the collective model of rights – namely that it avoids the problematic issues of what counts as a right-bearing group and the conflict with individual rights – it would seem that it is this model of groups and group rights that we should include in our bioethical framework.

Applying group models to bioethics

Such discussion leads to the conclusion that the collective model is less problematic than the corporate model and thus a preferable theoretical model. However, in order to conclude this we must consider the

[66] *Ibid.*, 65–6.   [67] *Ibid.*, 85.

effectiveness of such models, applying them to the collectives of UK
Biobank participants and the Hagahai. In short, we must answer the following questions. Is the collective model of a group sufficient to protect
the interests of both of these collectives? Or are there rights – or protections – which are available on the corporate model but not on the collective model? Does the corporate model give additional protections which
are important enough to justify arguing for some kind of corporate model
of group rights in at least some situations, despite all the difficulties this
entails? The answer to these questions would seem to be both 'Yes' and
'No': 'Yes' the collective model is sufficient to protect the group interests
of UK Biobank participants, but 'No' it is not sufficient for groups like the
Hagahai who have more substantial concerns.

The participants of UK Biobank fit with the fluid definitions of groups
adopted on the collective model; distinguished 'as a set only by their
shared interest in clean air, coastal defences, or community health measures [they] might possess collective rights to those goods, but they do
not constitute the sort of group that will possess corporate rights'.[68] For
the participants of UK Biobank, their group right does reduce to their
individual interests and they are a group in no other sense than in their
shared interest of being treated fairly by UK Biobank. They have no non-
contingent connection which makes them a group, but only a collective
interest (and on the collective model a group right) that UK Biobank uses
their material and information as promised, as entrusted, for the public
good. Thus the collective model, which is in line with bioethical thinking as it is derived from the individual model with the added advantage
of being able to accommodate groups, works well in this instance.

The difficulty comes when we consider the case of the Hagahai and
other indigenous groups. In these instances the collective construction of
the group and the attendant group rights do not appear to be enough to
protect the genetic material and information in question. Because, in the
case of groups with arguably valuable genetic make-ups or other issues of
this type, what they wish to protect does not simply equate with the interests of individual group members. For instance, as previously touched
upon, some rights – usually cited examples are of culture, ethnicity and
religion – are concerns which reach beyond the rights of currently existing individuals and 'imply a possessor that is not wholly identifiable with
a current set of individuals'.[69] This is true of certain political rights of
groups, most notably that of self-determination 'or rights to other forms of

[68] *Ibid.*, 87.   [69] Jones, 'Group rights', 367.

collective autonomy ... [which] ... cannot be convincingly disaggregated into the rights of individuals'.[70] Likewise this is true of indigenous groups and their claims to have property rights in their traditional knowledge and genomes, and is supported by the UN covenant that 'all peoples may, for their own ends, freely dispose of their natural wealth and resources without prejudice ... based upon the principle of mutual benefit'.[71] Such thinking has led to the recognition that there are some matters of fundamental importance which can only be protected by adopting substantial group models, as it is doubtful 'whether the concern and respect due to those minorities can be adequately secured merely by ascribing rights to their members individually'.[72] For example:

> Consider the right of a cultural group that its identity shall survive into the indefinite future. If there is such a right it is hard to see how it could be explained solely by reference to the interests of current members of the cultural group ... If a long-term right of cultural survival is claimed for a group it is more intelligibly claimed on the corporate than on the collective model. The same is true of some assertions of property rights. Nations are sometimes said to have rights over particular pieces of territory and tribes over particular tracts of land. Where those ownership rights are conceived as stretching back into the indefinite past and forward into the indefinite future, the 'owner' is more intelligibly conceived corporately than collectively.[73]

Such rights pertain to 'culture' but also to shared property or collective value – and here traditional knowledge and unmodified DNA would seem to fit well – where what is in question belongs not only to the individuals of the existing group but also to future generations. In addition, issues of cultural diversity and the value of preserving such diversity – the sense that there is something of value beyond the interests of existing individuals which should be protected and preserved – are also relevant. This type of ethical concern, for future generations and cultural diversity and heritage, are ethically significant and relevant to these cases; however, they are only visible on the corporate conception where the group *qua* group has moral status and rights. Likewise, as previously discussed, such groups can be harmed if their property, diversity and heritage is harmed, even if individuals within the group do not consider themselves

---

[70] *Ibid.*, 353.
[71] UN International Covenant on Civil and Political Rights, GA res. 2200A (XXI), 21 UN GAOR Supp. (No. 16) at 52, UN Doc. A/6316 (1966), 999 UNTS 171, entered into force Mar. 23, 1976, Art. 1(2).
[72] Jones, 'Group rights', 353.   [73] *Ibid.*, 367.

harmed as individuals. Such group issues are invisible on a collective model of rights just as they were on the individual models discussed at the beginning of the chapter. Thus groups which have more at stake than just contingent interests, such as the Hagahai, require a corporate conception of groups and their rights (at least in some instances) if what is ethically valuable is to be protected.

Furthermore, the corporate model gives such vulnerable groups a moral claim which cannot be outweighed by competing wishes. This is a danger for groups on the collective model as it determines which rights are granted in part by weight of numbers. For on the collective model 'the greater the number of people who share an interest, the stronger the case for that interest's grounding a right ... [and] ... the greater the number of people who enjoy a collective right in virtue of their shared interest, the weightier that collective right. Thus size matters.'[74] This is pertinent to this issue both within the group and with regard to interaction with other groups. Within the group it reduces the question of whether consent should be given to the patenting of DNA to a majority decision. This ignores, as we have discussed, myriad ethical issues pertinent to the debate (including those of power between groups, future generations and cultural identity), issues which cannot be properly addressed if rights are derived from individuals' interests. Likewise with regard to other cultures and groups, if it is the collective power of individual interests which creates rights, then small group rights will be less weighty than those of larger groups. Thus without other sources of justification (such as those granted on the corporate model which make other issues apart from individual interests ethically significant) small groups are unlikely to be adequately protected. Thus rather than the individual being overrun by the group, the fear is that small groups of individuals, such as the Hagahai, will be overrun by larger groups. The question of the weight of numbers on the collective model undermines at least some of the impetus in the initial search for group rights as it reduces the framework to individual concerns, again negating and reducing the import of the ethical issues which led us to seek group models in the first place. Thus it would seem that, despite the problems, we do need recourse to corporate models as part of our bioethical framework if we are to protect all of what is valuable to groups and to the individuals within groups.

[74] *Ibid.*, 369.

Conclusion

In sum then, if we are to protect what is valuable to groups and to address ethical issues currently neglected on individualist models of bioethics and counter actual and potential forms of injustice, group models are absolutely necessary for any comprehensive ethical framework. Moreover, our discussion of the patenting of indigenous groups' DNA suggests that, in some instances at least, we must adopt substantial models of groups and their rights which conceive of the group as an ethical locus in itself rather than just the individuals within the group. Without such corporate models bioethics will continue to be blind to concerns of groups especially when they do not reduce to concerns of individuals; for example, those connected to cultural diversity, future generations and the power of groups. This said, given the strong criticisms of such corporate models, we should be wary of overusing or giving undue priority to such corporate models and where appropriate adopt collective models of group rights. In many instances, for example that of UK Biobank, a collective model will be sufficient to provide group rights and ensure that group needs and entitlements are adequately recognised. Moreover, in all cases where group models are adopted, the fundamental insight of traditional bioethics, that of protecting the individual, arising as it did in the wake of the evils of Nazi research trials, must not be forgotten.

Thus we should attempt to use these models in parallel and balance the insights of the different conceptions so that we can clearly see, and thus be able to address, all the pertinent ethical issues – those of the individual, the family, shared interest groups and ethnic and cultural groups – and thus do justice to all the salient ethical features. Without a robust concept of groups and group rights we are unable to address instances directly when groups as well as individuals are harmed. For although harms to groups fundamentally impact upon individuals within the groups, without group models such issues can only be indirectly addressed, thus making group injustices appear obscure and less important than individual injustices, something our discussion of the communal models – from the family to the ethnic group – shows to be false.

The realities of the identifying and communal nature of genetic material, coupled with the practical needs of population genomic research, make considerations about how to structure such communal frameworks unavoidable. Rather than attempting to retain traditional models, this is an opportunity which should be embraced as an overdue moment to rectify the individualist concerns of traditional bioethics and the injustices which have followed from this model. Taken together, the traditional models and communal models should lead us to ethical frameworks which can accommodate both concerns for social and cultural justice as well as protect the individual. Therefore we must adopt sophisticated models which are capable of recognising the multifaceted nature of ethical dilemmas in the genetic and genomic context and thus see individuals, collectives and groups all as ethical loci.

5

Rights, responsibility and stewardship: beyond consent[1]

ROGER BROWNSWORD

With the prospect of an improved understanding of human genetics (as well as an accelerating application of that understanding), it is important that regulators should strike the right balance between support for the health care community (broadly conceived) and respect for the wider community's guiding values. Under conditions of ethical pluralism, this is no simple matter; for regulators will be presented with a variety of (often irreconcilable) demands.[2] For present purposes, let me focus on and contrast just two ethics – one prioritising private right, the other public good; one prioritising the autonomy of individuals, the other the good of the community; one putting a premium on informed consent, the other largely discounting or dispensing with consent (informed or otherwise).

The former ethic, strongly supported by the rights-respecting trajectory of mainstream modern bioethics, presents itself as an essential counterweight to medical paternalism and scientific ambition. So influential has this ethic become that it is now treated as axiomatic that individuals have, so to speak, a sovereign right to make informed choices about their treatment as well as about participating in research trials or studies.[3] According to this ethic, if patients or prospective participants

---

[1] A draft of this chapter, under the title 'Research and new technologies – rights overstated, responsibilities understated' was presented at the inaugural conference of the European Association of Health Law, held at the Royal Society of Edinburgh, April 10–11, 2008.

[2] Currently, the three principal competing ethical constituencies are utilitarian, human rights and dignitarian. Generally, see R. Brownsword, *Rights, Regulation and the Technological Revolution* (Oxford University Press, 2008), chs. 2–4 (on the challenge of regulatory legitimacy).

[3] See, e.g., Article 5 of the Convention on Human Rights and Biomedicine and Articles 6.1 and 6.2 of the UNESCO Universal Declaration on Bioethics and Human Rights. Council of Europe, Convention for the Protection of Human Rights and Dignity of the Human Being with regard to the Application of Biology and Medicine: Convention on Human Rights and Biomedicine CETS No 164 (Oviedo, Spain, 1997); http://conventions.coe.int/

say 'no', then medicine and science must be put on hold. By contrast, the latter ethic asserts itself in contexts where a gain can be made *either* without impinging on the 'interests' of an individual (for example, by conducting research on human embryos, or by retrieving cadaveric organs for transplantation),[4] *or* without impinging on the more important life-and-death interests of individuals (for example, by making body tissues removed in the course of surgery, biological samples or personal data more freely available to researchers). In such contexts, proponents of this latter ethic object that our obsession with individual right and with the obtaining of free and informed consent is counter-productive, allowing too many tails to wag the dog.

To a certain extent, this ethical tension is inevitable, for the former view is underwritten by an ethic of individual right and the latter by welfare-maximising utilitarianism. If rights theorists never contested utilitarian positions, and vice versa, we might well wonder what the world was coming to. We might also accept that, in the day-to-day skirmishing between these rivals, the purity of the ethic of rights will be challenged by utilitarian-inspired attempts to impose regimes that require only implicit or presumed consent, or that rely on third-party authorisation (for example, in relation to children), and the like.[5] However, *pace* Dr Pangloss, this is not the best of all possible worlds; and it is not so in two important respects. First, there is a danger that by caricaturing the significance of consent within the rights ethic, we will overstate the extent to which individual informed consent operates to constrain public interest health care projects. Secondly, if we omit to consider the responsibilities that both individuals and the state might have in a community of rights, we will understate the potential of the ethic of rights to support larger health care initiatives.[6]

---

treaty/en/treaties/html/164.htm; United Nations Educational, Scientific and Cultural Organisation (UNESCO), Universal Declaration on Bioethics and Human Rights (2005), 33C/Resolution 36.

[4] Recent examples include objections from leading scientists to explicit consent provisions in what was then the Human Fertilisation and Embryology Bill 2007–08 that might impede stem cell research (see M. Henderson, 'Ministers will rethink Bill that could block stem-cell experiments', *The Times*, 22 January 2008, 2; and proposals to introduce a presumed consent (opt-out) regime for organ donation (see BBC News Online, 'Backing for organ donor overhaul', 16 January 2008; http://news.bbc.co.uk/1/hi/uk_politics/7190168.stm).

[5] Compare R. Brownsword, 'Informed consent: to whom it may concern', *Jahrbuch für Recht und Ethik*, 15 (2007), 267.

[6] Compare M. Brazier, 'Do no harm – do patients have responsibilities too?' *Cambridge Law Journal*, 65 (2006), 397.

In this chapter, I want to begin to correct this dual tendency towards, on the one hand, overstatement and, on the other, understatement. Accordingly, my organising question is as follows: if we adopt the ethic of individual rights – which, I should emphasise, is the ethic to which Europeans are committed politically, legally and rationally[7] – and if we (i) correct for the caricaturing of the ethic of consent and (ii) tease out the full range of responsibilities implicit in such an ethic, then how far can we go towards meeting the concern that we should be doing more to support the healthcare interests of others and of the community at large?

The chapter is in two parts. In the first part, I seek to correct the tendency to overstate the constraints imposed by an ethic of rights. In particular, I seek to correct the absurd proposition that researchers may not either make use of or investigate a new technology unless those who have a view about such research have given their informed consent. To suggest that no action is legitimate unless it is backed by the consent of each and every individual who might be affected by that action, or who might have a preference for its performance or non-performance, is to commit the Fallacy of Necessity[8] – and the sooner that we eliminate this common cause of confusion, the better.

In the second part, I begin to draw out the extent of members' positive obligations to one another in a community of rights as well as considering the stewardship responsibilities of the state. My claim is that, once the ethic of individual right is fully elaborated, we will see that, beyond consent, there is the potential for larger health care activities and practices to be justified by reference to either the positive responsibilities of rights-holders or the stewardship responsibilities of the state. To be sure, such justificatory possibilities must be compatible with the guiding values of a community of rights; for it should not be thought that the object of the exercise is to compromise on rights commitments in order to effect an accommodation with utilitarianism.

That said, once we have corrected for caricature and then given due consideration to the responsibility dimension of the rights ethic, we might

---

[7] Politically, the activities of the Council of Europe speak to the commitment to human rights, all of which is given a focal legal expression in the European Convention on Human Rights (Council of Europe, The European Convention on Human Rights (Rome, 4 November 1950); www.hri.org/docs/ECHR50.html). As for rational commitment to rights, that is a much longer story but, seminally, see A. Gewirth, *Reason and Morality* (University of Chicago Press, 1978).

[8] See R. Brownsword, 'The cult of consent: fixation and fallacy', *King's College Law Journal*, 15 (2004), 223; and D. Beyleveld and R. Brownsword, *Consent in the Law* (Oxford: Hart, 2007).

all be surprised – defenders and critics of the ethic alike – at how far it might go in supporting research purposes that are designed to advance the public interest.

Overstating constraint

In some ethics, dignitarianism being the obvious case, the fact that an individual has consented to an action simply does not count: where the act in question is judged to compromise human dignity, it cannot be corrected by consent. By contrast, in those ethics that recognise that consent functions as a material authorisation, the obtaining of consent is a precondition to justified action. However, each of the ethical approaches in the latter category has its own distinctive take on consent – for example, whereas in a utilitarian ethic, consent is viewed as a tax on transactions and interactions, in ethics of individual right and duty, consent is integral to the background scheme of rights and duties. In what follows, I will focus on consent in what I call a community of rights,[9] this being the most natural home for an ethic that takes consent seriously.[10]

Consent in a community of rights

In a community of rights, the principal (but not exclusive) function of consent is to authorise an act that would otherwise constitute a violation of a right. Here, the consenting agent, A, is precluded from raising a complaint about the conduct of the recipient agent, B (B's 'wrongdoing' as it otherwise would be).

We can find a ready illustration in data protection law. This, it scarcely needs saying, is a field of law that is of particular relevance to researchers and, indeed, to many new technologies. It is also a body of law that has achieved some notoriety in the research community, where it is frequently perceived to be a source of ill-judged restriction, impeding legitimate research purposes.[11] It has even been suggested that compliance with data protection law is, in effect, 'killing patients'.[12]

---

[9] For my specification of a 'community of rights', see Brownsword, *Technological Revolution*, chs. 2–4.

[10] See Beyleveld and Brownsword, *Consent in the Law*.

[11] See, e.g., the concerns expressed in Academy of Medical Sciences, *Personal Data for Public Good: Using Health Information in Medical Research* (London, January 2006).

[12] For guidance, see Parliamentary Office of Science and Technology, 'Data protection and medical research', *Postnote*, 235 (2005). For relevant references and a sober assessment,

Turning to the legislation, in the first clause of Recital 33 of Directive 95/46/EC, we read:

> Whereas data which are capable by their nature of infringing fundamental freedoms or privacy should not be processed unless the data subject gives his explicit consent.[13]

This principle is articulated in Articles 7 and 8 of the Directive. So, to take the clearer exemplification, Article 8.1, which deals with the processing of what it calls 'special categories of data', requires member states to prohibit 'the processing of personal data revealing racial or ethnic origin, political opinions, religious or philosophical beliefs, trade-union membership, [or] … concerning health or sex life'. However, where 'the data subject has given his explicit consent to the processing of those data', then Article 8.2 lifts the prohibition. To express this more straightforwardly in rights terms: agents have a right which covers the processing of certain special categories of data; but, where an agent consents to the processing of such data, then that agent is precluded from asserting a wrongdoing (at any rate, so long as the processing is within the scope of the consent).

It is in this way that, in a rights-based regime, consent functions as a justifying reason. However, precisely because B relies on A's authorisation for the doing of x rather than on the rightness of the doing of x itself, it becomes clear that consent operates as a distinctive form of justification. In particular, we should note the following three distinguishing features of 'consent as a justification'. First, consent functions as a 'procedural' rather than as a 'substantive' (or, 'on the merits') form of justification. Secondly, as a procedural justification, consent amounts to a limited 'in personam' (or 'agent-relative') response. Consent does not comprehensively justify the action as such; rather, the consenting agent is precluded from asserting that he or she has been wronged. Thirdly, where consent is relied on as a shield, it justifies by way of negating a wrong rather than by way of overriding a right. Each of these features merits a word or two of explanation.

see D. Beyleveld, 'Medical research and the public good', *Kings Law Journal*, 18, 2 (2007), 286–7. For the official response, see P. Boyd, 'The requirements of the Data Protection Act 1998 for the processing of medical data', *Journal of Medical Ethics*, 29, (2003), 34; and UK Information Commissioner's Office: www.dataprotection.gov.uk/dpr/dpdoc.nsf.

[13] European Parliament and Council Directive 95/46/EC on the protection of individuals with regard to the processing of personal data and on the free movement of such data [1995] OJ L 281/31.

First, whereas a substantive (or, 'on the merits') form of justification refers to some set of background standards characterising (in the justificatory argument) particular acts as permitted (including required), a procedural justification refers to an authorising act or decision. For example, if agent B (an epidemiologist) contends that it is permissible to consult patients' medical records in a certain mining area because the information will contribute to our understanding of a particular dust disease, he relies on a substantive justification (resting on the permissibility of actions that are calculated to improve public health or develop therapies for a particular condition). By contrast, if agent B claims to be so entitled by reference to the consent of the patients or certain doctors or health officials, or his research sponsor, then the justification does not rest on background standards, contested or otherwise; rather the claimed justification is procedural in the sense that B relies on some authorising act or decision, not background standards, to assert the permissibility of the particular actions in question.

Secondly, where consent is relied on, it justifies 'in personam' (that is, only in an 'agent-relative' way). The consenting agent, but only the consenting agent, is precluded from asserting that he or she has been wronged. In other words, although agent A, who has consented to the doing of x by agent B, is precluded from asserting that the doing of x violates A's rights, this does not make the doing of x right *tout court* (i.e., right as against all comers). So, if the complaint about B's accessing of the medical records comes from those who have so consented, then B may respond that such complaints by such parties are precluded by their consent. However, none of this justifies the carrying out of the research as such. Other agents might have grounds for complaint to which it is no answer for B to rely on A's consent. In other words, even if A's consent gives B a complete answer to A, it might give B no answer at all to C (for example, to a patient who has not consented).

Thirdly, where B relies on A's consent as a justification, B does so in order to negate what would otherwise be a wrong in relation to A. To put this another way, given that A's consent *authorises* the action in question, it must follow that B, by doing the authorised act x, does no wrong to A. A's consent to B doing x entails that, as between A and B, the doing of x by B is permissible. This is to be distinguished from treating the doing of x by B as justified by reference to overriding rights, or all things considered as the lesser of two wrongs. In such a case, where A has not consented to the doing of x by B, and where the doing of x violates A's rights, then the doing of x, even if justified all things considered, involves a wrong to A. Now, if we return to our illustrative case, Articles 7 and 8 of the Directive, we find that the legislative scheme recognises the possibility of both procedural and substantive forms of justification. Thus, the prohibitions against data processing are disapplied where either (i) the data subject has consented to the processing, or (ii) one of the other justifying reasons (listed in the Directive) applies – for example, where B processes data without A's (the data subject's) consent, but this is necessary in order to save A's life or to save C's life.[14] In other words, data processors might seek to justify their actions procedurally, by relying on the data subject's consent, or substantively, by relying on a compelling, overriding reason.

Putting these three distinguishing features together we have the following. In a community of rights, consent functions as a procedural justification, giving the recipient of the consent (B) a complete answer to the consenting agent (A); no wrong is done to the consenting (authorising) agent (A) by the recipient agent (B); but it does not follow that the recipient agent (B) does no wrong to third-party agents (such as C). In the absence of consent, a wrong will be done to agents whose rights are violated even if, all things considered, the wrongdoing can be substantively justified as the lesser of two evils.

The attraction of consent as a justifying reason is not hard to understand. Quite simply, not only does consent provide the recipient, B, with a complete answer to the consenting agent, A, but it does so without the former having to engage contestable substantive justifications – or, at any rate, such 'on the merits' justifications do not have to be offered to the consenting party (even if such substantive justifications cannot be altogether avoided in relation to third parties).

Nevertheless, the lifeline offered by consent as a justification should not be abused. If we are to take consent seriously, at a practical level, we must guard against the 'routinisation' of consent; it will not do simply to direct a would-be consenting agent to 'sign here and here' or to 'just tick the box'. Nor, of course, will it do to treat the giving of notice (that data will be processed) and the absence of objection as if it were an informed consent that is properly signalled as such. Steps should be taken to ensure that the standards governing the adequacy of consent are fully articulated and stringently applied. The collection of consent, however commonplace, should not be approached in a mechanical or a perfunctory

---

[14] *Ibid.*, Articles 7(d) and 8(c) (processing necessary in order to protect the vital interests of the data subject), and Article 8.3 (processing required for the purposes of preventive medicine, medical diagnosis, the provision of care or treatment, and so on).

manner. Equally, we must discourage lazy or casual appeals to consent. Where substantive justification is called for, we should settle for nothing less; in particular, we should not be satisfied with artificial procedural justifications that are tendered in their place.[15] Conversely, where substantive arguments are called for to support condemnation of a particular act or practice, they should not be suppressed in favour of a more convenient, procedural objection to the effect that no adequate covering consents are in place. In every way, procedural justification should respect the ideals of transparency.

In sum, we begin to understand consent once we appreciate that it has an important role to play in justificatory arguments; and we refine that understanding once we distinguish between appeals to procedural and substantive considerations. However, we should not make the mistake of thinking that consent as a procedural justification is the whole justificatory story.

Caricature and the Fallacy of Necessity

If some communities undervalue and fictionalise consent, then others can overvalue it, becoming fixated with the twin ideas that consent is proof against any kind of wrong, and that an absence of consent is a cause for complaint. It is important not to get carried away with consent to the point where simple fallacies become written into our practical reason. Two fallacies are pervasive. One, the fallacy of treating consent as a sufficient justifying reason (the Fallacy of Sufficiency),[16] is not material to the present discussion. However, the other fallacy, the Fallacy of Necessity, is fundamental.

The Fallacy of Necessity, the fallacy of thinking that it is necessary to have an agent's consent before an action that impacts on the agent's plans or preferences can be justified, encourages two mistakes. One mistake is to think that where there is no consent there must be a wrong; and the other is to think that consent offers the only justification in response to a prima facie wrong.

The first articulation of this fallacy can be expressed very simply: if (as a matter of substantive justification) an act is morally permissible, if no right is engaged, then informed consent is simply not required. Crucially,

---

[15] For an egregious example, see *Strunk* v. *Strunk* 445 SW 2d 145 (Ky 1969); and, for general discussion, see Beyleveld and Brownsword, *Consent in the Law*, ch. 4.

[16] See Brownsword, 'The cult of consent'.

what determines whether an act is morally permissible is not the presence or absence of consent but the application of background rights and duties; if no right is infringed, then there is no wrong for consent to cure. So, for example, the claims made by the supermodel Naomi Campbell[17] and, more recently, by the author J. K. Rowling[18] that press photographers violated their privacy would not get to first base unless a relevant legal right (for example, the privacy right expressed by Article 8(1) of the European Convention on Human Rights (ECHR) or the common law right of confidentiality) was engaged. If such a right was not engaged, the fact that Campbell and Rowling had not consented to the coverage was irrelevant. If, however, the right to privacy was engaged, then for the press to proceed without the consent of the rights-holding celebrities would involve the commission of a prima facie wrong.

The second articulation of the fallacy holds that, where there is an unauthorised violation of a right (the right holder not having consented to the act in question), then the act simply cannot be justified. However, in a rights ethic, even an unauthorised violation might be justified exceptionally as the lesser of two evils, that is to say, where the (rights-infringing) act is designed to serve a more important (higher-ranking) right. Hence, to return to the Campbell and Rowling cases, if we assume that there was an unauthorised violation of a privacy right, the burden is transferred to the press to show that its coverage was justifiable all things considered, being a necessary and proportionate act designed to serve more compelling rights (such as the Article 10 ECHR right to freedom of expression). In other words, notwithstanding the lack of consent to the coverage, the press might have argued that the acts in question were legitimate, either because they were morally permissible *simpliciter* (no rights were engaged) or because, all things considered, they amounted to the lesser of two evils. To assume that Campbell or Rowling's lack of consent entails wrongdoing, without considering either the non-engagement of a right or the possibility of an overriding rights justification, is to commit the Fallacy of Necessity.

By way of further illustration, recall the alleged data misuse that was tested out in the *Source Informatics*[19] case. There, the question was whether the Department of Health had stated the legal position correctly in advising that there would be a breach of confidence if patients' prescription

[17] *Naomi Campbell* v. *Mirror Group Newspapers* [2004] UKHL 22.
[18] *Murray* v. *Express Newspapers plc* [2007] EWHC 1908 (Ch).
[19] *R* v. *Department of Health ex parte Source Informatics Ltd* [1999] 4 All ER 185; [2001] QB 424 (CA).

information, albeit in an anonymised form, was commercially exploited without their consent.[20] Simply pleading a lack of consent would not suffice; the patients would be wronged only if one of their rights was violated. At first instance, Latham J (seemingly attributing a proprietary right to the patients) ruled that the Department's advice was correct. However, this ruling was reversed by the Court of Appeal, where it was held that there would be a breach of confidence only if the prescription information was used unfairly against patients, which in turn hinged on whether the patients' privacy right was infringed; and, on this point, the Court, recognising only a narrowly conceived privacy right, held that the right would not be infringed provided that the information was anonymised. Had the information not been anonymised, the patients' lack of consent to the processing would have been decisive – not in a free-standing way, but by virtue of there being no consent-based cover for the infringement of the privacy right.[21]

To turn *Source Informatics* round, let us suppose that a claim were to be made by a patient who did not wish to be given information about his or her own genetic make-up. The claimant protests, 'I did not consent to this; I did not wish to know.' To get such a claim up and running, the claimant must focus, not on the absence of consent, but on the underpinning 'right not to know'.[22] Whether or not such an underpinning right is, or should be, recognised is not the present issue. Rather, the point is that, before we criticise the law or a particular court decision as making too much or too little of consent, we should check to establish whether a relevant right is engaged.

Once we are clear about the way in which consent functions interstitially within a framework of background rights and duties,[23] then

[20] For criticism, see, e.g., D. Beyleveld and E. Histed, 'Betrayal of confidence in the Court of Appeal', *Medical Law International*, 4 (2000), 277–311; D. Beyleveld, 'Conceptualising privacy in relation to medical research values', in S. A. M. McLean (ed.), *First Do No Harm* (Aldershot: Ashgate, 2006), 152–4; and G. Laurie, *Genetic Privacy* (Cambridge University Press, 2002).

[21] The patients' lack of consent would also have been decisive if, for example, the privacy right was understood more broadly, or if (as Latham J thought) a proprietary interest was implicated. Moreover, on any such analysis, the act of anonymising the information would be an unauthorised act and a prima facie breach of the patients' rights.

[22] Background support for such a 'right not to know' is provided by Article 10(2) of the Convention on Human Rights and Biomedicine, 1996, and by Article 5(c) of the UNESCO Universal Declaration on the Human Genome and Human Rights, (1997), 29 C/Resolution 16.

[23] Compare N. C. Manson and O. O'Neill, *Rethinking Informed Consent in Bioethics* (Cambridge University Press, 2007).

we should not make the mistake of treating an absence of consent as necessarily a constraint on either research or the application of new technologies. The prior question is whether the proposed action impinges on the rights of others. If it does, then consent becomes an issue; although, even then, there might be other justifications available. If the action does not impinge on a right, if the action is permissible, the ethic of right will regard it as justifiable irrespective of whether consent has been given.

Does it follow from this analysis that the research community is exercising too much restraint by being overrespectful of rights and the requirements of informed consent? The answer is 'possibly so' but we need to be very careful about how we understand this response. This response does not offer any encouragement to accord less respect to rights, *where rights are in play*; and, similarly, it offers no encouragement to be less attentive to the requirements of informed consent, *also when relevant rights are in play*. However, where relevant rights are *not* in play, the research community should treat itself as free to proceed without being concerned about consent clearance, or the like. There is the further possibility that the research community might tend to draw back from an initiative where rights are in play, even though such an initiative would be justified, all things considered, by reference to competing or conflicting rights. However, caution in such circumstances is a good instinct: for, even if there is an all things considered justification, care needs to be taken where an initiative involves the infringement of a prima facie right. In general, and whenever possible, it is probably better for regulators to signal priorities between rights rather than leaving the judgment to health care professionals and researchers.

Understating rights-based responsibility

Two questions that present themselves to a community of rights are: (i) whether (and, if so, which) positive rights should be recognised within the *background* set of standards; and (ii) whether the state has any kind of stewardship responsibility that requires, and authorises, it to take action that would not be justifiable if it were to be taken by an individual agent.

With regard to the first of these questions, if we want to take the ethic of individual right in a direction that is more responsive to the health care needs of others, it is not sufficient to intone that where there are rights there are also responsibilities. For the deontic logic of rights theory

already tells us as much: the correlative of A having a negative right, that
B does not act in ways that are harmful to A, is that B has a responsibility not to act in ways that are harmful to A; and, once we universalise
this standard, A, too, will have a responsibility not to act in a way that is
harmful to B. The aspect of responsibility that really matters is whether
it reaches beyond negative restraint to acts of assistance. In other words,
the question is whether the ethic of individual right implies positive as
well as negative responsibilities to others. If we assume that such an ethic
allows for individuals voluntarily to accept positive obligations to others
(most obviously by freely promising to assist others), the focal question
becomes whether positive responsibilities are recognised by such an ethic
as part of the (imposed) background obligations of rights holders. I will
argue that positive responsibilities are an important feature of the background commitments of rights holders.

With regard to the second question, the issue is whether, in a community of rights, the state stands in just the same position as one of its rights-
holding subjects, justifiably acting against prima facie rights only where
the right-holder has consented or where it has an overriding rights reason for so acting (and, even then, subject to limits of proportionality and
necessity). Against this restrictive view, it is arguable that rights-holders
need to make some allowance for the state's responsibility as steward for
the community – or, more precisely, as steward for those essential conditions without which the community cannot survive or function. For
example, where individual choices are cumulatively corrosive of the infrastructure (physical and moral) of such a community, it is arguable that the
state would be justified in taking preventive and precautionary measures;
but stewardship might also justify state-backed measures to support the
activities of researchers who are using or seeking to develop technologies
that contribute to the defence of these essential conditions.[24]

In this part of the chapter, I will start with the question of an
agent's positive responsibilities and then consider the question of state
stewardship.

Positive responsibilities

To what extent are agents required to offer aid and assistance to others?
I will respond to this question in two stages, first by setting out some

---

[24] For a conspectus of the conditions that are essential for the survival of civilised human
communities, see J. Martin, *The Meaning of the 21st Century* (London: Transworld
Publishers, 2007).

general guidelines for the recognition of positive obligations and then by applying these guidelines to a couple of test cases that arise in relation to the operation of UK Biobank.

To start with first principles, I take it that no community of rights would reject the very idea of background positive requirements. In which case, the real question concerns the conditions that the community would set for the recognition of background positive obligations. I suggest that the conditions set would reflect the community's understanding and application of three guiding considerations. First, there are considerations of rational prescription. In any community that accepts the basic canons of rational prescription, an agent will only be required to assist another where 'ought implies can' is satisfied. It follows that no agent will be burdened with a positive obligation unless they are capable of rendering assistance. If we are to prescribe that A ought to assist B, then the demands that we make of A should at least be within A's capabilities. Secondly, there are considerations of reasonableness. How much can we reasonably demand of A? We can imagine a hypothetical situation in which it would seem to be little more than a minor inconvenience for A to assist B. However, the circumstances might be very different. For example, if A would put his own life at risk by assisting B, would we *require* such a heroic act (or would this be a case of supererogation)? Thirdly, there are considerations of fairness. Even in a community that recognises positive rights, the default position is represented by 'can implies ought' – that is to say, the default expectation is that those who are capable of helping themselves should do so.

Arguably, drawing on these considerations, a four-stage test along the following lines might be formulated for the recognition of particular background prima facie positive rights and responsibilities:[25]

(i)   Is A in a position to assist B?
(ii) Does A have the capability to assist B in any material respect?
(iii) Even though A is in a position to assist B and has the relevant capability, would the burden of responsibility on A be unreasonable relative to A's own essential interests?
(iv) Even though A is in a position to assist B, has the relevant capability, and the imposition of responsibility on A would not be

[25] It should be emphasised that this test only takes the community as far as recognising prima facie responsibilities. Even if A is judged to have a prima facie positive obligation in relation to B, there might yet be competing or conflicting rights-based claims to be arbitrated.

unreasonable (relative to A's essential interests), would B be taking unfair advantage of A if A were required to assist B?

Quite clearly, there is still a great deal of interpretive work to be done on these general principles, particularly in relation to the pivotal notions of 'unreasonable imposition', 'essential interests' and 'unfair advantage taking'. Let us suppose that the community, recognising that these are slippery notions, tries to stabilise the four-stage test by focusing on the common needs of all agents, irrespective of their particular purposes, plans or projects – for example, the need of all agents for life and a level of basic physical and psychological well-being. With this focus, the community can say that A is not required to attempt to rescue B where this would jeopardise A's own life (this would be an unreasonable imposition) and, similarly, that A is not required to assist B where B is in no danger but simply wants A to assist him in relation to the fulfilment of some non-essential purpose (this would be an unreasonable demand that amounts to an example of unfair advantage taking).

Even with the test stabilised in this way, the community will also be mindful of a troubling pair of puzzles that threaten to undermine the practicability of any regime of positive rights. Stated shortly, one puzzle arises where A is not the only eligible rescuer. The question then is why we should single out A as the person responsible for assisting B. The converse puzzle arises where it is not just B, but B, C, and D who are in difficulty and A simply cannot assist all three. Here, the question is why we should single out, say, B as the agent to be assisted. For sure, the lesson to be taken from these puzzles is not that A is released from his positive obligation to assist (because, in the first case, others are also able to assist or because, in the second case, he cannot assist all three distressed agents). Rather, the lesson is that the community needs to articulate some principles of relative priority in relation to the bearers of positive duties (for the first kind of case) as well as those who are positive rights-holders (for the second kind of case).

In the light of these framework principles, we can turn to UK Biobank[26] as a test case for positive responsibility. Consider these two questions: (i) do agents have a positive obligation to offer to participate in UK Biobank (or to participate if called upon); and (ii) does UK Biobank have a positive obligation to feedback health information to participants?

---

[26] See www.ukbiobank.ac.uk; and J. V. McHale, 'Regulating genetic databases: some legal and ethical issues', *Medical Law Review*, 12 (2004), 70–96.

Following extensive criticism of the Icelandic model of biobanking, the culture is very much opposed to any kind of non-consensual participation. However, if the question were to be put to the test, what would be the view of a community of rights? Let us suppose that it was argued that, just as with jury service, a certain range of individuals might be required to participate in UK Biobank. Could this be plausibly treated as a matter of background positive obligation?[27]

We can take it that the obligation would be restricted to those who are in a position to assist and who have the relevant capability. As with jury service, this might narrow the field slightly; but, for the most part, agents would not be able to escape the imposition of positive responsibility on either of the first two grounds. To give up time, to give up samples, and to supply information for the benefit of UK Biobank is a little inconvenient; but it is an inconvenience of a minor nature that nowhere near approaches an agent's essential interests. On the other side, where UK Biobank is seeking a better understanding of life-threatening diseases, we are, by contrast, very much in the area of essential agency interests. Granted, if we treat participation in UK Biobank as a matter of positive responsibility, it might be objected that we are stretching the paradigm of positive obligation: for there is no guarantee that A's act of assistance will actually yield life-saving information, or life-saving treatment, for any agent B; and, if it does (happily) yield such information or treatment, it will be for an as yet unidentified B many years in the future. Even so, we might still think that such speculative acts of assistance are within the spirit of positive requirement. If so, and other things being equal,[28] we will judge that there is no unfair advantage taking by UK Biobank. In other words, we will judge that the third and fourth tests, too, are satisfied. So far so good for the research community: if researchers wished to take a stronger approach to public participation in UK Biobank, or similar projects, they might be justified in doing so.

What about the possibility of the UK Biobank itself having enhanced responsibilities? The Ethics and Governance Framework (EGF)[29] for the UK Biobank seeks to ensure that participants fully understand the

---

[27] Compare S. D. Pattinson, *Medical Law and Ethics* (London: Sweet and Maxwell, 2006) 345–7.

[28] If the data held by UK Biobank is to be commercially exploited, this might raise some complications: other things, then, might not be equal.

[29] UK Biobank Ethics and Governance Framework (version 2.0, July 2006). Available at www.ukbiobank.ac.uk.

purpose of UK Biobank, crucially that it is not a healthcare programme but a research resource. At enrolment, participants are to be provided with some very basic data concerning their blood pressure, body mass index, estimated amount of fat and the like.[30] However, the overriding message is that 'UK Biobank will generally not provide health information to participants …'[31] In the EGF, the rationale for this policy of non-disclosure is put in the following way:

> In normal healthcare settings, tests are conducted at the individual level immediately after sample collection; they search for specific conditions or outcomes; and, in the case of genetic tests, pre- and post-test counselling is provided. But, given the lack of knowledge at recruitment about the tests that might be done in this research context (and, hence, the inability to provide specific counselling beforehand), UK Biobank will not provide participants with information (genetic or otherwise) about their own individual results derived from examination of the database or samples by research undertaken after enrolment.[32]

So, on the side of the participants, there should be no therapeutic misconception. Nevertheless, one can imagine an exceptional and urgent case where the research team realises that a particular participant has a serious health problem of which the latter is unaware. What then? According to Alastair Campbell (the first Chair of the Ethics and Governance Council):

> There will be a provision for communication of initial seriously abnormal findings, for example, indicators of diabetes or advanced cancer, but this will only be exceptional, and recruitment materials will not mention it, since it could give the false impression that no communication from Biobank meant a 'clean bill of health'.[33]

Suppose, though, that this compromise comes unstuck. Suppose that an aggrieved participant claims that UK Biobank has a background responsibility to inform participants of life-threatening conditions. How might such a claim fare relative to the four-stage test?[34]

[30] *Ibid.*, p. 8, para. I.B.3.
[31] *Ibid.* The matter, however, continues to be under review: see UK Biobank Ethics and Governance Council: *Annual Review* 2007, 16 (under 'Enhancement of UK Biobank's protocol').
[32] UK Biobank Ethics and Governance Framework (version 2.0, July 2006), 9.
[33] A. V. Campbell, 'The ethical challenges of biobanks: safeguarding altruism and trust', in S. A. M. McLean (ed.), *First Do No Harm* (Aldershot: Ashgate, 2006), 208, note 15.
[34] For discussion of how such a claim might fare under current English tort law, see C. Johnston and J. Kaye, 'Does the UK Biobank have a legal obligation to feedback individual findings to participants?', *Medical Law Review*, 12 (2004), 239–67.

The first question, under the four-stage test, is whether UK Biobank is in a position to assist one of its volunteer participants. Plainly, it is.[35] There is also a short answer to the second question. UK Biobank has information that is material to the health and well-being of a participant. It has the capability to disclose that information; the question is whether it is required to do so.

The next step, the third stage, is to consider whether the demand made of UK Biobank is unreasonable relative to its own essential interests. Left to a subjective account of its essential interests, UK Biobank (conceived as an aggregate of agents) might well argue that it is in the business of research and that the reasonableness of any obligation to feed back clinical information should be judged relative to this fundamental mission. However, this is just the kind of special pleading that the community has neutralised by tying the notion of essential interests to those basic interests shared by all agents. No doubt, the burden of contacting and informing participants is more than trivial; but the imposition on responsible agents falls a long way short of being unreasonable.

Where, as we are assuming, the information relates to a serious medical condition, then the essential interests of participants are implicated. Hence, at the fourth stage, the demand to be informed is entirely reasonable and there is no hint of unfair advantage taking. Moreover, given that participants receive no significant material or financial inducement, they are immune to any accusation of free-riding, or the like.

Seemingly, then, UK Biobank has a prima facie background obligation to feed back to participants important personal medical information where it happens to have it. This is not to suggest that researchers should actively seek out such information for all participants or offer treatment to them; and nor does this discount the possibility that UK Biobank might face competing or conflicting rights claims advanced by the potential beneficiaries of its research activities. Nevertheless, relative to the four-stage test, a participant's claimed right to be informed where UK Biobank knowingly holds (and withholds) relevant medical information surely gets to first base.

Yet, is this not to overlook the steps explicitly taken by UK Biobank to caution participants against thinking that it has any kind of clinical function? How can UK Biobank possibly have a positive feedback responsibility when it disclaims very clearly any such obligation? This is an important

---

[35] Indeed, in the light of the emphasis placed by UK Biobank on building long-term and close relationships with its participants, it seems almost to have encouraged participants to believe that a special responsibility has been assumed.

question; but, when we recall the analysis of consent in the previous part of the chapter, the answer can be given quite summarily. If it is claimed that participants have a positive right to clinical feedback where life-threatening conditions are implicated, then we need to establish whether such a right is recognised within the background scheme of rights and responsibilities or whether it arises only by way of voluntary assumption. In other words, is clinical feedback covered by background or by foreground rights and responsibilities? The point just raised in defence of UK Biobank rather assumes that the feedback responsibility arises, if at all, only by virtue of (foreground) voluntary assumption – and that, on the facts, there clearly is no such assumption of obligation. If, however, as we have been arguing, the feedback responsibility arises by way of a background positive right, then it cannot be resisted simply by one-sided denial. In other words, if A has a (background) positive right that B undertake certain acts of assistance for A's benefit, B cannot avoid that responsibility simply by declaring that no such right or responsibility is recognised or assumed. Of course, B might still argue that no such responsibility arises because A has consented to B's release from the responsibility in question; and UK Biobank might follow this lead by arguing that participants have consented to a release of the relevant feedback responsibility. However, before we would accept that a right-holder has consented to a release of either a negative or a positive responsibility, we would want a much clearer signal than a sequence of acts, one of which is a disclaimer of responsibility or notice of non-responsibility by the agent(s) who bears the relevant background negative or positive obligation. Accordingly, a simple declaration, denial or confession of non-responsibility on the part of UK Biobank is unlikely to be regarded as sufficient to preclude the rights-holder asserting and insisting upon the former's responsibility.

This analysis of positive rights and responsibilities is not entirely good news for the research community. In a community of rights, the stakes are raised all round. Agents might be judged to have enhanced positive responsibilities to assist researchers; but researchers in turn are likely to be judged to have enhanced responsibilities to their research participants – at any rate, this will be so unless they make special efforts to obtain the consent of the agents, not simply to participate, but specifically to waive the benefit of the protections that they have by virtue of the background regime of positive rights and responsibilities.[36]

[36] Compare R. Brownsword, 'The ancillary-care responsibilities of researchers: reasonable but not great expectations', *Journal of Law, Medicine and Ethics*, 35 (2007), 679.

State stewardship

Even if we judge that, in a community of rights, background positive responsibilities are engaged only exceptionally, essentially in life-and-death emergencies, we still need to consider the state's stewardship responsibilities. If the state has (stewardship) responsibilities for the collective well-being of the community, this might involve some extension of the positive obligations of citizens.

We can introduce the possibility of state stewardship by considering the Nuffield Council on Bioethics' recent report on the ethics of public health.[37] Here, the Council takes as its guiding standard Millian liberal principles modified by a principle of state stewardship.[38] While the liberal principles resist the idea that coercion may be legitimately applied against an agent unless their conduct creates a clear and present threat of harm to others, stewardship extends the range of legitimate state intervention (although, according to the Council, coercive measures should be treated as a last resort). The resulting stewardship model holds that legitimate public health interventions should:

- aim to reduce the risks of ill health that people might impose on each other;
- aim to reduce causes of ill health by regulations that ensure environmental conditions that sustain good health, such as the provision of clean air and water, safe food and decent housing;
- pay special attention to the health of children and other vulnerable people;
- promote health not only by providing information and advice, but also with programmes to help people to overcome addictions and other unhealthy behaviours;
- aim to ensure that it is easy for people to lead a healthy life, for example by providing convenient and safe opportunities for exercise;
- ensure that people have appropriate access to medical services; and
- aim to reduce unfair health inequalities.[39]

Although the legitimacy of these interventions is not predicated on obtaining each individual's informed consent, the Council recognises that, wherever possible, it is better to respect personal choice and individual consent, as well as avoid coercive measures. Accordingly,

---

[37] Nuffield Council on Bioethics, *Public Health: Ethical Issues* (London: Nuffield Council on Bioethics, 2007).
[38] *Ibid.*, ch. 2.   [39] *Ibid.*, para. 2.44.

the stewardship version of liberalism specifies that public health programmes should:

- not attempt to coerce adults to lead healthy lives;
- minimise interventions that are introduced without the individual consent of those affected, or without procedural justice arrangements (such as democratic decision-making procedures) which provide an adequate mandate; and
- seek to minimise interventions that are perceived as unduly intrusive and in conflict with important personal values.[40]

Some of these extensions of Mill are relatively easy cases for stewardship – for example, interventions that address the care of children, that provide information about the risks to health associated with certain foods, drinks, or lifestyles, that offer facilities that are designed to help to overcome addiction, and the like. Few, too, would question the state's responsibility for ensuring the basic environmental conditions that are essential for public health. However, this aspect of the state's responsibility is given a subtle twist once we extend it to a self-conscious staging of everyday circumstances so that they are defaulted in a way that is conducive to public health. Nevertheless, provided that the default setting (say, for walking or using stairs) co-exists with alternatives (say, for riding or using lifts or escalators), this seems to keep faith with Millian liberal principles while exercising stewardship in a way that tilts conditions towards public health.[41] More controversially, the Council also relies on stewardship to reduce unfair health inequalities. Clearly, any manifesto that aspires to equalise the conditions of public health or to eliminate unfairness in access to health resources is open to interpretation. However, in so far as these extensions relate closely to the conditions that are judged to be essential for any prospect of agency, this seems to me to be entirely defensible relative to the broad commitments of a community of rights.

We might, however, take the idea of stewardship beyond matters of public health and safety, and indeed the integrity (for health purposes) of the environment. Elsewhere, I have suggested that, in a community of rights, there will be support for the state being entrusted with a

---

[40] *Ibid.* These constraints are open to a number of interpretations. In a community of rights, they would be expressed in a more focused rights-respecting way.
[41] Compare the idea of 'libertarian paternalism' elaborated by C. Sunstein (with R. Thaler) in *Laws of Fear* (Cambridge University Press, 2005), ch. 8.

stewardship responsibility for the *moral* welfare of the community.[42] At its most profound, the state's stewardship responsibility is to ensure that the enthusiasm that regulators begin to display for technological instruments of control does not insidiously undermine the conditions that give moral life its meaning.[43] However, if the state is not to tilt from its liberal disposition to a more authoritarian form, it is imperative that we are clear about both the basis and the boundaries of stewardship.

To start with the basis of stewardship: in a community of rights, we can assume that the state will need special reasons for interfering with acts that are to be treated as prima facie permissible – whether because they do not obviously impinge on the rights of others or because the relevant others have consented and there is no impingement on non-consenting third parties. Moreover, we can assume that where individual agents act, alone or in concert, in ways that seem to be permissible, the state has the burden of justification if it is to intervene against such acts. As Han Somsen has rightly pointed out,[44] to license the state to intervene on the grounds that the acts in question *might* be damaging to rights-holders or *might* be damaging to the community is to put a considerable trust in both the sound judgment and the good faith of the state. In *a community of rights*, we can define away this particular difficulty; for it is an analytical truth that, *in such a community*, the state simply will not act in bad faith or in a way that is clearly incompatible with the community's rights commitments. Once we remove this safety net, however, there is no guarantee that stewardship, like precautionary restriction, will not serve as a Trojan Horse for disreputable regulatory purposes. Lacking such a guarantee, it is an open question how far we might want to go with the idea of a stewardship responsibility.

To take a step back, if it is agreed that the state needs special reasons for interfering with prima facie permitted acts, we might argue for a lower or a higher threshold for legitimate state intervention. If we argue for the higher threshold, we are, in effect, treating the state as no different from an individual agent. In the absence of consent, the state should not

---

[42] See, e.g., R. Brownsword, 'Happy families, consenting couples, and children with dignity: sex selection and saviour siblings', *Child and Family Law Quarterly*, 17 (2005), 435–73.

[43] For extended discussion of this issue, see Brownsword, *Technological Revolution*, chs. 8–10.

[44] H. Somsen, 'Cloning Trojan Horses: precautionary regulation of reproductive technologies', in R. Brownsword and K. Yeung (eds.), *Regulating Technologies* (Oxford: Hart, 2008), 221.

prohibit or otherwise impede an agent's act unless this is necessary for the sake of more compelling rights.[45] By contrast, if we argue for a lower threshold, our view is that, in addition to the reasons that are adequate relative to the higher threshold, the state may (indeed, should) exercise a stewardship responsibility. Quite possibly, those who view the state as an unwelcome extension of private relationships will tend towards the former view, while those who start with a public law perspective will tend towards the latter view. Clearly, though, whether our mindset is private or public, we will want to see the boundaries of stewardship closely defined.

What, then, are the boundaries of stewardship? I suggest that, in a community of rights, there are three circumstances in which stewardship might legitimately be invoked. Briefly, these conditions are: (i) where state intervention is required in order to settle doubts (at least provisionally) about the application of the rights regime; (ii) where state intervention is required in order to maintain the physical conditions that are essential to the community's survival; and (iii) where state intervention is required in order to maintain the conditions that are essential to the community's self-perception as an aspirant moral community. A few words of elaboration about each of these conditions is in order.

First, if we suppose (as I do) that the members of a community of rights do not regard themselves as morally omniscient, the state has some margin to cater for the fallibility of the community. Accordingly, if it is argued that an action should be prohibited because it might put at risk the interests of *possible* rights-holders or because it might *indirectly* be damaging to rights-holders, the state may intervene (if only temporarily) on stewardship grounds. The question of how far the community will permit the state to intervene on such speculative grounds is moot. For, example, if the state proposed to prohibit the use of human embryos for research on the precautionary ground either that human embryos might just be locked-in agents or that such a practice might indirectly lead to brutalisation and a diminishing of respect for the rights of fellow agents, the community might judge this to be an overreaching of stewardship. Or, again, if the state proposed to compromise its concerns by permitting the research but not actively encouraging it (hence, withdrawing patent protection for research processes or products of this kind), the community might judge this to be unacceptable. Even in a community that is

---

[45] Compare the insightful analysis in F. G. Du Bois, 'Rights trumped? Balancing in constitutional adjudication', *Acta Juridica* (2007), 155–81.

self-consciously sceptical, we are likely to find that there is a sense of where the limits of plausibility lie and, with that, where the limits of stewardship are to be drawn.

Secondly, the state has a responsibility to protect and promote the physical conditions that are conducive to flourishing agency; and, to this extent, a community of rights might well judge that it is legitimate for the state to exercise stewardship by requiring participation in programmes that are intended to improve the conditions of, say, public health. In this light, let us think again about UK Biobank, not in its formative years but perhaps fifty years from now, as a major source of our public health intelligence. The data and analysis in UK Biobank, let us suppose, reveal clear and important linkages between certain lifestyles, particular genetic markers and serious disorders. What should the stewardship state do with this information? How far may it legitimately act upon the information with a view to improving public health? So long as we recognise, as the Nuffield Council does, that individuals have a right not to be coerced into leading a healthy life, then the state's responsibility is to draw on the findings by providing public information and focusing on the defaults that now seem to be conducive to public health.[46] Beyond this, let us imagine that, in fifty years' time, the state of public health is challenged by such rudimentary factors as overpopulation and food shortages. In such circumstances, a community of rights might judge that, as an exercise in stewardship, the state is justified in restricting the reproductive rights that individuals are recognised as having.

Thirdly, the state has a stewardship responsibility to protect and promote the conditions that are constitutive of a meaningful moral community. In saying this, I do not mean that the community of rights, qua an aspirant moral order, is challenged if there is a breakdown in the moral order such that there is far too much immoral (rights-infringing) conduct. What I mean is that it is challenged if the context for a moral way of life is threatened. There are, in other words, certain preconditions before the enterprise of a moral community makes any kind of sense. For example, if there were an abundance of resources available to a community, supply always far exceeding demand, it would make no sense to debate principles of distributive justice – because, under such conditions, the practical position would be one of 'to each according to his or her wants'. Similarly, if our biology had a protective and instantly regenerative capacity so that

---

[46] Compare R. Brownsword, 'Making people better and making better people', *Journal of Academic Legal Studies*, 1 (2005), online.

we could never be physically harmed, and if we were also immortal, it would make little sense to debate such matters as the right to life and the right to physical integrity. Particular moral debates presuppose a particular context; and I suggest that moral community, too, presupposes a certain kind of context.

What are the key features of such a context? Let me suggest two such features and their correlative conditions. One relates to the vulnerability of members of the community and the other relates to their perception of control, choice and responsibility.

The first feature of a moral community, any moral community, is that members understand what it is to respect one another. They understand that each member has interests that are protected by the moral code; and they understand that, where other-regarding moral standards are breached, harm is occasioned. It follows that one condition of moral community is that members are vulnerable, that they bleed, that they are mortal, that they are not so thick-skinned that they cannot be humiliated, that they are not immune to being instrumentalised, and so on; in short, that they have interests that are capable of being adversely affected.

The second feature is that members view themselves as agents who are sufficiently in control of their actions to make their own choices and to be held to account for the choices that they make. Moral community, in other words, presupposes a degree of freedom and personal responsibility. For members of such communities, the burden of responsibility is significant but not crippling. Paradigmatically, members will strive to do the right thing; the choices that they make will reflect their best judgment of what doing the right thing is in particular circumstances; and, if called to account, their response will be that they judged, in good faith, that what they chose to do was the right thing to do.[47]

If we focus on this second condition, then all aspirant moral communities, concerned for moral sustainability, need to be careful about actions or practices that challenge (directly or insidiously) the sense that members make and are responsible for their own choices. In the light of this, we can anticipate a number of anxieties (about possible corrosion of this condition of moral community) that might be prompted by the development of modern technologies. For example, those who are so concerned might point to genetic engineering (if and when we are able to engineer a particular genetic make-up that we know to be associated with particular

---

[47] It follows that, where members recognise the limitations of their own moral understanding, practice will focus on agent-morality rather than act-morality.

aptitudes or abilities) and, similarly, to rapid recent developments in the new brain sciences.[48] The question is whether such prospects and developments present a special threat to the preconditions for moral community.

Famously, Jürgen Habermas[49] has raised the possibility that genetic enhancement (or positive genetic engineering), if not fundamentally altering the extent to which humans have 'free will'[50] and the extent to which the predicates for human responsibility are met, nevertheless might affect our perception of such matters. The thought is that, to the extent that the idea of free will rests on a phenomenology of choice and responsibility, genetic modification could make a huge difference to the way in which we perceive ourselves, our 'achievements' and our 'failures'. If we come to see our genetic make-up as a programme that runs us, it will be tempting to think (against free will and responsibility) that we could not have acted otherwise; and, where our particular genetic make-up has been specified by others, if there is any responsibility left in the world, it seems to be with the specifiers rather than ourselves.[51] In other words, genetic enhancement threatens to alter the context by either undermining notions of free will and responsibility or by inviting the transfer of responsibility.

In our life and times, it is surely inconceivable that geneticists will understand enough about genetic pathways and interactions (both within the genome itself and with the natural and social environment) for selection or engineering of this kind to be achieved. Nevertheless, the thought that our particular dispositions and characteristics are strongly influenced by a genetic make-up over which we have no control already hints at an excuse or a degree of mitigation: if we act as we do because this is how we are genetically coded, then why should we be held responsible for our actions?[52] Moreover, in a future in which some enjoy the

---

[48] See D. Rees and S. Rose (eds.), *The New Brain Sciences – Perils and Prospects* (Cambridge University Press, 2004).

[49] J. Habermas, *The Future of Human Nature* (Cambridge: Polity Press, 2003). See, too, B. McKibben, *Enough: Genetic Engineering and the End of Human Nature* (London: Bloomsbury, 2003).

[50] For a very helpful and accessible review of the impact of genetics and brain science on our thinking concerning free will and responsibility, see P. Lipton, 'Genetic and generic determinism: a new threat to free will?' in Rees and Rose, *The New Brain Sciences*, 88.

[51] Similarly, see R. Dworkin, *Sovereign Virtue* (Cambridge, MA: Harvard University Press, 2000), 445.

[52] See, further, N. Rose, *The Politics of Life Itself* (Princeton University Press, 2007), ch. 8, esp. 233–4, for discussion of the case of Stephen Mobley, a young man who was convicted

'benefits' of genetic enhancement, those who have been less fortunate will argue that they should not be held responsible for 'wrongdoing' that can be attributed to their disadvantaged genetic inheritance.

This is not say that all expressions of modern biotechnology threaten the fabric of moral community. Far from it: green biotechnology presents no obvious threat to the viability of *moral* community and nor does therapeutic cloning, stem cell research, germ-line therapy, or the like. Even cytoplasmic hybrid embryos seem to be ethically clean on this score. Of course, such technologies might have a radical impact on the community (these are disruptive technologies), the life and times of the community might change, and some members might hanker after the good old days. However, so long as the community continues to function as a moral enterprise, its sustainability is not threatened in a relevant sense. Accordingly, if the state is to have a stewardship responsibility, in a community of rights, it cannot be treated as a licence for conservatism (with a small c); the state's responsibility is not to freeze the status quo but to monitor developments that might undermine the conditions that give its moral aspirations some sense and purpose.

State stewardship, like positive responsibilities, might signal that, in relation to some research endeavours, public cooperation is a matter of requirement. However, it also signals that the research and development, and utilisation, of new technologies need to be sensitive to the conditions that are essential not only for the community's physical survival but also for its cultural (moral) coherence.

Conclusion

In this chapter, I have suggested that regimes of individual rights and, concomitantly, of informed consent are not only less obstructive of health care research than is sometimes thought but also much more supportive.[53] To counter the *overstatement* of obstruction, we need to get the ethic of rights and consent more clearly into focus. In particular, we need to weed out the Fallacy of Necessity. To counter the *understatement* of support for research, we need to attend much more closely to the

---

of shooting the manager of a pizza store but who (unsuccessfully) pleaded a genetic inheritance by way of mitigation – Mobley's lawyers pointed to a four-generation family history of violence, aggression and behaviour disorder.

[53] Compare U. Baxi, *Human Rights in a Posthuman World* (New Delhi: Oxford University Press, 2007), esp. 211, where a certain expression of human rights is seen as a necessary (if not sufficient) constitutive condition of techno-scientific development.

cooperative responsibilities – the positive responsibilities of individuals and the stewardship responsibilities of the state – that are implicit in the idea of a community of rights.

However, this is not a one-sided manifesto in favour of researchers. With the ethic of rights and consent properly in focus, first, there is no longer an excuse for perfunctory attention to consent; secondly, where full substantive justification is required (e.g., in the treatment of children), we should not resort to inappropriate procedural justification; and, thirdly, as a corollary of enhanced responsibilities for potential research participants, we should understand that researchers, too, might have increased obligations. In short, our modern commitment to individual rights and informed consent is an important thread in the narrative that has it that, for regulators and researchers alike, the technologies of the twenty-first century present both a challenge and an opportunity.[54]

[54] See Brownsword, *Technological Revolution*, ch. 11.

6

Who decides what? Relational ethics, genetics and well-being

SARAH WILSON

This chapter addresses issues relating to genetic information and genetic technologies by asking what principles should guide the framework for the development of appropriate governance mechanisms. The chapter considers individualist and communitarian accounts, and addresses both specific technologies and broad theoretical frameworks. Genetic information is considered in the context of health related genetic technologies, as being the 'end point' of genetic research, where the development of genetic technologies and interventions requires the collection of genetic samples, the extraction of and collection of genetic information, and the storage of such information.

There is evidence of an emerging (or converging) rhetoric of community and social solidarity in policy and politics, and in academic commentary. Discussions of genetic information and technologies are both reflecting and developing this rhetoric, in highlighting the concepts of the shared nature of genetic information and of the human genome as the common heritage of mankind, and using notions of public goods and of benefit sharing.[1] The implication of this 'relational turn' for the governance of genetic technologies is itself problematic in that it has tended to manifest either as a privileging of the collective over the individual, or by extending individualist concepts outwards to the family or the community. The philosophical frameworks which may underpin these accounts remain largely unspecified and unexplored. This chapter explores the application of one such framework to the governance of genetic information and technologies, as contemporary moral and political philosophy also reflects a turn towards more relational accounts of central philosophical concepts. Relational ethics in particular presents a view of society as consisting of embedded, interconnected, interdependent selves,

---

[1] R. Chadwick and S. Wilson, 'Genomic databases as global public goods?', *Res Publica*, 10, 2 (2004).

as contrasting with the independent, separate selves of traditional moral and political theory. The particular theoretical framework adopted here is informed by feminist ethics, specifically feminist care ethics, adapted for use as a critical tool and a theoretical framework, identified here as the 'care perspective'.

In relation to the governance of genetic information, this 'care perspective' is helpful in at least two ways. In presenting an alternative perspective on individualist accounts of the implications of genetic technologies, the perspective broadens the issues under discussion. At the same time, it can bring into focus the need for a close analysis of relational concepts which are being put forward as an alternative.

The chapter begins by outlining some of the key points of the care perspective, illustrating its relational basis and how it developed in opposition to traditional individualist theory. A care perspective is then applied in developing a critical analysis of both individualist and more communitarian accounts of issues relevant to genetic technologies, through a consideration of a broadly liberal individualist account of potential enhancement technologies, and the 'emerging trends' identified by Bartha Maria Knoppers and Ruth Chadwick.[2] The chapter discusses how a care perspective might be applied to questions of the governance of genetic information and genetic technologies more generally, and how this may bring forward new issues, concluding with suggestions for an alternative approach. Drawing on previous work in developing an account of one such alternative framework, I will make the tentative suggestion that certain key principles may provide a way to respond to the issues identified, and suggest how the principles can be adapted to shed light on the complex issues surrounding the implications of genetic technologies.[3]

The ethic of care and the care perspective

The ethic of care is of particular relevance to the discussion here, being linked to liberal individualism through its original positioning

[2] B. M. Knoppers and R. Chadwick, 'Human genetic research: emerging trends in ethics', *Nature Reviews Genetics*, 6 (2005).

[3] My PhD thesis developed an account of the care perspective, and its application as both a critical and a creative tool. The creative element of the work reconstructed Rawls's theory from a perspective informed by both justice and care, particularly in reworking the hypothetical device of the original position, which included the development of a list of principles presented as an alternative to Rawls's principles of justice. S. E. Wilson, 'The ethic of care and Rawlsian social justice: critique and reinterpretation', unpublished PhD thesis, Lancaster University (2003).

in opposition to such accounts, and to the relational turn through its foundational relational concepts. Carol Gilligan's work on the psychology of moral development[4] is foundational to an ethic of care, describing a new model of moral development, which has been profoundly influential in the development of the ethic of care. Gilligan's work identified a 'different' voice, a mode of moral reasoning that was contextual rather than abstract, with an emphasis on the preservation of existing relationships and on dialogue. Originally Gilligan posited this 'ethic of care' against an ethic of justice, suggesting that the two approaches reflect two different perspectives, with differing views on, amongst other things, self, relationships, mode of moral reasoning and autonomy. Gilligan suggested that the ethic of care represents 'a shift in perspective that changes the meaning of the key terms of moral discourse – such as the concept of the self, the idea of relationship, and the notion of responsibility'.[5] Work then developed to explore the possibilities of a synthesis of care and justice,[6] although the contrast between mainstream approaches and a feminist care perspective continues to provide new ways of exploring problems. A recent example is Ruth Groenhout's work[7] which develops an account of care theory based upon a view of human nature which Groenhout suggests is implicit in the ethic of care, and which she demonstrates has connections with the theories of Augustine and Levinas. Groenhout applies the theory to assisted reproductive technologies, and to cloning, with the caveat that '[t]he book intends to provide resources for thinking about various issues, not a set of absolute rules with which to solve every moral problem'.[8]

Examining issues through the perspective of care highlights the narrow focus of mainstream arguments. In particular, the emphasis on relationships and connection, an original emphasis of Gilligan's work, offers perhaps the most recognisable contrast between the ethic of care and justice reasoning. Justice reasoning is seen as concerned with resolving conflicts in terms of individual interests, whereas care emphasises the need to resolve conflicts within the terms of relationships. This presents a

[4] C. Gilligan, *In a Different Voice: Psychological Theory & Women's Development* (Cambridge, MA and London: Harvard University Press, 1982).
[5] C. Gilligan, 'Reply by Carol Gilligan', *Signs*, 11, 2 (1986), 326.
[6] See, e. g., the collection of essays in 'Symposium on Care and Justice' (a special edition), *Hypatia*, 10, 2 (1995).
[7] R. E. Groenhout, *Connected Lives: Human Nature and an Ethics of Care* (*Feminist Constructions*) (New York: Rowman & Littlefield, 2004).
[8] *Ibid.*, 136.

particularly clear contrast with a care-based account, where an emphasis on the situated, concrete nature of people's lives leads to a mode of moral reasoning which places emphasis on attention to the specific context of moral dilemmas. This is one of the original contrasts identified by Gilligan, in that while justice reasoning was based on principles to be followed ('sort of like a math problem with humans'),[9] the care ethic was based on attention to context.

Key elements of a care perspective reflect an alternative view of the self, relationships and moral reasoning: most notably, the notion of the situated self, of persons embedded in relationships, inevitably connected to others, in contrast to a view of persons as primarily separate, independent individuals. The care perspective recognises and takes seriously the notion of persons as existing along a continuum of care, where one end of the continuum represents extreme dependence, and the other relative independence. It also demands recognition of *care* itself, the fact that people care both for and about other people, both practically and emotionally. Whilst the precise nature or role of 'care' may remain undefined, the contribution of caring labour and the existence of positive emotional connection are acknowledged as central to persons' lives. Although developments in care theory take many different forms, the notions of connection, interdependence and care are common threads in these differing accounts.

The ethic of care and, more broadly, the care perspective have served as a useful critical lens through which to illuminate the exclusions of more traditional theories, not only of women, but in particular the way in which the role of care and carers is largely unaccounted for. The care perspective can also provide an alternative framework for considerations of social justice, in offering a way to consider the circumstances in which needs are defined and met. The following section draws upon the framework of the care perspective in examining arguments relating to genetic enhancement, arguments which can be broadly labelled as liberal individualist.

Enhancement technologies[10]

The following section presents an alternative account of the core issues at stake in relation to genetic enhancement, in order to bring into focus

[9] Gilligan, *Different Voice*, 26.

[10] The arguments in this section have developed from S. E. Wilson, 'Social perspectives and genetic enhancement: whose perspective? Whose choice?', *Studies in Ethics, Law, and Technology*, 1, 1 (2007).

issues that are frequently left unexamined. There is inevitably some simplification in the representations discussed here, which serves to illuminate the differences in emphasis. The mainstream arguments are identified as being associated with reproductive autonomy, individual choice and a 'neutral', passive interpretation of technology. The alternative account is associated with the perspective of 'woman' or child-bearer, with a fundamental concern for social justice, and an understanding of society in both a global and a contextual sense.

The arguments relating to genetic enhancement are frequently made using the language of individual choice and of individual or parental rights. This might take the form of claims to reproductive autonomy, the freedom of persons to make their own reproductive choices, or it may be framed in terms of the rights of the child – the child's right to an 'open future'. Such arguments emphasise individual rights and freedoms above any other value and, where used in discussions of reproductive technologies, imply – or assume – that the technologies themselves (or indeed the development of those technologies) are a neutral matter, value-free. Such reductionist arguments obscure the multiple arenas for concern raised by the issue of genetic enhancement. These include matters of social justice, and questions of access and inequality, in particular as they relate to the specific place occupied by women as bearers of children in relation to these technologies. The perspective of care foregrounds 'maternal' thinking, thinking for and about families, and emphasises the interdependence and social constitution of persons. This alternative framework supports the critique of current individualistic approaches, as well as offering signposts towards alternative solutions.

Whilst a care perspective is not unique in providing the foundation for a critique of the individualist approach, the contrast between care and justice approaches can be clearly seen in the case of genetic enhancement. This is evident in the way in which arguments for enhancement tend to be made. Four particular instances of this are identified here and briefly discussed:

(i)   the way in which conflicts and tensions are presented as being between the rights or freedoms of individuals, rather than being set in a wider social context;
(ii) the individualism in the account is a competitive one, rather than set in a co-operative framework;
(iii) the use of examples which tend to the abstract, removing the social, familial and emotional context;

(iv) the use of binary oppositions in argument, rather than a more complex positioning of the issues under consideration.

As previously suggested, the emphasis on relationships and connection which is central to a care perspective highlights the different foci of care and mainstream arguments, where justice reasoning is seen as concerned with resolving conflicts in terms of individual interests, whereas care emphasises the need to resolve conflicts within the terms of relationships. Pro-genetic enhancement arguments are frequently made using the language of individual rights, even where those rights are situated within a family context. So, for instance, the right to reproductive freedom is reduced to the rights of individual potential parents, free from interference. In other forms of individualist argument, the rights of the child and the rights of the potential parent are placed in tension. This may take the form of justifying the use of enhancement by extending Feinberg's arguments of the rights of the child to an open future.[11] Alternatively, the right of the child not to be harmed is argued to be the overriding value. A similar adversarial model can be seen in representations of disagreements between health care professionals and patients – or patients' carers – where there are differences in opinion about appropriate care. Relational accounts, based on resolving such dilemmas whilst maintaining the various relations of care, might provide the basis for a new model of governance, enabling a wide range of factors to be taken into account.[12]

The mainstream models in arguments relating to genetic enhancement are individualistic in more than the explicit use of arguments in terms of individual rights and freedoms. These models are in fact characterised by an emphasis on the individual *in competition*, both in relation to rights and freedoms, and in the broader social setting. Rather than any notion of equality, or of cooperation, claims for genetic enhancement are frequently underscored by a notion of competition: so in the case of genetic enhancement, the aim of enhancement is frequently to gain some advantage which others do not have. This competitive underpinning is also

---

[11] J. Feinberg, 'The child's right to an open future' in J. Feinberg, *Freedom and Fulfillment, Philosophical Essays* (Princeton University Press, 1992), 76–97.

[12] Whilst not specifically developed from care ethics, in *The Patient in the Family* (Routledge: London and New York, 1995) Hilde and James Lindemann Nelson emphasise the importance of caring responsibilities and relationships; and in ' "Family matters": a conceptual framework for genetic testing in children', *Journal of Genetic Counselling*, 13, 1 (2004), 9–29, Allyn McConkie-Rosell and Gail A. Spiridigliozzi respond to tensions arising from a focus on principlism.

evident in the way that arguments tend to be framed in terms of binary oppositions, simplifying arguments into either/or statements where one claim or position will 'win out' over the other.[13] These arguments tend to focus on the abstract, and any exemplars are usually presented simplistically and largely context-free. Even though case-based examples are now commonly used to illustrate particular arguments, they are presented in such a way as to offer restricted understandings – and restricted resolutions. This presents a particularly clear contrast with a care-based account, where an emphasis on the situated, concrete nature of people's lives leads to a mode of moral reasoning which places emphasis on attention to the specific context of moral dilemmas. This attention to context is evidenced in the work relating to IVF technologies discussed shortly. As previously noted, this is one of the original contrasts identified by Gilligan, in that while justice reasoning was based on principles to be followed, the care ethic was based on attention to context. The various ways in which the individualist argument is made combine to narrow the range of the arguments, and do not therefore address some other fundamental issues.[14]

Whilst Buchanan et al.'s thorough work[15] emphasises the social and political aspects of genetic technologies, such an approach tends to be in the minority. The individualist framework is very much still the dominant paradigm, represented by, for example, Nicholas Agar, who introduces his notion of eugenics as 'primarily concerned with the protection and extension of reproductive freedom'.[16] This emphasis on the individual is frequently defended as a safeguard against the 'old', 'bad', eugenics, as Agar puts it: '… switching attention from races and classes of humans

[13] For an example of how these issues appear in bioethical debate, see J. Leach Scully, 'Drawing a line: situating moral boundaries in genetic medicine', *Bioethics*, 15, 3 (2002), 189–204, in which she suggests that genetic technologies be assessed for impact on both social equality and individual freedom, and alludes to the narrowing of focus that occurs through the use of oppositional reasoning.

[14] In *Liberal Eugenics, In Defence of Human Enhancement* (Oxford: Blackwell Publishing, 2004) Nicholas Agar quotes Lee Silver's liberal argument that 'Anyone who accepts the right of affluent parents to provide their children with an expensive private school education cannot use "unfairness" as a reason for rejecting the use of reprogenetic technologies.' (The quote is from L. Silver, *Remaking Eden: Cloning and Beyond Brave New World* (New York: Avon Books, 1997), 9, as quoted by Agar on page 138.) This argument suggests there are only two possibilities, that one must either accept all such unfairness, or reject it, closing down discussion of a range of possibilities.

[15] A. Buchanan, N. Daniels, D. Wikler and D. W. Brock, *From Chance to Choice: Genetics and Justice* (Cambridge University Press, 2000).

[16] Agar, *Liberal Eugenics*, vi.

to individuals provides a version of eugenics worthy of defence'.[17] The individualist perspective is also said to safeguard against a dystopian future: 'The liberal view I have described takes away from social planners responsibility for choices about what kinds of human beings there will be and gives it to parents, who are unlikely to want children subservient by design.'[18] These examples illustrate the earlier point about the use of binary oppositions, implying that the individualist perspective is the obvious 'good' choice. Yet what is obvious is that, in this case as in many others, it does not have to be an either/or choice, the responsibility need not lie solely with either 'social planners' or parents. Indeed, the choice should not lie solely with either, for ideally, as Groenhout suggests, 'The social context into which a child with special needs will be born is a matter of collective decision making.'[19]

These examples show how a care perspective can provide the basis for a close critique of the mainstream liberal arguments for enhancement. They support the need for a more comprehensive and context sensitive assessment of genetic enhancement technologies, and consequent implications for appropriate governance mechanisms. Whilst the mainstream liberal framework continues to be the dominant paradigm, the method of argument employed tends to make invisible other concerns relating to genetic enhancement. A care perspective provides one alternative framework within which to ask other questions about genetic enhancement and genetic technologies more generally.

In this case, such an approach leads to an emphasis on the concrete situations in which technologies are being developed and how they are – or may be – put into use. Further, attention to the interdependence and related nature of everyday lives brings into focus the potential impact of enhancement technologies on the individuals and societies involved. Specific questions about genetic enhancement may include asking how the enhancement will actually take place, and what would be the impact of this on persons directly or indirectly involved? Exploring this issue means paying attention to the processes involved in performing enhancement, and the following discussion considers enhancement which requires in-vitro fertilisation (IVF) technology.

---

[17] *Ibid.*, 5.   [18] *Ibid.*, 133.
[19] Groenhout, *Connected Lives*, 175. Indeed Agar actually seems to accept this viewpoint with the closing sentence of his book, when he suggests that parents would be granted 'a limited prerogative to use enhancement technologies to choose their children's characteristics' (Agar, *Liberal Eugenics*, 175).

Taking IVF technologies as an illustration is in keeping with a contextual approach, in part because IVF is one of the technologies necessary for genetic enhancement to be put into practice. It is also because the site of IVF technologies, where the technology is put into practice, is in the body of the woman. Research into the impact of IVF technologies offers an insight into the impact such technologies have on women in particular, and the responses women have to them. This contrasts with many of the discussions of genetic enhancement in which the technology is either invisible, or not subject to serious consideration: the methods of delivery, and the differential impact upon women, are not discussed.

It has been said of IVF that it is 'too cumbersome, expensive, and risky to the woman's health to use for sex selection alone'.[20] It is certainly true that IVF technologies have a major impact on women, both psychologically and physically, as well as being very disruptive and time consuming. IVF technologies also have a high failure rate. Furthermore, as Sarah Franklin has identified, many women do not experience new technological approaches as an expansion of choice: 'the existence of new technological options takes away the choice simply to accept infertility ... new technological options produce a forced choice; once a choice exists it must either be pursued or refused'.[21] Women express the need to try all possible options, to try and obtain 'peace of mind'.

These illustrations, directly drawn from the context of women's experiences with IVF, highlight the need to consider the impact of enhancement technologies on women as it may affect their physical well-being, their psychological well-being, and any practical impact on their day-to-day lives. The stresses of undergoing IVF treatment are likely to be greater on the mother than on the father, although the stress fathers undergo should not be dismissed. Such an understanding highlights the ways in which the burdens of new technologies may fall more heavily on women. The examples given also imply a need to question the concept that more options always equate to better choices.

Further questions are raised by feminists who are against reproductive technologies, because they see such technologies as inherently patriarchal. That is, they are seen as a function of a particularly male approach to technologies, to reproduction – or more specifically to

[20] D. Davis, *Genetic Dilemmas: Reproductive Technology, Parental Choices, and Children's Futures (Reflective Bioethics)* (New York: Routledge, 2001), 91.
[21] S. Franklin, 'Making miracles: scientific progress and the facts of life', in S. Franklin and H. Ragone (eds.), *Reproducing Reproduction* (Philadelphia, PA: University of Pennsylvania Press, 1998), 108.

proving paternity – and to women. It has been suggested that '[w]omen's objectives for birthing a healthy baby or for better birth management are subjugated goals often employed as rhetorical alibis for the application of new birth technologies, but rarely considered in their own right'.[22] Whilst we may not want to follow the line of argument that rejects reproductive technologies *because* they are seen as inherently patriarchal, the raising of questions about healthy births and mothering may help to inform discussion of genetic enhancement. Asking questions about the underlying objectives of genetic enhancement, rather than restricting the discussion to an issue of permissibility, may be illuminating. The objective of happier, healthier children and families may have nothing (or little) to do with genetics anyway. A consideration of the objectives of enhancement follows towards the end of this section.

In applying a care theory analysis to assisted reproduction techniques (ARTs), Groenhout identifies problems relating to sperm donation, suggesting that it is premised on a denial of relationship, 'because it involves, in most cases, a deliberate lack of relationship between genetic father and child'. In relation to surrogacy, Groenhout is critical of contractual surrogacy, as being likely to destroy relations of care, and presenting the possibility of exploitation, as surrogacy contracts 'represent practices of control over another's body that are incompatible with minimal concern for the other's well-being or autonomy'.[23] In discussing the ways in which ARTs may be seen as leading to the commodification of children, and the essentialising of women's role as mother, she suggests that '[s]ocial practices that entrench problematic social constructions need to be challenged, not endorsed'.[24] She also makes some interesting points arising from the definition of ARTs as commercial services rather than health care, particularly how the justification for such services frequently relies upon arguments which may be appropriate to the health care context but are not so in commercial contexts.

In terms of the actual technologies, the development and achievement of the technologies is not neutral. It has already had, or will have, an impact on the direction of research, the lack of funds for other projects etc. Clearly there are ethical issues, value judgements, and vested interests in developing the technologies. Further, each technology does not exist in isolation but in the context of other choices or routes of action. While

---

[22] A. Balsamo, *Technologies of the Gendered Body* (Durham, NC: Duke University Press, 1999), 95.
[23] Groenhout, *Connected Lives*, 146.   [24] *Ibid.*, 150.

the question may seem simple if one considers one particular technology at a time, if the question is on the balancing of two or more options, or of resources in general, the matter is more complex. Broadening the discussion away from a focus on individual rights therefore allows us to consider a range of different perspectives and potential areas of impact of genetic enhancement, from the use and impact of the relevant technologies, to the pursuing of a particular research agenda.

Thinking about the notion of enhancement itself raises more questions: a more contextual approach may destabilise the emphasis on physical factors – appearance or abilities – which is often a focus of enhancement discussions. Further, recognising caring labour and the continuum of care brings to the foreground that the process of enabling maturity and relative independence is not so much about 'static' physical factors as about environmental factors and interactions between the two. A recognition that not all are able to reach relative independence anyway brings into focus issues about the whole aim of enhancement, and demands a recognition of the full range of human functioning. Recognising *all* members of society, rather than only independent, fully functioning persons, enables us to consider the value of all lives and the social aspects which impact on the fulfilment of people's life plans. This approach asks whether it may be more effective to enhance the environment in which people live, or to enhance the social context, rather than to focus on individuals. This obviously has comparisons with claims that disability is primarily a social construct, and with the objections from some disability rights supporters to the use of genetic technologies.[25] Such considerations demonstrate how reproductive and life choices are already not simply an individual matter: other interests are always and inevitably involved. The state is already and inevitably involved in reproduction. Acknowledging that this is the case illustrates the inappropriateness of arguments which claim that genetic enhancement is a matter of reproductive freedom and individual rights.

Foregrounding the social context enables a consideration of issues of injustice and inequalities that is clearly central to social justice, and confirms the differential impact of enhancement technologies on women (and children). This is particularly true in a global context: as the majority of the world's poor are women and children, they are also likely to suffer differentially from any increasing inequalities which genetic

[25] Tom Shakespeare discusses such objections in 'Disability, genetics and global justice', *Social Policy and Society*, 4 (2005), 87–95.

enhancements may bring. Thinking from a care perspective, that is thinking of persons as embedded in a web of relationships, not primarily as independent autonomous persons, supports a move away from a competitive, individualist framework. Whereas current arguments frequently appeal to the individual's particular interests – 'Would I want this for myself/my children?', a broader perspective asks 'What sort of opportunities/society would I want to support, and does this help to achieve this?' Asking questions is one way to explore the complexity of issues raised by genetic enhancement that are closed off when the arguments are focused on reproductive freedoms. It is obviously particularly relevant to ask what is the purpose of genetic enhancement? Advantage over others? Happiness? Success? And who, or what, is it for? Should the questions be addressed at the level of 'society' rather than the individuals who make up society? Would the answers look different in either case? Addressing these issues, particularly in asking what enhancement under a less, or non-, competitive framework would look like, may lead to other questions. Rosemarie Tong has suggested that this is an issue about how we want to perceive ourselves: 'The question, then, is not "What kind of people should there be in the future?" but "What kind of people do we want to be now?" '[26] Inevitably linked to questions of the enhancement of children is the question of what reproduction itself is for. For example, is it about the opportunity to be a parent? To be the best parent? To do the best for 'our' children? If we take a perspective informed by concerns with global social justice, and with the particular vulnerability of women and children, doing the best for 'our' children may mean doing the best for all children – and the most effective form of enhancement may therefore not be genetic at all.

With genetic enhancement as the focus, the above discussion demonstrates how the care perspective can be critically applied, and how it widens the discussion from a focus on individual rights and choice, and brings in a range of benefits and burdens which should be taken into account when assessing the potential risks (and benefits) of genetic enhancement. The perspective presents a way for *individuals* to assess the merits of enhancement for society as a whole, rather than the argument being framed as an opposition between individual rights and 'social planners'.[27] It also demands that attention is paid to the processes involved

---

[26] R. Tong, *Feminist Approaches to Bioethics. Theoretical Reflections and Practical Applications* (Boulder, CO: Westview Press, 1997), 242.

[27] Agar, *Liberal Eugenics*, 175.

in performing enhancement, to explore the potential differential impact of the technologies on women, and the ways in which the technologies are being developed, to dispense with the notion that technology is value neutral. Finally, in exploring the issue of what enhancement is for, the space is open for a wide range of alternative accounts and aims, and consequently alternative ways of meeting these aims. Governance mechanisms will therefore need to be able to respond to these challenges, by attending to sensitivities of gender and context, and to social as well as individual issues.

Emerging trends

The above discussion focused on the application of genetic technologies, but there is also much debate about the appropriate ethical response or principles relating to genetic information itself. Much of this debate centres around the shared nature of genetic information, as well as concerns over inappropriate use of such information. These bring into question issues relating to the governance of research, including both the priority given to the individual in consent procedures, and the appropriate role of participants and publics in research governance and procedures. Such critiques have brought to the fore some of the problems arising from a focus on individuals, particularly relating to consent and unsought information, as well as responding to public concerns over commodification and private profiteering. They have stimulated debate about both philosophical and practical concerns and can be seen reflected in discussions around benefit sharing and the potential for genetic technologies to be viewed as public goods.[28] Contemporary bioethical debates on advances in genetics often address the ways in which the potential social impacts of genetic technologies and the 'shared' nature of genetic information challenge mainstream individualist ethical perspectives. Indeed, Ruth Chadwick and Bartha Maria Knoppers have suggested that an underlying shift from individual to more communitarian models has taken place – as evidenced by the five general trends they outline, namely, those of reciprocity, mutuality, solidarity, citizenry and universality.[29] However, as Heather Widdows has identified, there remains a

---

[28] See, e.g., the suggestions for benefit sharing mechanisms in G. Haddow, G. Laurie, S. Cunningham-Burley and K. Hunter, 'Tackling community concerns about commercialisation and genetic research: a modest interdisciplinary proposal', *Social Science and Medicine*, 64, 2 (2007), 272–82.

[29] Knoppers and Chadwick, 'Emerging trends'.

'conceptual gap' to be filled, and current models tend to remain focused on individualist approaches, extending individualist concepts out to the family, or the community, rather than presenting an alternative model.[30] Such an individualist focus is problematic not only in relation to issues such as consent and confidentiality, but also as it tends to obscure the multiple influences and arenas for concern that are involved in the use and development of genetic technologies. In outlining the 'emerging trends', Knoppers and Chadwick suggest that these are not 'at odds with' contemporary debates about ethics, including feminist ethics.[31] In paying close attention to the meanings of the trends they identify, the following section raises concerns which suggest that this connection is not a wholly coherent one. Although the article itself identifies five key trends, the discussion here will concentrate upon three: reciprocity, mutuality and solidarity.

Reciprocity

This is defined by Knoppers and Chadwick as reflecting 'recognition of the participation and contribution of the research participant'.[32] They note the development of this notion: 'This trend towards reciprocity not only recognizes autonomy but also respects the personal and cultural values of the individual participant ... a more recent extension of reciprocity expands the concept from exchange with the individual or his/her family to the community or population.'[33]

Although in the article itself benefit sharing is not specifically linked to reciprocity (being linked to universality and equity), it is likely that debates concerning governance mechanisms for benefit sharing arrangements can be interpreted as representative of this developing account of reciprocity. This concept of reciprocity might be taken as offering an alternative model to encourage participation in research, in contrast to either altruistic participation in research or participation in research based on self-interest (i.e., the hope that one will directly benefit from the results of such research). However, dependent on how the lines of 'community' or 'population' are drawn, it is possible to see it as simply an extension of the appeal to self-interest. That is, the hope that members of a particular community, or population group, will benefit as a result of participating

---

[30] H. Widdows, 'Genetic challenges to ethics', paper presented at EACME Conference, Barcelona, August 2005.
[31] Knoppers and Chadwick, 'Emerging trends', 75.   [32] Ibid.   [33] Ibid., 76.

in the research. The extent and interpretation of the concept is open to interpretation, depending upon the underpinning conceptual framework. If this concept of reciprocity is based upon standard contractual models of reciprocity, as is suggested by the notion of 'exchange', then it may continue to exclude the wider community. So, Rawls's account of reciprocity, under which '[f]air terms of cooperation specify an idea of reciprocity: all who are engaged in cooperation and do their part as the rules and procedure require, are to benefit in an appropriate way', applies only to those who are participating, and does not provide space for the non-participant to be considered.[34] However, feminist interpretations of reciprocity, underpinned by the theoretical framework of care, move away from the notion of exchange, and thus present the possibility of a more inclusive account. In elucidating this relational concept of reciprocity, care theorists draw upon caring relations themselves as illustration. Nel Noddings writes of reciprocity in the relationship between parent and child, where 'this reciprocity is not contractual, that is it is not characterised by mututality',[35] and Eva Kittay offers the concept of *doulia*, taken from *doula*, a person who cares for a new mother whilst the mother cares for her new-born.[36] As Kittay notes, this is captured by the common aphorism, 'What goes around comes around.'[37] In the context of Kittay's usage, that is caring labour, she explains this as 'just as we have required care to survive and thrive, so we need to provide conditions that allow others – including those who do the work of caring – to receive the care they need to survive and thrive'.[38] This is a non-mutual, non-contributory and broader concept of reciprocity which is able to encompass various interests. Although this expanded account of reciprocity allows for the consideration of a range of interests, it seems to return us to the argument which supports participation in research as an altruistic act – as long as it is believed that there is a real chance that *someone* will benefit from the research.

Clearly an expanded concept of reciprocity needs some further work in order to clarify what responsibilities and duties might come into play. Not least in this account is the necessity for a full consideration of the notion of benefit. Here it will be important to consider questions relating

[34] J. Rawls, *Political Liberalism*, new edn (New York: Columbia University Press, 1996), 16.
[35] N. Noddings, *Caring: A Feminine Approach to Ethics and Moral Education* (Berkeley, CA: University of California Press, 1984), 150.
[36] E. Feder Kittay, 'Human dependency and Rawlsian equality' in D. T. Meyers (ed.), *Feminists Rethink the Self* (Boulder, CO: Westview Press, 1997), 233.
[37] Kittay, 'Human dependency', 233 [38] *Ibid*.

to the use of the deficit model, particularly given the claim that the public would participate in research if only they understood the benefits it may bring: 'These studies offer no immediate personal benefits. Much groundwork is required to explain to the public the goals of this genotyping research.'[39] It would also be necessary to ensure that a concept of reciprocity linked to a generalised, hoped-for benefit would not lead to an erosion of an individual's right to, or, less formally, opportunity to, decline to participate in research.

Mutuality

The concept of mutuality is intended to capture the ways in which genetic information is common amongst family members, and two particular ideas are put forward. The first is the notion that there is 'an ethical (distinct from a legal) duty to warn at-risk family members' (under certain conditions), and, secondly 'there is the approach that views the family as a distinct social unit ... justified by the familial nature of genetic information and therefore by the need for mutuality or sharing within families, rather than discretionary physician control over access'.[40] This notion of mutuality is descriptive of the difficulties associated with the shared nature of genetic information, but it does not clearly present a possible solution. As with the concept of reciprocity, there appear to be different possible underpinning frameworks, which create further problems. A principle of mutuality may be seen to be resting on a public health model, creating a duty to warn at-risk family members. Alternatively, it may be seen as foregrounding an individual's right to access information about themself. This would seem to privilege the validity or power of the genetic information over and above 'family' understandings of how, or indeed if, such information should be shared. The need or duty to share such information not only overrides any right of the initial individual 'patient' to keep their own information confidential, but also the right of other family members to choose not to know such information. Consideration of the governance mechanisms necessary to put such mutuality into practice throws up some practical issues, and a possible contradiction. If genetic information belongs to all in a family, whose responsibility would it be to let them know it is available? Surely the gatekeeper to the decision that an ethical duty exists is still the clinician?

[39] Knoppers and Chadwick, 'Emerging trends', 76.   [40] *Ibid.*

Solidarity

The issue of the right not to know is picked up in the discussion of solidarity:

> In the case of the right to know or not to know debate, the issue is whether
> individuals have a responsibility to know their genetic make-up to then
> make responsible decisions (for example, whether to have a predictive
> test, or for making reproductive decisions). Some bioethicists believe
> that this is the case and that the basis of this is a kind of solidarity that
> can be expressed as a willingness to share information for the benefit of
> others.[41]

A distinction is made between communal solidarity and constitutive solidarity. Communal solidarity arises from 'shared human vulnerabilities' which create shared moral responsibility, whereas constitutive solidarity is 'the pursuit of advantage: individuals have an interest in common and get together to protect it through joining an insurance scheme'.[42] Both accounts of solidarity, based on common interest or interests in common, emphasising either *shared* moral responsibility, or mutual self-interest, seem a long way from the alternative, perhaps colloquial, sense of solidarity as all people standing together, where those who are stronger and not vulnerable have a moral responsibility to lend their support to the vulnerable. There is a developing literature around contemporary feminist accounts of solidarity which emphasises not only the motivational aspect of solidarity but also captures this account of solidarity in the concept of *normative solidarity*.[43] Defining solidarity as being about challenging oppressive social structures would seem to throw into question the application of this concept in isolation.[44] As an illustration, the 'Emerging trends' article gives a particular example of human genetic databases, where it is suggested that what is at stake is constitutive solidarity, that is: 'In so far as it can be argued that the establishment of human genetic databases is a means towards the provision of more effective therapies, individuals might perceive that they have an interest in common, namely better health care, and they might collectively choose to get together to create a genetic database for the public good.'[45] This revisits the discussion

---

[41] *Ibid.*   [42] *Ibid.*, 77.

[43] C. C. Gould and S. J. Scholz (eds.), *Journal of Social Philosophy* (Special Issue on Solidarity), 38, 1 (Spring 2007).

[44] Indeed, as solidarity, whether motivational or normative, may itself be oppressive, a context-sensitive and reflexive account is essential.

[45] Knoppers and Chadwick, 'Emerging trends', 77.

in the earlier section relating to underlying objectives. If the underlying objective is better health care, then individuals might collectively choose many different ways of achieving that aim. A developed concept of normative solidarity may provide a framework from which to develop governance mechanisms, rather than an assumption of solidarity which might silence opposing voices as being against the common good.

The above discussion gives some idea of the way in which the 'emerging trends' seem appealing in offering an alternative to individualist accounts, yet are problematic in themselves. The remaining concepts of citizenry and universality similarly present both opportunities for, and challenges to, inclusivity in developing the governance of genetic technologies. The notion of citizenry includes both the increasing involvement – or at least rhetoric of involvement – of the public, for example on advisory committees, as well as a concept of collective identity. Regarding universality, Knoppers and Chadwick note that '[c]urrent ethical rhetoric emphasizes universality on the basis of the characterization of the genome itself (rather than, for example, shared human vulnerabilities) as a shared resource'.[46] Whilst the concepts of citizenry and universality both provide opportunities to develop inclusive accounts, there is an inevitable tendency towards genetic exceptionalism, and an increasing geneticisation of areas of life where other issues might equally be prioritised. Thinking from a care perspective inevitably leads to asking 'Why not take shared human vulnerability as a universal?'

The preceding sections illustrate the range of issues that come into focus when a care perspective is drawn upon to critique existing accounts. The section on enhancement technologies drew attention to the narrowing of focus which tends to occur in individualist arguments, to the exclusion of other relevant considerations. Specifically, the analysis highlighted the potential differential impact of genetic technologies on women and children, the need to consider the implications for and impact on social practices, and how a consideration of the underlying aims and objectives opens up alternative ways of meeting these aims. The discussion of the emerging trends showed that the trends themselves do not necessarily support a more communitarian or relational approach, as Knoppers and Chadwick note when suggesting that appeals to solidarity can 'be made by both sides in the debate'.[47] The principles they identify appear to require further supporting frameworks, and may in fact be interpreted as individualistic. Even if the trends are not wholly

---

[46] Ibid.   [47] Ibid., 76.

set within an individualistic framework, they do seem to be 'atomised', dividing consideration of ethical issues into smaller units, in a similar way to the individualist arguments relating to enhancement which were discussed in the preceding section. Where communitarianism is the strongest framework, there is a concern that adopting these emerging principles might result in the potential removal of individual liberties with little or no corresponding benefit, for example with calls for a duty to participate in research.[48]

Developing a critical analysis drawing on the framework of care has highlighted problems with the more mainstream frameworks within which the governance of genetic information and technologies is discussed. This chapter concludes with a brief exploration of alternative principles, and some comments on how these might offer the potential for a more holistic approach.

Alternative principles

Can a set of principles developed in the contexts of gender justice and social justice provide a framework for developing appropriate governance mechanisms? This preliminary idea is based on Nancy Fraser's work on principles of gender equity, which is a philosophical and political analysis of the connection between the welfare state and models of 'gender order'.[49] Adapting these from a perspective informed by care enables the development of an account related to social justice and justice in public institutions. Although Fraser's work is specifically focused on gender equity within a welfare state, the emphasis on principles relating to the way in which needs are met, rather than focusing on individual rights and entitlements, is compatible with the critical perspective taken here. The preceding analysis drew attention to the importance of the context in which principles are applied, and the frameworks within which they are supported and debated. Fraser's work presents a way of addressing these issues, as it puts forward a comprehensive and holistic view. Fraser identifies principles of gender justice, which are then used to assess two idealised versions of the welfare state based on two different models of gender order. All the principles are given due consideration, and whilst neither model meets all principles equally, the process highlights problems and successes. What is particularly interesting for

---

[48] Clearly it is somewhat ironic that the criticism here *defends* individualism.
[49] N. Fraser, 'After the family wage', *Political Theory*, 22, 4 (1994).

the context to be applied here is the way in which alternative ways of meeting each principle are possible, and these are assessed against all the principles, ensuring that one principle is not met at the expense of others. Clearly there are difficulties with balancing principles, but this method does demonstrate potential for developing a mechanism which addresses a wide range of interests. Fraser puts forward five key principles and three sub-principles: and the discussion here focuses on the principles of antipoverty, antiexploitation, antimarginalisation, and antiandrocentrism, and the sub-principle, equality of leisure time. In the analysis here these principles are suggested as a way of responding to the concerns identified in the earlier discussion. This concluding section makes only brief comment on how these principles might be used to develop more responsive governance mechanisms. The principles are not intended to replace mainstream concepts such as autonomy (self-definition rather than self determination), equality, privacy and justice.

The *antipoverty* principle requires that the prevention of poverty should always be under consideration. The principle is concerned with the distribution of income, but also, more broadly, provides a way of accounting for basic material needs. When thinking about the potential impact of genetic technologies, this principle would lead to a consideration of whether – or in what ways – it might make people worse off. The principle might also be used to consider whether people would be worse off than in another possible situation, and may be applied in order to maximise benefit-sharing arrangements, or to prevent bio-piracy.

Fraser's principle of *antiexploitation* is developed from the concept of exploitable dependency, that is, where an asymmetric relationship exists in that the subordinate party in a relationship stands to lose a great deal if they were to withdraw from the relationship, whilst the other party, the superordinate, has little to lose.[50] In Fraser's original context it primarily relates to individual relations of exploitable dependency (within families, on employers and supervisors, on state officials), and the aim is in part to ensure the subordinate has realistic 'exit options'. In a genetic context this notion of exploitation as exploitable dependencies may provide a basis to assess and prevent the exploitation of vulnerable groups. This might encompass those made vulnerable by actual or potential genetic illness,

---

[50] Fraser credits Robert Goodin with this definition of exploitable dependency: R. Goodin, *Reasons for Welfare: The Political Theory of the Welfare State* (Princeton University Press, 1988).

impacting on their access to insurance, or the incentive to participate in research programmes.

As a 'sub-principle' of equality, Fraser posits the principle of *equality of leisure time*. As Fraser emphasises, leisure time is not simply the opposite of waged work, and takes into account the time spent on various forms of 'care' work. This has implications for the arrangements by which services are provided and accessed, in that they must be as time-efficient as possible. In terms of genetic technologies, this presents a concrete way to assess the impact of the practice of the technologies, for example the differential time requirement of IVF technologies on women outlined in the preceding section on genetic enhancement.

All the above principles may be met, and some groups may still be marginalised, or subject to marginalisation. The principle of *antimarginalisation* requires that people are able to participate in all areas of social and civil life, by ensuring access to such opportunities. This principle may come into play in supporting public participation in deciding research governance mechanisms, or indeed research trajectories. It may also provide for a consideration of the impact of research trajectories and new and emerging technologies on particular groups, in ensuring that they will not be subject to marginalisation or discrimination.

The principle of *antiandrocentrism* deconstructs the notion of there being one acceptable idealised standard or norm, assumed to be representative. It offers a reminder that equality does not mean sameness, and that people must be free to pursue their own conceptions of the good life without having to conform to a (frequently male) norm. Applied to the context of the governance mechanisms related to genetics, this principle mandates for the consideration of a range of interests, to be considered in relation to, for example, research design, research trajectories and research priorities more generally.

Do these principles expand our understanding of the emerging trends, and can they provide guidance on appropriate governance mechanisms?

If the principle of reciprocity is interpreted as an extension of benefit sharing, and a response to the perceived unfairness and exploitation by the pharmaceutical industry, then the alternative principle of antiexploitation is the most obvious principle to draw upon to support such an interpretation. That is, to ensure that a conception of reciprocity does not take for granted the contribution of the more vulnerable party, the relationship must not be one which exploits the vulnerabilities of individuals, families or communities. This principle, along with those of antimarginalisation and antiandrocentrism, may also be able to address concerns relating to mutuality. That is, whilst mutuality represents recognition that a family member is responsible for the sharing of genetic information, the alternative principles would provide support for a choice not to share that information. This would imply that access to genetic information may be restricted where there is the potential for stigmatisation, and would prevent potentially exploitable dependencies upon health care workers and providers. Similarly, any claims to a principle of solidarity may be assessed against the alternative principles, to ensure that the practical application of the concept will not marginalise or exploit the vulnerable.

The alternative principles then do seem to offer a way to assess existing accounts of principles and concepts relating to genetic information and genetic technologies, and thus may provide a useful tool in developing comprehensive and responsive governance mechanisms. Developing an analysis and alternative concepts informed by a care perspective seems to offer a promising way forward in managing some of the complexities associated with developments in genetic technologies. In the examples presented here, such an approach leads to an emphasis on the concrete situations in which technologies are being developed and how they are – or may be – put into use. Attention to the interdependence and related nature of everyday lives brings into focus the potential impact of genetic technologies on the individuals and societies involved. Broadening the discussion away from a focus on individual rights therefore allows us to consider a range of different perspectives and potential areas of impact, from the use and impact of the relevant technologies, to the pursuing of a particular research agenda. Whereas current arguments frequently appeal to the individual's particular interests ('Would I/we want this for myself/my children?'), a broader perspective asks 'What sort of opportunities / society would I/we want to support, and does this help to achieve this?' Asking questions is one way to explore the complexity of issues raised by genetic technologies that are closed off when the arguments are focused on individual or even group freedoms.

Exploring these questions widens the discussion from a focus on individual rights and choice, and brings in a range of benefits and burdens which should be taken into account when assessing the potential risks and benefits of genetic technologies. The perspective presents a way for *individuals* as well as groups to assess the merits of these technologies for society as a whole, rather than the argument being framed as an opposition between individual rights and potential eugenic controls. It also demands that attention is paid to the processes involved, to explore the potential differential impact of the technologies on women, and the ways in which the technologies are being developed, to dispense with the notion that technology is value neutral. Finally, in exploring the issue of what these technologies are for, the space is open for a wide range of alternative perspectives and aims, and consequently alternative ways of meeting these aims.

SECTION III

Redesigning governance

Involving publics in biobank governance: moving beyond existing approaches

KATHRYN G. HUNTER AND GRAEME T. LAURIE[1]

This chapter examines the crucial issue of how to include people *well*[2] in biobank governance. We use the example of UK Biobank to illustrate our discussion because it is ground-breaking in its approach to governance and because, in terms of public engagement, the project has been criticised for its approach to public consultation. In reaction to these perceived failings there have been calls for greater participant involvement in the running and oversight of UK Biobank.[3] More particularly, and more recently, Winickoff has proposed a 'shareholder model' which seeks to '… move beyond public consultation to embrace participatory forms of resource entitlement'.[4] Winickoff draws on corporate modelling to argue for more direct representation of UK Biobank participants in the project's decision making and governance processes. As such, he argues that public engagement must move from consultation to representation. In other realms, representation itself is found wanting, with writers such as Pimbert and Wakeford arguing that engagement exercises 'in the design of technologies' should embrace deliberative democratic practices to '… democratize [sic] policy making by moving beyond representative democracy and traditional forms

---

[1] We should, at this stage, declare a particular interest, which is that one of us, Graeme Laurie, is currently Chair of the UK Biobank Ethics and Governance Council – a key element of the novel governance framework (as we discuss below). That said, Laurie writes here in an entirely personal academic capacity and nothing herein should be taken to reflect the views of the Council.

[2] We borrow liberally here from Marilyn Strathearn. See M. Strathearn, 'Afterword: accountability and ethnography' in M. Strathearn (ed.), *Audit Cultures: Anthropological Studies in Accountability, Ethics, and the Academy* (London: Routledge, 2000), discussed at 292–4.

[3] R. Tutton, J. Kaye and K. Hoyer, 'Governing UK Biobank: the importance of ensuring public trust', *Trends in Biotechnology*, 22, 6 (2004), 285.

[4] D. E. Winickoff, 'Partnership in U.K. Biobank: a third way for genomic property?', *Journal of Law, Medicine & Ethics*, 35, 3 (2007), 451.

of consultation'.[5] We examine these calls to move beyond consultation to representation and from representation to more deliberative and inclusive processes of participation. Perhaps ironically, we agree with Winickoff that there is value in models from the corporate sphere; not on a shareholder approach, however, but on a stakeholder approach which goes beyond even that which is proposed in the discourse on deliberative democracy. Moreover, and despite early criticisms of UK Biobank, we find valuable evidence within that model of what it means to involve people *well*.

UK Biobank and its Ethics and Governance Council

UK Biobank is a not-for-profit charity (a company limited by guarantee). It consists of a Board of Directors (with representatives from the funders), a Steering Committee (led by a Chief Executive Officer) and an International Scientific Advisory Board. Its central objective is to build a major research resource containing lifestyle, physical and genetic information, as well as samples, from 500,000 people in the UK, aged between 40 and 69. The overarching purpose of UK Biobank is to support *health-related research*, nationally and internationally. In governance terms, UK Biobank is subject to the same set of complex regulations as any other life sciences project involving human participants. Notwithstanding, upon the initiative of the two principal funders of UK Biobank – the Wellcome Trust and the Medical Research Council – processes were put in place to consider the need for *additional* governance and these were explored in parallel with development of the scientific protocol.[6] Consultations played a central role.

An Interim Advisory Group (IAG) was established to advise the funders, which undertook various public consultations in tandem, and the recommendations of the IAG were in turn put out to public consultation and ultimately accepted. We return to the consultation processes below, but for now it is important to note two key features of the

[5] M. Pimbert and T. Wakeford, 'Deliberative democracy and citizen empowerment: an overview', *PLA Notes*, 40 (February 2001), 24.
[6] We explore these processes and their outcomes more fully elsewhere: see G. Laurie, A. Bruce and C. Lyall, 'The roles of values and interests in the governance of the life sciences: learning lessons from the "Ethics+" approach of UK Biobank', in C. Lyall, J. Smith and T. Papaioannou (eds.), *The Limits to Governance: The Challenge of Policy-making for the New Life Sciences* (Aldershot: Ashgate, 2009) 51–7.

IAG's recommendations. These were that UK Biobank should adopt and be subject to an Ethics and Governance Framework (EGF) and that it be overseen by an independent Ethics and Governance Council (EGC).

The Ethics and Governance Framework is an instrument of UK Biobank.[7] As a living document, which outlines the commitments to participants, researchers and society at large, it is designed to be revised as necessary as new or unforeseen challenges arise and/or as social attitudes change. The EGF is explicit that the commitment is to manage the resource for the public good, in keeping with UK Biobank purposes, and while honouring the participants' original consent. More particularly, it identifies a very full range of stakeholders and the interests considered to be at stake; this obviously includes participants and potential users of the resource, but Section III of the EGF also addresses the 'relationship with society'. It is telling that the tag line on UK Biobank's corporate logo reads: 'Improving the health of future generations'.

The Ethics and Governance Council was established in November 2004 with a specific remit to:[8]

- act as an independent guardian of the UK Biobank EGF and advise on its revision;
- monitor and report publicly on the conformity of the UK Biobank project with the EGF; and
- advise more generally on the interests of research participants and the general public in relation to UK Biobank.

The mantra of the EGC is to speak *about UK Biobank, not for UK Biobank*. The EGC meets quarterly, holds regular public meetings, reports annually on its work, commissions research, maintains a public profile through its website, seeks to engage actively with participants and other sectors of the public, and is ultimately accountable to the funders and the public. We comment on the Council's work in due course, but it is important to note that there was strong public support during consultations about the need for, and value of, such a body. None the less, much criticism has been levelled at these consultations in terms of their values as public engagement exercises.

---

[7] www.ukbiobank.ac.uk.   [8] www.egcukbiobank.org.uk.

UK Biobank consultations

The principal funders organised a series of public consultations and workshops during the project's development.[9] These involved a variety of groups, including publics and stakeholders, health professionals and industry. A number of different 'engagement' methods were used, including surveys, focus groups and a people's panel; in addition, lay members were included on the IAG and on the committee devising the scientific protocol.[10] Considering this 'extensive consultation process',[11] UK Biobank might, as Levitt has commented, 'be seen as a model for public involvement'.[12] Yet, these consultations have been widely criticised for being 'too politically tailored by biobank planners';[13] for avoiding contentious issues (such as the establishment of a UK-wide biobank in the first place);[14] for 'the validity of the science for which the database is being created';[15] and for ignoring public concerns.[16] Wakeford and Hale have suggested, for example, that in the 'BioBank UK: A Question of Trust' consultation in 2002, there was 'a subtle steering of public responses … in order to produce insights that were useful to those promoting the biobank', and that participants were treated as 'reactive members of the public rather than as citizens in any more active sense of the word'.[17] While the report contains 22 recommendations, Godard et al. have noted that it 'does not indicate whether any of these recommendations

---

[9] The various consultation and workshop reports may be found at: www.ukbiobank.ac.uk/ethics/consult.php. See also M. Levitt, 'UK Biobank: a model for public engagement?', *Genomics, Society and Policy*, 1, 3 (2005), 78.

[10] Levitt, 'UK Biobank', 78.

[11] See UK Biobank website at www.ukbiobank.ac.uk/ethics/consult.php.

[12] Levitt, 'UK Biobank', 78.

[13] Winickoff, 'Partnership in U.K. Biobank', 445, citing H. Wallace, 'The development of U.K. Biobank: excluding scientific controversy from ethical debate', *Critical Public Health*, 15, 4 (2005), 323–33.

[14] T. Wakeford and F. Hale, *Generation Scotland: Towards Participatory Models of Consultation* (University of Newcastle, Policy Ethics and Life Sciences Research Institute (PEALS), 2004), 9. http://129.215.140.49/gs/Documents/Consultation.pdf. See also Levitt, 'UK Biobank', 79.

[15] B. Godard, J. Marshall, C. Laberge and B. M. Knoppers, 'Strategies for consulting with the community: the case of four large-scale genetic databases', *Science and Engineering Ethics*, 10, 3 (2004), 468.

[16] Godard et al., 'Strategies for consulting with the community', 465, 468.

[17] Wakeford and Hale, *Towards Participatory Models of Consultation*, 9–10. The authors note that these 'tensions' are similar to those identified by Irwin in his critique of the DTI Public Consultation on Developments in the Biosciences (PCDB). See A. Irwin, 'Constructing the scientific citizen: science and democracy in the biosciences', *Public Understanding of Science*, 10 (2001), 13.

are being seriously examined'.[18] In the absence of any perceptible policy impact, commentators have pointed to the fact that the consultation appears to have succeeded only in a change of name from BioBank UK to UK Biobank, as it sounded 'less commercial'.[19] Less cynically, the consultations offered evidence of support for the proposed governance mechanism, but it is certainly true that there was an absence of transparency of process in terms of tracing the impact that consultation responses had on UK Biobank's set-up and management. Moreover, the consultations may be criticised for having adopted an expectation of a 'passive public' rather than one which would be more involved in UK Biobank's governance and decision making.

Perhaps in reaction to these perceived failings, there have been calls for greater participant involvement on decision making bodies. Subsequent to the publication of UK Biobank's Ethics and Governance Framework, for example, Tutton, Kaye and Hoyer urged funders 'to consider the inclusion of representatives of the participants in the EGC and other management bodies as a way of securing public trust and support'.[20] Recognising the potential limitations of 'public involvement initiatives', the authors maintain nonetheless that 'given the opportunity, the general public can contribute well-considered views to policy discussion'.[21]

The shareholder approach: from consultation to representation

More recently, David Winickoff has asked how projects such as UK Biobank might 'move beyond public consultation to embrace a participatory model of resource entitlement'.[22] He notes that '[i]n the wake of the well-documented failures of the Human Genome Diversity project, community participation in research governance of population genetics emerged as a central concern'.[23] While bioethicists have argued for group consent or community consultation, Winickoff eschews these forms of participation in favour of 'developing representational forms for the donor collective in biobanking'.[24] Winickoff maintains that 'if donors had some form of real representative power then project goals would be better achieved'.[25] In particular, 'some meaningful representation for the donor collective could greatly enhance both participation rate, participant

[18] Godard et al., 'Strategies for consulting with the community', 468–9.
[19] Wakeford and Hale, Towards Participatory Models of Consultation, 10.
[20] Tutton, Kaye and Hoyer, 'Governing UK Biobank', 285.   [21] Ibid.
[22] Winickoff, 'Partnership in U.K. Biobank', 451.
[23] Ibid., 449.   [24] Ibid.   [25] Ibid.

trust, and by extension, project sustainability'.[26] Winickoff notes that
'[m]ounting evidence suggests that there may be a divide between public
expectations [and values] and those of biobank managers, thereby creating an agency gap with potential destabilizing effects'.[27]

For Winickoff the core problem underlying the challenges of biobanks – both as to governance and arm's-length oversight – is one of
agency; that is, the problem of representing the interests of the donor collective, which provides crucial biological and informational material to
the resource.[28] While he notes that Fortun's idea of 'using the analogy of
labor for the organization of donors is ... a creative possibility', he rejects
it on the grounds that '[t]he labor analogy imagines an interest-based
form of relations which may not promote the very trust and goodwill that
both sides, researchers and donors, seek. Unionism also tends to move the
discourse away from charity and towards an interest in politics that can
undermine reciprocity and productive deliberation.'[29] Reconceptualising
labour as capital, he suggests instead that 'project planners and potential
research participants ought to consider new forms of "partnership governance" that draw upon the legal logic of corporate governance to solve
the agency problems involved in the management of collective genomic
assets'.[30]

The form of 'partnership governance' Winickoff favours is based on
a corporate shareholder model which, he suggests, may be 'less strange'
than it first seems: 'UK Biobank, after all, is a legal corporation.'[31]
Winickoff proposes 'constituting a committee of direct representatives
of the research participant group', which would play a formal governance role in UK Biobank.[32] During the consent process, potential donors
could voluntarily choose to sign on to a donor association. Association
members would elect the donor association leadership who would sit on
the UK Biobank Board of Directors, 'akin to how a major institutional
investor would sit on a commercial corporate board'.[33] The association
could also fill seats on the EGC. For the cohort of 500,000 participants,
the donor association might have 10,000 members. The association leadership would organise meetings to assess attitudes and preferences and

---

[26] *Ibid.*, 446.   [27] *Ibid.*   [28] *Ibid.*, 450.
[29] *Ibid.*   [30] *Ibid.*, 449.   [31] *Ibid.*, 451.
[32] *Ibid.*, 450. The idea of a committee of direct representatives of donors was developed by
Winickoff and Neumann elsewhere. See D. E. Winickoff and L. Neumann, 'Towards a
social contract for genomics: property and the public in the "Biotrust" model', *Genomics,
Society and Policy*, 1, 3 (2005), 8–21.
[33] Winickoff, 'Partnership in U.K. Biobank', 451.

deliberate policy choices regarding resource distribution, and would be bound to represent any collective decisions reached (e.g., guiding criteria for preferable research topics) on the Board of Directors and on the EGC. Although Winickoff acknowledges the operational challenges, he maintains nonetheless (1) that it might solve 'the agency gap between biobank donors and managers [which] may work towards solving the well-documented trust problem'; and (2) that it will provide direct representation for the donor group which is required 'if the social project of biobanking is to move forward fairly and sustainably'.[34]

Winickoff has contributed considerably to the debate by providing a practical attempt to turn the rhetoric of 'participation' into practice; he correctly identifies trust as a central problem, and that there may be an 'agency gap' between public expectations and those of biobank managers: we suggest, however, that his proposed model is problematic both conceptually and in practical terms. Furthermore, we are not persuaded that attempts to create a form of representation are necessarily the optimal means to involve publics and participants in biobank governance.

A shareholder approach: practical issues

There is an initial question of how far Winickoff's approach should be taken literally – as a wholesale proposal to transplant a corporate model into the biobank context – or whether his shareholder modelling should be seen as a metaphor for how participants should be involved in governance and decision making. He states: 'The idea that shareholders will be represented in corporate decision-making is one of the pillars of the corporate concept. Why should the same concept not apply in the realm of biobanks?'[35] Well, first, and most obviously, although UK Biobank is a company, it is a company limited by guarantee; more importantly, it is a registered charity. A company limited by guarantee is most commonly used for not-for-profit companies and 'is normally the only corporate structure that can be used for a registered charity'.[36] This entity has some features in common with public limited companies and private companies limited by shares (for example, limited liability and a separate legal personality from its members, so that it can hold

---

[34] *Ibid.*, 452.   [35] *Ibid.*, 451.
[36] R. Smerdon, *A Practical Guide to Corporate Governance*, 2nd edn (London: Sweet & Maxwell, 2004), 315. See also D. J. Hayton, *The Law of Trusts* (London: Sweet & Maxwell, 1998), 105; and P. L. Davies, *Gower and Davies' Principles of Modern Company Law*, 7th edn (London: Sweet & Maxwell, 2003), 7.

property and enter into contracts),[37] but it also has notable differences. The most important difference is that it has no share capital and therefore no shareholders.[38] The very notion of 'shareholders' is antithetical to this form of company. Moreover, UK Biobank's purpose is for 'public benefit', and all the powers of the company, like all charitable companies, 'can only be exercised in pursuance of the charity's objects and not for any other purpose'.[39] As Campbell has argued, 'to create some sort of participant *control* ... would be contrary to the stated aims of such projects, which is to enhance the health of all, not just participants'.[40] Indeed, although Winickoff speaks of biobanking as a 'social project', the shareholder model accommodates the donor collective only; the wider public is conspicuously absent. The model thus fails to take adequate account of the central question any system of governance must answer: 'What is the objective of the corporation and for whose benefit is it to be run?'[41] UK Biobank has an extremely wide constituency of concern which clearly includes its participants and their interests but which extends far beyond too; it is a resource to be managed for the public good and, ultimately, for the health of future generations.

Second, and something Winickoff himself raises, is the important question of whether any body 'could adequately represent the donor collective of UK Biobank, which will be a collection of 500,000 heterogeneous donors without a clearly shared goal'.[42] A body that purports to represent the donor collective would, we assume, need to reflect the diverse interests and views of the whole collective, including those of historically excluded and marginalised groups.[43] However, since the sign-up process for the donor association would be self-selecting,[44] it would be difficult to ensure that it included a broad range of 'voices',

---

[37] Hayton, *Law of Trusts*, 105.   [38] Smerdon, *A Practical Guide*, 316.   [39] *Ibid.*, 319.

[40] A. V. Campbell, 'The ethical challenges of genetic databases: safeguarding altruism and trust', *King's Law Journal*, 18 (2007), 242.

[41] UN Secretariat of the Economic Commission for Europe, 'Corporate governance in the ECE Region' in *Economic Survey of Europe 2003 No. 1* (Geneva: United Nations, 2003), 103–21, 109.

[42] Winickoff, 'Partnership in U.K. Biobank', 449.

[43] Traditionally marginalised groups include the economically disadvantaged, disabled and non-literate, as well as divisions based on gender, race and ethnicity. See Wakeford and Hale, *Towards Participatory Models of Consultation*, 11; and N. Urbinati and M. E. Warren, 'The concept of representative democracy in contemporary democratic theory', *Annual Review of Political Science*, 11 (2008), 394.

[44] See J. Burgess and J. Chilvers, 'Upping the *ante*: a conceptual framework for designing and evaluating participatory technology assessments', *Science and Public Policy*, 33, 10 (2006), 718, where the authors comment that many regard the major failing of

and it is unlikely that this group would be 'genuinely representative' of the 500,000 donor cohort. More worrying is the lesson to be learned from other realms where vocal minorities have exerted disproportionate influence on supposedly democratic and representative processes. Tait's commentary on the GM crops debacle is particularly illuminating in this regard:

> The value of a democratic governance process lies in its ability to prevent powerful vested interests from dominating decision making. There are many who regard the European GM crops regulatory outcome as an example of this process in action, the triumph of advocacy groups acting in the public interest, over the power of multinational companies. However, the European outcome could equally be seen as the replacement of one vested interest (the agro-biotechnology industry) by another more recently influential group, at least in the EU (public interest advocacy groups), with equally negative outcomes for democratic decision making on risk issues.[45]

There is, then, a danger that vocal minorities might come to dominate within the shareholder model, especially if connected to groups that are already well organised, resourced and mobilised (e.g., patient or advocacy groups)[46] and which have strong preconceived and fixed preferences about the use of the resource and/or the distribution of resources. It might also lead to a presumption that a model of representation is truly representative and that no further engagement is required.

These potential dangers also lead us to question whether a shareholder approach would necessarily address the trust problem that troubles Winickoff and others. In a report on a series of focus groups around UK Biobank, Levitt and Weldon note that:

> There was a general suspicion of all vested interests, not just commercial ones. 'People with an axe to grind' included patient groups and scientists themselves, who would try to orientate research to their particular interests.[47]

the GM debate to be that participants were self-selecting and therefore 'biased' and unrepresentative of wider UK publics.

[45] J. Tait, 'Risk governance of genetically modified crops: European and American perspectives' in O. Renn and K. Walker (eds.), *Global Risk Governance: Concept and Practice using the IRGC Framework* (Dordrecht, Netherlands: Springer Science and Business Media, 2008), 146.

[46] Wakeford and Hale have noted that social inclusion is problematic for engagement exercises also. See *Towards Participatory Models of Consultation*, 11.

[47] M. Levitt and S. Weldon, 'A well placed trust?: Public perceptions of the governance of DNA databases', *Critical Public Health*, 15, 4 (2005), 318.

A similar sentiment was echoed in a recent project undertaken by Tutton, Kerr and Cunningham-Burley[48] where focus groups discussed the possibility of participation in the governance of UK Biobank. Tutton notes that 'there was quite a degree of ambivalence' about 'lay' or 'public' membership on the Ethics and Governance Council:

> There were concerns among some focus groups with how individuals would be recruited, and these stressed the importance of ensuring their independence and having no conflicting interests.[49]

Thus, while Winickoff has suggested that a model of direct representation 'may work towards solving the well-documented trust problem', it could, in fact, have the opposite effect. Winickoff himself acknowledges some of these limitations:

> Donors are unlikely to agree in their preferences, and new forms of representation will always be just that, representations. Somebody has to speak for somebody else, and it will be specific donors who take these positions, and they will hold particular views, which could equally be said of any form of political representation.[50]

Although it is true that these observations could well 'be said of any form of political representation', this remark speaks to a far deeper concern with the very concept of 'representation' itself which has been challenged in democratic theory,[51] in particular the capacity of elected representatives to 'speak for' or 'act in the name of' the people they claim to represent'.[52] Democratic theorists have argued that representative government can be discriminatory and can exclude many groups from the political decision-making process.[53] Indeed, representation does not necessarily involve nor lead to wider participation in decision making processes. As Pimbert and

---

[48] R. Tutton, A. Kerr and S. Cunningham-Burley, 'Myriad stories: constructing expertise and citizenship in discussions of the new genetics' in M. Leach, I. Scoones and B. Wynne (eds.), *Science and Citizens: Globalization and the Challenge of Engagement* (London: Zed Press, 2005), referenced in R. Tutton, 'Constructing participation in genetic databases: citizenship, governance, and ambivalence', *Science, Technology & Human Values*, 32, 2 (2007), 174.

[49] Tutton, 'Constructing participation', 185–6.

[50] Winickoff, 'Partnership in U.K. Biobank', 452.

[51] See D. Runciman, 'The paradox of political representation', *Journal of Political Philosophy*, 15, 1 (2007), 100, where he comments that 'The ability of individuals to express their views, and to have those views heard, is a central feature of any kind of "genuinely" representative politics: no use of the term "representative" to describe a political system in which individuals are denied the ability to express their views would be plausible.'

[52] Urbinati and Warren, 'The concept of representative democracy', 390–1.

[53] *Ibid.*, 394.

Wakeford note, 'representative democracy has been heavily criticised for its inability to protect citizens' interests', and in particular the interests of marginalised groups, who 'often do not participate effectively in such representative democracy', and are 'ill served by the organisations that mobilise their votes and claim to represent their interests'.[54]

One of the central problems with representative democracy is that 'representation is understood as a principal-agent relationship, in which principals [constituencies] ... elect agents to stand for and act on their interests and opinions, thus separating the sources of legitimate power from those that exercise that power'.[55] In a very real sense, then, this approach may not address Winickoff's central concern, viz. the agency gap. It may, indeed, merely widen that gap by placing additional actors within governance mechanisms and do little more than provide a pastiche of participation. Williams has argued that we must think 'beyond principal-agent models of representation in which principals are presumed to be formally equal individuals'.[56] Urbinati and Warren note that much democratic theory has moved in this direction, 'conceiving democracy as any set of arrangements that instantiates the principle that all affected by collective decisions should have an opportunity to influence outcomes'.[57] This, the authors point out, 'enables us to avoid reduction of "democracy" to any particular kind of institution or decision-making mechanism'.[58] In turn, it leads us to question whether a form of representation such as that proffered by Winickoff is appropriate as a means of engagement. It may be neither necessary nor sufficient in providing a mechanism which allows an opportunity for *all* relevant parties to participate.

A shareholder approach: conceptual issues

In addition to the practical issues outlined above, there are fundamental conceptual issues with the shareholder analogy, particularly as it relates

---

[54] Pimbert and Wakeford , 'Citizen empowerment', 23.
[55] Urbinati and Warren, 'The concept of representative democracy', 389; and G. Brennan and A. Hamlin, 'On political representation', *British Journal of Political Science*, 29 (1999), 110. See also H. Pitkin, 'Representation and democracy: an uneasy alliance', *Scandinavian Political Studies*, 27, 3 (2004).
[56] Urbinati and Warren, 'The concept of representative democracy', 394, citing M. S. Williams, *Voice, Trust and Memory* (Princeton University Press, 1998).
[57] Urbinati and Warren, 'The concept of representative democracy', 392, 395 and the references cited therein.
[58] *Ibid.*, 395.

to the notion of 'partnership governance'. For Winickoff, 'the notion of "partnership" … connotes a form of cooperative human relations with respect to shared conditions and aims';[59] this, however, is manifestly different from the relations between shareholders and managers in the corporate world. As Winickoff himself notes, the relationship between shareholders and managers in corporations 'is fraught with the potential for mistrust and misappropriation'.[60] The various provisions under corporate law which Winickoff identifies as being aimed at solving the agency problem – for example, the fiduciary duties incumbent on managers and rules against self-dealing – are not just about 'closing the gap' between the expectations of shareholders and those of managers, they are about ensuring that managers serve the interests of the shareholders to the exclusion of the interests of all other stakeholders, and in particular their own.

The analogy of 'shareholders' or 'shareholding', like that of labour, suggests an interest-based form of relations, moving the discourse – and any resultant model – away from charity towards economics and private (property) rights. A shareholder model does not embody the ideal of 'partnership' either in theory or in practice, and, we suggest, would be equally likely to 'undermine reciprocity and productive deliberation'.[61] This is not to suggest that nothing of value can be gleaned from the corporate world, but it is important first to explore its landscape and to determine what lessons can, and cannot, be usefully learned.

Historically, '[s]hareholder supremacy [has been] the cornerstone of Anglo-American corporate governance'.[62] There are two predominant theories of the modern corporate form of organisation: as property, and as a nexus-of-contracts.[63] The property view conceives shareholders as the 'owners' of corporate assets, who have 'a moral and legal right that the corporation is run solely in their interests'.[64] The nexus-of-contracts model views the *firm* as a base for contracting, the ultimate aim of which is to make the firm an optimal base for contracting, thereby maximising

[59] Winickoff, 'Partnership in U.K. Biobank', 443.
[60] *Ibid.*, 451.   [61] *Ibid.*, 450.
[62] S. Kiarie, 'At crossroads: shareholder value, stakeholder value and enlightened shareholder value: which road should the United Kingdom take?', *International Company and Commercial Law Review*, 17, 11 (2007), 329.
[63] C. Mason, J. Kirkbride and D. Bryde, 'From stakeholders to institutions: the changing face of social enterprise governance theory', *Management Decision*, 45, 2 (2007), 287.
[64] *Ibid.* Although shareholders are 'conceived' of as owning corporate assets, they do not in law 'own the company'. See in this regard S. Deakin, 'The coming transformation of shareholder value', *Corporate Governance*, 13, 1 (2005), 11.

benefit to shareholders through increased residual income.[65] In both, the defining feature is the primacy of shareholders.[66] Under American law, 'the purpose of the corporation ... is to make profits and the beneficiaries of those profits are the shareholders'.[67] The duty of managers is to act in the interests of, and to maximise returns (i.e., profit) for, the shareholders as a whole.[68] Shareholders alone, to the exclusion of all other stakeholders, have the right to hold managers and directors accountable.[69]

Both of these theories take their starting point from what has been termed the 'separation of ownership and control' in the modern public company,[70] whereby control of the company is delegated to managers, who act as agents for the shareholders (principals).[71] Since control is in the hands of managers there is a 'moral hazard' that the agents will not always act in the shareholders' interests.[72] At the heart of agency theory is the assumption that both the principal (shareholder) and the agent (manager) are motivated by self-interest – what Davis *et al.* refer to as 'individualistic utility motivation' – which is likely to result in a diversion of interests between the principal and agent.[73] Where there is interest diversion between shareholders and managers, the objective of agency theory is to reduce the cost to shareholders of managers' 'self-interested opportunism', by realigning the interests of management with those of the shareholders.[74] This is accomplished through a set of controls, including monitoring and incentives or sanctions, carried out by the board

[65] Mason *et al.*, 'From stakeholders to institutions', 287.　[66] *Ibid.*

[67] UN, 'Corporate governance in the ECE Region', 109.

[68] *Ibid.* See also A. Gamble and G. Kelly, 'Shareholder value and the stakeholder debate in the UK', *Corporate Governance*, 9, 2 (2001), 113.

[69] Deakin, 'The coming transformation', 12.

[70] Gamble and Kelly, 'The stakeholder debate', 111, referencing A. Berle and G. Means, *The Modern Corporation and Private Property* (New York: Macmillan, 1932). Gamble and Kelly suggest that it 'is more accurately described as a fragmentation of ownership'.

[71] Because of its association with the separation of ownership and control, the relationship between shareholders and managers of the company has been described as the 'pure agency relationship'. See J. H. Davis, F. D. Schoorman and L. Donaldson, 'Towards a stewardship theory of management', *Academy of Management Review*, 27, 1 (1997), 21, citing M. C. Jensen and W. H. Meckling, 'Theory of the firm: managerial behaviour, agency costs and ownership structure', *Journal of Finance Economics*, 3 (1976).

[72] D. W. Anderson, S. J. Melanson and J. Maly, 'The evolution of corporate governance: power redistribution brings boards to life', *Corporate Governance*, 15, 5 (2007), 781.

[73] Davis *et al.*, 'Towards a stewardship theory', 20, 22.

[74] J. Roberts, 'Agency theory, ethics and corporate governance', paper prepared for the Corporate Governance and Ethics Conference, Macquarie Graduate School of Management, Sydney, Australia, 28–30 June 2004, 2. www.le.ac.uk/ulsm/research/cppe/levinas/pdf/roberts2.pdf.

of directors on behalf of the shareholders.[75] Agency theory, then, when applied to corporate governance, is not merely about the agent 'representing' the principal's interests: it is about how the principal (shareholder) can ensure that his or her agents (company managers) will serve the shareholders' interests and not their own.[76] Deakin has gone so far as to suggest that under agency theory 'the function of shareholders is to *discipline* corporate management' (emphasis in the original).[77]

The 'shareholder' analogy envisions not 'partnership' or 'co-operation' but, rather, *self-interest* and *control*. There is something inherently antagonistic about the relationship between shareholders and managers, which neither embodies nor reflects an 'ethos of trust' or 'goodwill'.[78] Moreover, the shareholder model of governance firmly places shareholders at the centre of the company, which 'is conceived as being managed primarily in their interests'.[79] Thus, the notion of 'shareholding' is antithetical to the purpose of UK Biobank which is aimed at benefiting the wider community or society. More explicitly, whereas the objective of the corporation in a shareholder model of governance is to 'maximise profits for its shareholders',[80] the objective of UK Biobank is to 'maximise benefits' (in the form of improved prevention, diagnosis and treatment of illness) for society, and not the donors specifically. This language and conceptualisation therefore clearly sit extremely awkwardly with an entity like UK Biobank.

We acknowledge that the shareholder analogy might work better in the context of a private biobank such as PXE International,[81] an example Winickoff points to as a model in which some rare disease groups have 'leveraged … control of the biobank *qua* biocapital' to achieve 'their own research goals'.[82] We believe, however, that the analogy breaks down

[75] Anderson *et al.*, 'The evolution of corporate governance', 781; and Davis *et al.*, 'Towards a stewardship theory', 23.
[76] Roberts, 'Agency theory', 2.
[77] Deakin, 'The coming transformation', 15.
[78] Winickoff, 'Partnership in U.K. Biobank', 450.
[79] Gamble and Kelly, 'The stakeholder debate', 110.
[80] UN, 'Corporate governance in the ECE Region', 109.
[81] PXE International has negotiated a contract with researchers in which the foundation retains ownership rights in any patent application arising from the research, thereby enabling the foundation to share in any revenues, to influence future licensing agreements and to ensure widespread and affordable genetic tests. See D. Gitter, 'Ownership of human tissue: a proposal for federal recognition of human research participants' property rights in their biological material', *Washington & Lee Law Review*, 61 (2004), 262, 315.
[82] Winickoff, 'Partnership in U.K. Biobank', 450.

in the context of large public-oriented resources such as UK Biobank. Whereas UK Biobank does not have one overriding research goal, PXE International does – to encourage researchers to study the genetic basis of PXE to develop therapies.[83] Since donors to the PXE biobank are those affected by the rare disorder and their families,[84] it is easier to conceptualise them as 'shareholders', with a direct, tangible and shared interest both in the research conducted using the resource and its benefits. It is far less easy and less appropriate to conceptualise the participants in UK Biobank as 'shareholders', as they will have varied and potentially conflicting goals, will be unlikely to benefit directly from any research conducted using the resource, and have contributed to the resource explicitly for the benefit of others.[85]

To conclude this section, we welcome Winickoff's contribution for opening up the debate and the possibilities when it comes to addressing two key issues of concern in biobank governance, namely, the agency gap and the fostering and maintaining of trust. We are not convinced, however, that a shareholder paradigm is either necessary or sufficient to address the concerns. Representation might move beyond mere consultation in carving out an active role for a happy few, but given evidence of public suspicion around the prospect of *any* vested interests, it is not obvious that the inclusion of 'a small set of' self-selected donor representatives in the governance framework of UK Biobank would necessarily enhance public trust. Moreover, the very idea of 'shareholders' in UK Biobank suggests a privileged position, notably for participants, when the very purpose of UK Biobank is for the benefit of all. If participation in such a public endeavour should be opened up – as we agreed that it should – then it is not at all clear that a shareholder approach goes far enough: we must move beyond its corporate confines. Finally, we would point out that a model of representation does nothing to ensure that 'the right sort of deliberations'[86] take place within either the UK Biobank Board of Directors or the EGC, with the donor collective as a whole, or

---

[83] D. E. Winickoff, 'Governing population genomics: law, bioethics, and biopolitics in three case studies', *Jurimetrics*, 43 (2003), 223.

[84] S. F. Terry, 'Learning genetics', *Health Affairs*, 22, 5 (2003), 171.

[85] Winickoff himself has recognised this in part elsewhere: see 'Governing population genomics', 226.

[86] See N. Daniels and J. Sabin, 'The ethics of accountability in managed care reform', *Health Affairs*, 17, 5 (1998), 61, where the authors note, in the context of managed care plans, that 'Consumer participation might improve deliberation about some matters, but ... Simply being accountable to a "board" containing consumer representatives would not ensure that the right sort of deliberation took place at appropriate levels in the plan.'

indeed with wider constituencies such as society itself. Without robust, inclusive and transparent processes, the legitimacy of decisions would remain open to question.

Of relevance here are recent developments in political democratic theory, which have given rise to an increase in the use of 'Deliberative and Inclusive Processes' in a variety of different fields, including policy making and technology assessment.[87] This 'deliberative turn' has had a substantial influence on the design of engagement processes in emerging areas of science and biotechnology generally,[88] and in the context of biobanks specifically. Burgess et al., for example, have convincingly argued that the use of deliberative methods of engagement 'is a necessity if we are to meaningfully consider diverse "public interests" during the development of biobanks'.[89] Because of the potential 'impact' of biobanking on society and individual rights, the authors argue that 'biobanking policy must consider the informed and deliberative input of a range of perspectives within the citizenry'.[90] They note that current policy approaches manifest 'democratic deficits, including a lack of representation of diverse public interests'.[91] 'Representativeness' is used here in a different sense from that used by Winickoff, in that it is concerned with providing a reflection of a wide range of interests, rather than speaking on behalf of such interests. It is concerned with social representativeness as opposed to statistical representativeness.[92] The value of such deliberative democratic mechanisms is that they provide a potential evidence base for decision making,[93] yet they say little about how the process might be translated into policy or concrete decisions. Research undertaken into public views on biobanking may be instructive, but it remains at arm's-length to those managing

---

[87] Pimbert and Wakeford, 'Citizen empowerment', 23. See also S. Chambers, 'Deliberative democratic theory', *Annual Review of Political Science*, 6 (2003), 307, where she notes that deliberative democratic theory is being applied in a number of research areas, including policy studies and empirical research.

[88] See generally Burgess and Chilvers, 'Upping the *ante*'; and J. Chilvers, 'Deliberating competence: theoretical and practitioner perspectives on effective participatory appraisal practice', *Science, Technology & Human Values*, 33, 3 (2008), 421–51.

[89] M. Burgess, K. O'Doherty and D. Secko, 'Biobanking in British Columbia: discussions of personalized medicine through deliberative public engagement', *Personalized Medicine*, 5, 3 (2008), 285.

[90] *Ibid.*, 286.   [91] *Ibid.*, 285.

[92] Burgess and Chilvers, 'Upping the *ante*', 719.

[93] Burgess and Chilvers, e.g., have said that 'Not only should the inclusion of a wider range of voices assist in the development of more robust decisions, it should also contribute to the political legitimacy of the outcome on the basis of the representativeness of the participants.' *Ibid.*, 718.

biobanks, and the practical impact is unclear. Moreover, engagement exercises, especially in the biosciences, are often 'one-off' events which further limits their impact over time. It is for these reasons that we contend that we must consider mechanisms of on-going participation that place the organisation, and more particularly management, at the centre of the process, and that this requires a shift to a stakeholder approach.[94]

The stakeholder approach – from representation to participation

We have already suggested that the corporate world might hold valuable lessons for biobank governance, albeit that we reject a shareholder model. A more fitting approach is a stakeholder model of governance, which is widely used in the not-for-profit company sector[95] and 'has become one of ... management theory's most encompassing concepts'[96] since Freeman's landmark book, *Strategic Management: A Stakeholder Approach* in 1984. Of particular relevance is the social orientation of the stakeholder approach, with its emphasis on inclusion and accountability, as is the recent trend in the conduct of stakeholder relationships towards interactive and on-going engagement.[97] In this regard, there are some interesting parallels between a stakeholder approach and notions of 'participatory democracy' prevalent in the social science literature. Although much of the discussion below is drawn from corporate governance, the general concepts are applicable to all types of organisations.

Stakeholder theory draws its basic ideology from communitarian philosophy and is connected with broader 'philosophical and political arguments about creating a "stakeholder society"';[98] i.e., a society based on 'fairness and a move towards social responsibility and respect for others'.[99] The basic premise is that organisations should be 'run for the benefit of,

---

[94] The stakeholder approach to management is to be distinguished from stakeholder analysis. While stakeholder analysis may be part of a stakeholder approach to management, it is not synonymous with it. See J. Chevalier, *Stakeholder Analysis and Natural Resource Management* (Ottawa: Carlton University, 2001). http://http-server.carleton.ca/~jchevali/STAKEH2.html.

[95] See C. Low and C. Cowton, 'Beyond stakeholder engagement: the challenges of stakeholder participation in corporate governance', *International Journal of Business Governance and Ethics*, 1, 1 (2004), 45–55.

[96] M. Morsing and M. Schultz, 'Corporate social responsibility communication: shareholder information, response and involvement strategies', *Business Ethics: A European Review*, 15, 4 (2006), 324.

[97] See generally *ibid*.

[98] B. Pettet, *Company Law*, 2nd edn (Harlow: Pearson Education Limited, 2005), 61.

[99] C. E. Metcalfe, 'The stakeholder corporation', *Business Ethics*, 7, 1 (1998), 34.

and be accountable to, all their stakeholders'.[100] The model 'aims at inclusion and broader accountability';[101] it is a 'search for social consensus, for community'.[102] Metcalfe has said that '[s]takeholding's aim is to benefit an organisation's wider community – i.e., society'.[103] In the corporate context, stakeholder theory is '[t]he theory that a firm should be run in the interests of all its stakeholders rather than just the shareholders'.[104] In exploring the potential breadth of stakeholder involvement, Freeman and McVea have noted that 'the [stakeholder] approach sought to broaden the concept of strategic management beyond its traditional economic roots, by defining stakeholders as "any group or individual who can affect or be affected by the achievement of the organization's objective"'.[105] This is premised on the principle that an organisation has responsibilities to a broad range of stakeholders. Evan and Freeman have suggested that this responsibility is fiduciary in nature and that management must act in the interests of stakeholders, as well as the organisation, in order to 'safeguard the long-term stakes of each group' and 'ensure the survival of the firm'.[106]

For Freeman, the 'survival of the firm' is 'the achievement of an organization's objectives'.[107] One of those objectives is to understand *stakeholder relationships* – that is, how the firm might affect others and gain support from those who can affect the firm in the long term (for better or worse).[108] Freeman and McVea have argued that 'in a world of ... accelerating change ... [t]he interests of key stakeholders must be integrated into the very purpose of the firm, and stakeholder relationships must be managed in a coherent and strategic fashion'.[109] A stakeholder approach thus requires 'the simultaneous attention to the legitimate interests of all appropriate stakeholders, both in the establishment of organisational structures and general policies'.[110] On this view, stakeholders are treated

---

[100] *Ibid.*, 30, citing W. Hutton, *The State We're In* (London: Jonathan Cape, 1995).

[101] Kiarie, 'At crossroads', 332.   [102] Pettet, *Company Law*, 62.

[103] Metcalfe, 'The stakeholder corporation', 34.

[104] G. Vinten, 'Shareholder versus stakeholder – is there a governance dilemma?', *Corporate Governance*, 9, 1 (2001), 37.

[105] R. E. Freeman and J. McVea, 'A stakeholder approach to strategic management', in M. A. Hitt, R. E. Freeman and J. S. Harrison (eds.), *The Blackwell Handbook of Strategic Management* (Oxford: Blackwell Publishing, 2001), 189.

[106] W. M. Evan and R. E. Freeman, 'A stakeholder theory of the modern corporation: Kantian capitalism', in T. L. Beauchamp and N. Bowie (eds.), *Ethical Theory and Business*, 3rd edn (Englewood Cliffs, NJ: Prentice Hall, 1988), 103, cited in B. Langtry, 'Stakeholders and the moral responsibilities of business', *Business Ethics Quarterly*, 4, 4 (1994), 433.

[107] Freeman and McVea, 'A stakeholder approach', 194.   [108] *Ibid.*   [109] *Ibid.*, 193.

[110] T. Donaldson and L. E. Preston, 'The stakeholder theory of the corporation: concepts, evidence and implications', *Academy of Management Review*, 20, 1 (1995), 67. The

'as ends unto themselves', rather than simply as '*means to a corporate end*' (emphasis in the original).[111]

It should be self-evident that this approach has significant resonance with the current UK Biobank governance framework, not least in the EGF's explicit commitment to participants, users *and* society. But on this view, potentially anyone, or everyone, could be a stakeholder – *how* is this term defined and *what* does it mean? Is such a broad commitment workable, and if so, *how*? More particularly, *what* does a stakeholder approach mean in terms of engagement and *how* can an organisation like UK Biobank effectively involve its stakeholders in governance and decisionmaking?

Identifying stakeholders

Freeman's definition of 'stakeholder' as 'any group or individual who can affect or is affected by the achievement of the organization's objective' is the most widely accepted.[112] Commonly identified stakeholders in the corporate context include shareholders and investors, employees, customers and suppliers, special interest groups, competitors, the natural environment, the state, local communities and society-at-large.[113] Applying Freeman's definition to UK Biobank, stakeholders would include (among

---

requirement that the interests of all legitimate stakeholders must be given simultaneous attention falls on anyone who manages or affects corporate policies.

[111] Freeman and McVea, 'A stakeholder approach', 196. This neo-Kantian principle has been developed by Evan and Freeman elsewhere. See Evan and Freeman, 'Kantian capitalism'; R. E. Freeman and W. M. Evan, 'Corporate governance: a stakeholder interpretation', *Journal of Behavioural Economics*, 19, 4 (1990), 337–59; and R. E. Freeman, 'The politics of stakeholder theory: some future directions', *Business Ethics Quarterly*, 4, 4 (1994), 415. See also Donaldson and Preston, 'The stakeholder theory of the corporation', 67, where the authors argue that the fundamental basis of stakeholder theory is normative and involves accepting that '[t]he interests of all stakeholders are of intrinsic value'.

[112] R. E. Freeman, *Strategic Management: A Stakeholder Approach* (Boston, MA: Pitman, 1984), 46, cited in A. Kolk and J. Pinkse, 'Stakeholder mismanagement and corporate social responsibility crisis', *European Management Journal*, 24, 1 (2006), 60.

[113] See A. J. Hillman and G. D. Keim, 'Shareholder value, stakeholder management, and social issues: what's the bottom line?', *Strategic Management Journal*, 22, 2 (2001), 126–7 and the references cited therein; Metcalfe, 'The stakeholder corporation', 30, citing J. Argenti, *Your Organization: What Is It For?* (New York: McGraw Hill, 1993); A. B. Carroll, 'The pyramid of corporate social responsibility: toward the moral management of organizational stakeholders', *Business Horizons* (July-August 1991), 43; and N. K. Kakabadse, C. Rozuel and L. Lee-Davies, 'Corporate social responsibility and stakeholder approach: a conceptual review', *International Journal of Business Governance and Ethics*, 1, 4 (2005), 294.

others) participants; UK Biobank's Board of Directors; the EGC; funders and members of the company; researchers; communities; the wider public or society and, arguably, future generations whose health the resource is intended to improve.

It is interesting to note that, in much of the literature on public engagement processes related to the biosciences, 'the public' are often positioned as 'other' than a stakeholder.[114] MacLean and Burgess, for example, classify 'stakeholders' along with 'experts' as 'groups [that] have topically related expertise and are invested in the advancement of research in certain areas'.[115] Similarly, Sheremata has suggested that a non-exhaustive list of stakeholders in biobanking would include: 'the participants (and their relatives or fellow "group" members), the researchers and the research community, health care providers, agencies that fund research, regulating bodies, other users of data, special interest groups and the media'.[116] Neither the public, communities nor, indeed, society are viewed as 'stakeholders'.[117] This is very curious considering, as Burgess has noted, the potential 'societal impact' of biobanking. The longitudinal nature of a project like UK Biobank means necessarily that wider groups such as potential participants, potential beneficiaries and future generations – amorphous as they may seem – are as crucial to the success of biobanking projects as more easily identified stakeholder groups.

Winickoff dismisses the involvement of the 'British taxpaying public' in the governance of UK Biobank on the ground that it 'enjoys indirect representation on the Board of Directors' through the Department of Health and Medical Research Council.[118] While we might quibble about how far this is true, it is undeniable that the British public has a stake in the project in numerous senses, not least because it is funded partly with public money but also because 'the public' is an explicitly identified beneficiary in the EGF. On the other side, large sectors of the British public can affect the success of UK Biobank by choosing to participate or not. Although

[114] There are, of course, exceptions. See, for example, Laurie et al., 'The roles of values and interests', forthcoming.
[115] S. MacLean and M. M. Burgess, 'Biobanks: informing the public through expert and stakeholder presentations', Health Law Review, 16, 4 (2008), 6.
[116] L. Sheremata, Population Biobanking in Canada: Ethical, Legal and Social Issues, Report for the Canadian Biotechnology Advisory Committee (2003), 15.
[117] One report on the GM Nation? debate commented that participants at an open 'public' meeting 'approached the status of stakeholders', because they held strong pre-existing views, knowledge and interest (emphasis added). See Burgess and Chilvers, 'Upping the ante', 719.
[118] Winickoff, 'Partnership in U.K. Biobank', 444.

UK Biobank has recruited almost 190,000 participants to date,[119] there are still over 300,000 *potential* participants. This is a substantial stakeholder group, and although it is impossible to identify who a potential donor might be, Biobank's policies and the actions it takes will have a significant impact on this group's willingness (or otherwise) to participate. This is true at recruitment *and* throughout the project because participants can withdraw at any time and because new participants might be sought in the future. It is, therefore, crucial that UK Biobank's policies reflect social norms and ethical values and adequately take account of public concerns as these are now and as these might shift over time.[120]

Unlike the shareholder model, which would directly involve a handful of donors (at most) in decision making and governance, the stakeholder model envisions the involvement of *all* legitimate stakeholders. Considering the vast number of stakeholders (both individuals and groups) who might have a legitimate 'stake' in UK Biobank, however, how could this be achieved in practice?

Involving stakeholders

Kakabadse *et al.* have argued that a major 'flaw' in the stakeholder approach is that, since 'everyone' could theoretically be a stakeholder, 'then the notion of accountability becomes valueless because it is too broadly set and useless from a managerial point of view'.[121] Their solution is the need for a clear classification of stakeholder groups, but arguably this already exists for UK Biobank and it is drawn extremely widely.

Fundamentally, we must ask what does it mean to involve stakeholders (and how to do so *well*)? In response, we would point out that direct involvement in decision-making through notional representation, as envisioned by Winickoff, is but one way to conceive of stakeholder involvement. Diversity and fluidity among the amorphous communities in question render attempts at statistical representation disingenuous and social representativeness impractical; equally, direct involvement in decision making is also unrealistic. It does not follow, however, that this diversity and fluidity cannot be mapped and taken into account in decision

---

[119] As of 22 September 2008 UK Biobank reported recruitment of 186,484 participants.

[120] See further Laurie *et al.*, 'The roles of values and interests', 72–3.

[121] Kakabadse *et al.*, 'Corporate social responsibility and stakeholder approach', 293, referencing H. Hummels, 'Organizing ethics: a stakeholder debate', *Journal of Business Ethics*, 17, 13 (1998), 293; and G. Vinten, 'The stakeholder manager', *Management Decisions*, 38, 6 (2000), 377–83.

making and governance; indeed, Morsing and Schultz have argued that what is required is a clear strategy for engagement with stakeholders with frequent and systematic interaction.[122] Central in this process is the role of management: 'Leadership is a determinant in shaping and orienting the organisational climate so that the expectations of organisational constituents match more socially accepted norms of behaviour.'[123]

The following section outlines two different approaches to stakeholder involvement in the corporate and not-for-profit sectors, and evaluates their applicability to UK Biobank.

The stakeholder participation strategy

Low and Cowton have noted that a stakeholder 'participation model', which seeks to move beyond 'engagement'[124] and involve stakeholders in a more active governance role, is most commonly achieved through representation on boards or other management bodies.[125] This approach might be seen as a hybrid accommodation between Winickoff's shareholder model (which privileges participants) and a stakeholder model which includes a wider range of players. Certainly, while this model may be appealing in that stakeholder views cannot be 'pushed aside once representatives have been granted a place on the board',[126] it is 'plagued by the issue of which stakeholder groups should be included'[127] in the first place. Referring to Freeman's definition of 'stakeholder', Low and Cowton point out that 'theoretically a huge range of stakeholders could be ... recruited to the governance function. Clearly this would make the management of such initiatives unworkable.'[128] They suggest that for organisations operating beyond a single sector, large numbers of stakeholders 'may be best accommodated by the formation of a stakeholder council which would not strictly be part of the board but that could have representatives that were elected to the board'.[129] Again, this is much like Winickoff's 'shareholder model', but with three important differences: first, representatives would be drawn from a wider constituency

[122] Morsing and Schultz, 'Corporate social responsibility', 328.
[123] Kakabadse et al., 'Corporate social responsibility and stakeholder approach', 296.
[124] The 'engagement model' of stakeholder management involves activities such as meetings with key stakeholder representatives and public meetings in the locality of the corporation's activities. This model 'keeps stakeholders at arm's-length from any corporate level decision-making'. See Low and Cowton, 'Beyond stakeholder engagement', 48.
[125] Kiarie, 'At crossroads', 333; and Mason et al., 'From stakeholders to institutions', 288–9.
[126] Low and Cowton, 'Beyond stakeholder engagement', 49.
[127] Ibid.   [128] Ibid.   [129] Ibid., 52.

(that is, from the wider public and not just from the donor collective); second, participation would not be conditional on representatives having donated 'biocapital' to the resource; and finally, representatives would be 'recruited', rather than self-selected. None the less, this approach raises many of the same concerns as the shareholder model. While the inclusion of 'diverse voices and opinions' in board processes[130] might theoretically translate into greater 'representativeness', as Daniels and Sabin have commented, although in a different context, there is no 'realistic mechanism' for making representatives 'truly representative' of the population as a whole.[131] Moreover, it would not necessarily ensure openness and accountability. And, as we have argued, we are not convinced that representation is necessarily the correct approach, especially if this shifts the onus from managers or a board to engage proactively with a broad range of stakeholders effectively and over time.

The stakeholder involvement strategy

Whereas stakeholder theory has focused traditionally on how companies might 'manage' stakeholders,[132] with all of the negative connotations associated with that term, there has been a shift towards long-term 'interactive, mutually engaged and responsive relationships' between companies and stakeholders, which 'create the groundwork for transparency and accountability'.[133] 'This', as Morsing and Schultz comment, 'brings the notion of participation, dialogue and involvement to the centre of stakeholder theory, with clear inspiration (and aspiration) from democratic ideals'.[134] Indeed, as Goodjik notes, this more democratic approach envisions a '*partnership* between management and stakeholders, a partnership as a real dynamic and changing process of dialogue' (emphasis added).[135]

[130] W. A. Brown, 'Inclusive governance practices in nonprofit organizations and implications for practice', *Nonprofit Management and Leadership*, 12, 4 (2002), 372.
[131] Daniels and Sabin, 'The ethics of accountability', 61.
[132] Morsing and Schultz, 'Corporate social responsibility', 325. See also S. Waddock, 'Parallel universes: companies, academics and the progress of corporate citizenship', *Business and Society Review*, 109, 1 (2004), 25.
[133] J. Andriof, S. Waddock, B. Husted and S. S. Rahman (eds.), *Unfolding Stakeholder Thinking: Theory, Responsibility and Engagement* (Sheffield: Greenleaf, 2002), 9, cited in Morsing and Schultz, 'Corporate social responsibility', 325.
[134] Morsing and Schultz, 'Corporate social responsibility', 325.
[135] R. Goodjik, 'Partnership at corporate level: the meaning of the stakeholder model', *Journal of Change Management*, 3, 3 (2003), 237.

In this regard, Morsing and Schultz have commented that by engaging in frequent and systematic interaction with multiple stakeholders, the organisation 'ideally ensures that it keeps abreast not only of its stakeholders' concurrent expectations but also of its potential influence on those expectations, as well as letting those expectations influence [the organisation] itself'.[136] This form of interaction – 'stakeholder involvement strategy' – 'invites concurrent negotiation with its stakeholders to explore their concerns ... while also accepting changes when they are necessary'.[137] This approach requires organisational commitment both to put in place mechanisms for on-going dialogue with multiple stakeholders and to respond and adapt to their concerns. As Harrison and St John have emphasised, an organisation must make a commitment to and be proactive about forming strategic partnerships with stakeholders.[138] Moreover, they warn that to avoid difficulties over the long term, organisations must avoid acting 'contrary to societal values'.[139] This can be achieved by 'listening and involving stakeholders in organisational processes'.[140]

Finally, Carroll has noted that, in terms of corporate social responsibility, companies have certain ethical responsibilities to their stakeholders. These are:

1. To perform in a manner consistent with expectations of social mores and ethical norms.
2. To recognise and respect new or evolving ethical/moral norms adopted by society.
3. To prevent ethical norms from being compromised in order to achieve corporate goals.
4. To define good corporate citizenship as doing what is expected morally or ethically.
5. To recognise that corporate integrity and ethical behaviour go beyond mere compliance with laws and regulations.[141]

In contrast to the shareholder model, a stakeholder model genuinely resonates with democratic notions of 'participation', 'involvement' and 'inclusion'. This not only reflects the growing trend towards more deliberative and participatory mechanisms for involving publics in governance processes generally, but also accords with UK Biobank's and the

[136] Morsing and Schultz, 'Corporate social responsibility', 328.   [137] *Ibid.*
[138] J. S. Harrison and C. H. St John, 'Managing and partnering with external stakeholders', *Academy of Management Executive*, 10, 2 (1996), 58.
[139] *Ibid.*, 56.   [140] *Ibid.*, 58.
[141] Carroll, 'The pyramid of corporate social responsibility', 41.

EGC's own commitments to 'seek active engagement' with a variety of stakeholders, including 'participants, research users and society in general over the lifetime of the resource'.[142] It is also underpinned by a strong normative core, which recognises that ethics cannot be separated from an organisation's activities.[143]

The EGF embodies UK Biobank's commitments to its stakeholders and it is a living document. The expectation and the reality is that it will evolve in response to changing circumstances, including changes in stakeholder expectations. We would suggest that the processes necessary to allow this to happen effectively could be informed by the five points outlined above, and more particularly through specific exercises in stakeholder engagement which would inform biobanking decision-making and governance. UK Biobank itself has not engaged in any such exercises to date, but useful first steps have been taken by its EGC in discharging its role in the spirit of transparency, openness and reflexive governance.[144]

The EGC is committed to making explicit the basis for much of its reasoning and what informs its advisory and monitoring role: for example, it has produced documentation that explores and explains its approach to *advising in the public interest*. The Council also holds regular public meetings from which a list of Frequently Asked Questions is developed and updated on its website. It has also commissioned research on public attitudes in the important area of access and commercialisation to inform itself and UK Biobank about potential public concerns and possible ways forward.

A commitment to garnering an evidence base of stakeholder perspectives on an on-going basis represents a form of stakeholder involvement which does not reduce the exercise to a one-size-fits-all model nor mere tokenism which may undermine rather than foster public trust. By the same token, this form of engagement cannot realistically expect to satisfy the entire range of diverse views that it will generate; but then this should neither be its purpose nor should it be the expectation raised among stakeholders. It is reasonable and appropriate, however, for stakeholders to expect that their views and perspectives will be taken into account in decision making and governance, and that these processes are transparent with clear explanations and justifications for decisions reached or advice given. As Daniels and Sabin have argued, the overall

[142] UK Biobank Ethics and Governance Framework, Version 3.0 (October 2007), 3. www.ukbiobank.ac.uk/docs/EGF20082.pdf.
[143] See in this regard Freeman, 'The politics of stakeholder theory', 412.
[144] See generally Ethics and Governance Council, www.egcukbiobank.org.uk/.

aim should be to produce a process in which decisions are reached that are acceptable to (all) reasonable persons because the reasons and means by which they have been reached can be understood, even if they are not agreed with.[145]

Conclusion

There is much value in Winickoff's shareholder model for its attempt to turn the rhetoric of participation into reality, but it is problematic both practically and conceptually. In particular, we take issue with Winickoff's description of the problem underlying biobank governance as one of agency; that is, of representing the interests of the donor collective. To give participants alone a 'voice' would not only be contrary to Biobank's charitable purpose (which is for public benefit), but would also be unlikely to address the issue of public trust. Moreover, the inclusion of a few participants on UK Biobank's Board of Directors and the EGC might well become merely tokenistic – a quick institutional fix[146] – that could forestall productive deliberation. We have argued instead that the fundamental challenge is a commitment to engage with and take account of the views of stakeholders through processes which are robust, transparent and endure throughout the life of the project.

Accordingly, we contend that a more appropriate alternative is a stakeholder approach, which envisions direct and on-going dialogue between all legitimate stakeholders and management. This approach reflects both UK Biobank's purpose and its commitment to engage with a wide variety of stakeholders. However, the stakeholder approach requires not only a commitment to engage frequently and systematically, but also a willingness to respond and adapt to stakeholder concerns over time. It must be an iterative process, in which management both identifies stakeholders (or stakeholder groups) and develops strategies to manage these relationships actively and promote shared interests.[147] In this regard, deliberative engagement mechanisms might enhance such processes, but it falls to

---

[145]   For the full argument, see N. Daniels and J. Sabin, *Setting Limits Fairly: Can We Learn to Share Medical Resources?* (New York: Oxford University Press, 2002).

[146]   Irwin has said that we should not be looking for 'institutional fixes, but rather the development of an open and critical discussion between researchers, policy makers and citizens'. See Irwin, 'Constructing the scientific citizen', 16.

[147]   See Freeman and McVea, 'A stakeholder approach', 192 where the authors note that 'A stakeholder approach emphasizes *active* management of the business environment, relationships and the promotion of shared interests.'

management to ensure that engagement moves beyond mere consultation and mere representation and is, rather, a genuine commitment to involve stakeholders.

Acknowledgements

The authors would like to thank Heather Widdows, Caroline Mullen and two anonymous reviewers for their extremely helpful comments on earlier drafts; and David Winickoff for his valuable contribution to the debate and for inviting us to think outside the box.

8

Genetic information and public opinion

ANDREW EDGAR

The purpose of this chapter is to explore the nature of public debate in the field of genetics. Focusing on the issue of developing DNA biobanks, it will be argued that public consultation and involvement are crucial to the process of sustaining and legitimating such projects. However, it will be suggested that consultation processes are readily distorted, due to the complexity of the science involved, and the ideological distortions that are inherent in much of the language and imagery that is available to think about genetics. It will therefore be suggested that public consultation must proceed in the spirit of an ideology critique – that takes both the scientific and public understandings of genetics seriously, but recognises that such understandings may be symptomatic of deep-seated cultural fears and imbalances of power.

Genetic information and biobanks

Einsiedel argues that the completion of the mapping and sequencing of the human genome in 2001 was not the end of a project, but the beginning.[1] The human genome is not, in itself, meaningful. Mapping and sequencing merely serve to identify the chromosomal site of each gene, and to identify the gene's molecular composition (of deoxyribonucleic acid (DNA) base pairs), respectively.[2] Genes are expressed in the production of proteins.[3] Understanding and making sense of the role that this fundamental organic chemistry plays in the formation and behaviour of any organism, let alone the complex cultural being that is the modern human, is daunting, both as a project within the natural sciences,

[1] Edna Einsiedel, *Whose Genes, Whose Safe, How Safe? Publics' and Professionals' Views of Biobanks* (Ottawa: Canadian Biotechnology Advisory Committee, 2003), 1.
[2] Timothy F. Murphy, 'Mapping the human genome' in H. Kuhse and P. Singer (eds.), *A Companion to Bioethics* (Oxford: Blackwell, 1998), 198.
[3] See R. Twyman, 'Gene expression', (2003) http://genome.wellcome.ac.uk/doc_WTD020757.html.

and as one within the social sciences and humanities.[4] In the light of this, Einsiedel suggests a distinction between 'genetic information' and 'genetic knowledge'. The Human Genome Project (HGP) provides mere 'information', which is to say, it offers a resource that requires interpretation, before it can be turned into 'knowledge'. Even within natural science, further forms of inquiry are needed in order to understand any links that may exist between the human genome and disease, behaviour and any other human qualities and potentials. More broadly, and within the context of the humanities, the HGP provides the raw material for posing anew the question, 'What is it to be human?' For Einsiedel, the twenty-first century will then be dominated by this quest for this 'genetic knowledge'.

Traditional approaches to the understanding of the genetic grounding of disease, and thus the generation of some part of genetic knowledge, required a 'backwards' approach that began with inherited patterns of disease, and sought to trace, through studies of families, the genetic variations that contributed to the disease. In contrast, the HGP and its associated interpretation and exploitation in biotechnology promise a more comprehensive and subtle understanding of the nature of genetic variation, and the complex interaction of genetics, environment and behaviour in the determination of disease.[5] It may nonetheless be noted that the realisation of much of this genetic knowledge still remains in potential only. Again, reflecting the distinction between genetic information and genetic knowledge, Murphy notes that 'the genetic atlas to be achieved by the HGP will identify a great deal of data without describing its function or tying it to useful clinical interventions'.[6]

A key method for making genetic knowledge available focuses upon the compilation and exploitation of biobanks, or collections of human biological material, from which DNA information can be extracted. The Canadian Biotechnology Advisory Committee defines a biobank 'as a collection of physical specimens from which DNA can be derived, the data that have been derived from DNA samples, or both'.[7] Crucially, such biobanks typically involve the collection and storage of samples

---

[4] Y. Egorova, S. Pattison and A. Edgar, 'The meanings of genetics: accounts of biotechnology in the work of Habermas, Derrida and Baudrillard', *International Journal of the Humanities*, 5, 3 (2006), 97–103.

[5] Einsiedel, *Whose Genes*, 1.

[6] Murphy, 'Mapping the human genome', 199.

[7] CBAC, *Population Biobanking in Canada: Ethical, Legal and Social Issues* (2003), http://cbac-cccb.ca/epic/site/cbac-cccb.nsf/en/ah00589e.html#1.

from populations of hundreds of thousands of individuals. In addition, the collection of biological material is complemented by the collection of information about lifestyles, medical histories and other personal data. As Einsiedel argues, such biobanks provide potentially very powerful research resources, for they allow the direction of scientific inquiry to be reversed, and thereby made far more effective. Examples of large-scale biobanks include the Iceland Biobank, that collected 270,000 blood samples from Icelandic citizens; UK Biobank, that seeks to collect DNA samples, medical records and lifestyle information from 500,000 volunteers aged between 45 and 69 (with the subjects being followed for 30 years); and the Estonian Genome Project, collecting DNA samples and health and genealogical data from one million Estonian adults and children. Further such population-based projects are being run in Canada, Latvia, Singapore and Japan.[8]

The compilation of DNA biobanks has stimulated intense ethical debate. A series of key moral issues may be seen to be associated with their development, centring on the possibility of the contributor to the biobank being able to give genuinely informed consent.[9] While the individual participant in the project typically undertakes no significant risk or inconvenience in the provision of their genetic material (a mouth swab or blood sample merely being required), it has been noted above that many of the benefits of genetic research remain in potential only. Indeed, the short-term outcome of some genetic research may be merely to allow the diagnosis of conditions for which there is currently no therapy.[10] While the person who donates their genetic information to the biobank may not expect a personal benefit, the notion of some collective benefit may, at least in the foreseeable future, remain vague. This concern about consent is compounded by the fact that genetic samples and information will be stored for considerable periods of time. They provide a long-term resource for research. However, the nature of any future research cannot be predicted in advance. The contributor cannot then meaningfully give informed consent to that future research, thereby violating what may be regarded as a fundamental principle of research ethics. Yet, if too

---

[8] K. J. Maschke, 'Navigating an ethical patchwork – human gene banks', *Nature Biotechnology*, 23, 5 (2005), 540.

[9] T. Caudfield, R. E. G. Upshur and A. Daar, 'DNA databanks and consent: a suggested policy option involving an authorization model', *BMC Medical Ethics*, 4, 1 (2003); www.biomedcentral.com/1472–6939/4/1.

[10] Murphy, 'Mapping the human genome', 201.

strenuous an interpretation of informed consent is imposed, potentially useful future research will be curtailed.[11]

The potential misuse of the data provided is equally of significance. Biobanks, as noted, typically require not merely biological material, but also personal information about lifestyles and health. The biological and lifestyle information must remain linked during research, in order to explore, for example, the interaction of genetics and the environment in the expression of any susceptibility to disease. While personal identifiers will typically be removed from samples,[12] the risk remains that the misuse of the data, or violation of security, will make personal information available to third parties. Einsiedel notes examples of this violation from Sweden, the UK and the US.[13] In particular, concern focuses upon insurance companies becoming aware of genetic information, and using this to discriminate against individuals or groups.[14] Protecting the confidentiality of genetic information is therefore paramount.

This problem is compounded by the complex nature of genetic information. As Knoppers argues, DNA is at once what all humans share in common (and thus the 'normal' genome that the HGP sought to map), and what distinguishes each individual (with the exception of identical twins).[15] Between these extremes, genetic information links the individual, not merely to their species, but to their family and ethnic group. Thus, on the one hand, genetic information may be significant in establishing one's very identity, and the groups and families to which a person considers themselves to belong. On the other hand, genetic information is significant not merely for the individual who contributes their sample, but potentially also for their kin (living, dead, and yet to be born), and all with whom they identify as biological beings. A potential for a disease may be shared between the individual and all those closely related to them. In providing DNA information, the individual therefore provides it, not merely upon their own behalf, but potentially upon behalf of many others.

A further problem for the provision of informed consent rests upon the very possibility of a public, that lacks specialist training in the

---

[11] Maschke, 'Ethical patchwork', 542.
[12] See B. M. Knoppers, 'DNA banking: a retrospective-prospective', in J. Burley and J. Harris (eds.), *A Companion to Genethics* (Oxford: Blackwell, 2002), 380–1.
[13] Einsiedel, *Whose Genes*, 22.
[14] See L. Low, S. King and T. Wilkie, 'Genetic discrimination in life insurance: empirical evidence from a cross sectional survey of genetic support groups in the United Kingdom', *British Medical Journal*, 317 (1998), 1632–5.
[15] Knoppers, 'DNA banking', 379.

genetic sciences, being able fully to understand the nature of the research involved. This is not merely a question of the divide that may exist between 'lay' and 'expert' understanding, but rather rests upon the status of genetic science itself. Collins and Evans's typology of normal science, golem science and historical science helps to explicate this point.[16] In normal science, core scientific debates have been resolved within the scientific community. The picture that this science presents to the public is thus one of near certainty and fundamental agreement, and this allows the scientist to perform a largely undisputed role as an 'expert' in the application of scientific knowledge to public policy. The scientist here is accredited with an expertise that, in effect, trumps that of the 'lay' person. An example might be the dispute over MMR vaccines in the UK that began in 2001.[17] In effect, poor scientific research (and inappropriate publication of it) by a single scientist, while receiving a great deal of publicity, did not in fact disrupt the condition of normal science. The core scientific community continued to accept the safety and efficacy of MMR vaccines. It may therefore be suggested that there existed a case for that scientific expertise to overrule the demands of worried parents either to forgo vaccinations altogether, or to use three separate and thus less effective vaccines. It follows that, in the case of normal science, informed consent may entail an acceptance of the arguments of the core scientist as being reliable information. To make a decision diverging significantly from that scientific understanding is to act irrationally.

A golem science is such that it may become a normal science, but has not yet achieved that level of agreement amongst core members of the scientific community. The examples of the effect of genetically modified foodstuffs on the animals that eat them, and the causal link between BSE and Creutzfeld-Jacob disease are given by Collins and Evans.[18] The problem here lies in the fact that much public policy relies upon golem science. Governments are required to introduce policies, for example, to regulate the commercial sale of genetically modified organisms (GMOs), or to control the spread of Creutzfeld-Jacob disease. However, precisely because that policy is based upon science that is not yet settled, it is highly problematic, not merely in terms of its efficacy, but also in terms of its public legitimacy. As Collins and Evans summarise this, golem 'science

---

[16] H. Collins and R. Evans, 'The third wave of science studies: studies of expertise and experience', *Social Studies of Science*, 32, 2 (2002), 235–96.

[17] L. Smeeth *et al.*, 'Measles, mumps, and rubella (MMR) vaccine and autism', *British Medical Journal*, 323 (2001), 163–9.

[18] Collins and Evans, 'The third wave of science studies', 268.

becomes visible before it becomes certain'.[19] Precisely because the HGP offers the potential for genetic research and the advancement of genetic technologies, it may be suggested that its exploitation through biobanks is, necessarily, an example of a golem science. The precise agreement upon the genetic knowledge that is to be derived from the human genome lies in the future.

Historical sciences are such that agreement within the scientific community cannot be expected in the foreseeable future. Collins and Evans's examples include that of the effect of GMOs on the environment as a whole, rather than upon a signal organism.[20] Such environmental effects, and the causal mechanisms that underpin them, will only be revealed in the natural world slowly and gradually. It may be suggested that it is unnecessary to place biobank-based research in this category, at least in so far as that research is concerned with the genetic determination of discrete diseases. The problem is not that those mechanisms have yet to manifest themselves in nature. It is rather that long-term study (such as the 30-year follow-up of participants in the UK Biobank) is necessary to reveal them.

However, Collins and Evans do offer a further category, that of reflexive historical science. In this case, the long-term effects will be realised only in conjunction with human action (and indeed, as humanity responds to a growing understanding of the science itself). Thus, the long-term manifestation of global warming is dependent upon governmental policy and individual human action that itself responds to the work of environmental and climate scientists.[21] If genetics is bound up with our understanding of what it is to be human, then it may be suggested that genetics too shares the characteristics of a reflexive historical science. Certain forms of genetic knowledge will depend upon how humanity, or how certain individuals or groups, come to understand the relative place of their genetic inheritance alongside the cultural and environmental factors in shaping them. The emergence of genetic essentialism within popular culture might, for example, lead to the pursuit of radically different technologies, forms of knowledge and social policies than would be found in a culture more comfortable with environmental explanations.

If the pursuit of genetic knowledge is either a golem science or a reflexive historical science, then the general public will be confronted, not with agreement and certainty within the scientific community, but rather with a sometimes puzzling and disturbing fragmentation and disagreement.

[19] *Ibid.*, 248.   [20] *Ibid.*   [21] *Ibid.*, 269.

The possibility of informed consent is thus made problematic, precisely because the very nature of the information available is contested. The genetic scientist does not seem to be in a position to trump the decision made by the member of the general public. This position does not, however, render the non-scientist's perception of genetics random or purely subjective. On the contrary, following Collins and Evans's argument, the experience of the non-scientist may play an important role in developing golem and reflexive historical sciences, and crucially in enacting them in social policy. Collins and Evans offer the example of the contribution that Cumbrian sheep farmers could have made to the understanding of the impact of the Chernobyl nuclear reactor disaster.[22] Such an example suggests that 'lay' people may have experience and factual knowledge (here of the ecology of sheep and the fells) that the scientist lacks. It may be suggested that genetics demands a somewhat different form of experience and expertise. At the core of this lies the transition from genetic information to genetic knowledge, which is to say, from the raw data of the human genome to a practically exploitable understanding of the part that genetics plays in human life. This transition is not merely a process of natural scientific extrapolation, but also one of humanist understanding, precisely because, to repeat, it poses the core humanist question of what it is to be human, in the light of genetics. If, as noted above, genetics comes to be bound up with our sense of personal, group, and even species, identity, then the everyday cultural or lifeworld resources and competencies that ordinary people use to respond to that question may be incorporated into the development of the science, and in its application in social policy. The contention here is, then, that this lifeworld needs to be scrutinised carefully and critically, in order to understand not merely its role in influencing the development of genetic science and its regulation by governments, but also the degree to which the very nature of the lifeworld may inhibit or systematically distort a humanist interpretation of genetic information.

Public consultation

In order to resolve, or at least manage, the ethical and humanistic problems of biobanks, it has become common to use processes of public consultation to frame the scientific project, and thus, it might be hoped, to draw upon and explicate precisely the lifeworld resources that contribute

---

[22] *Ibid.*, 255.

to the humanist interpretation of genetic information. Examples of such formal consultation include that carried out by the Medical Research Council and Wellcome Trust, in support of the UK Biobank;[23] the MORI study commissioned by the Human Genetics Commission on public attitudes to genetic information in the UK,[24] as well as work commissioned by the European Union and individual European nation states, the Canadian CARTaGENE project,[25] and work carried out by private market research companies. The methods employed in such public consultation have ranged from public opinion surveys and focus groups, through consultation with stakeholders and broader communities, to web-based consultation and the inclusion of lay representatives on expert committees.[26] Other national projects, such as those in Iceland and Estonia, have generated more informal, and sometimes heated, public debate.[27]

Scepticism over the purposes and efficacy of public consultation may readily be expressed. In part, as Levitt notes, such scepticism arises from the belief, on the part of the scientific expert, that the general public lacks sufficient knowledge or experience to contribute to the debate.[28] While the suggestions developed above from Collins and Evans may seem readily to challenge this, the precise nature of that challenge is not yet clear. Members of the general public may have experience and expertise that complements that of the science community, but that experience can only be brought into dialogue with science through some degree of common understanding. Public consultation thus, in practice, is frequently concerned with eliciting the degree of public understanding of the genetic sciences, and crucially in enhancing that understanding.[29] The results of public consultation may play a crucial role in preparing explanatory material for potential participants, and in general in presenting biobanks to the general public. However, if it is assumed that the educational role of

---

[23] MRC and Wellcome Trust, *Biobank UK: A Question of Trust: A Consultation Exploring and Addressing Questions of Public Trust* (London: People Science & Policy Ltd, 2002).

[24] UK Human Genetics Commission, *Public Attitudes to Human Genetic Information. People's Panel Quantitative Study Conducted for the Human Genetics Commission* (London: HGC, 2001).

[25] B. Godard, J. Marshall and C. Laberge, 'Community engagement in genetic research: results of the first public consultation for the Quebec CARTaGENE Project', *Community Genetics*, 10 (2007), 147–58.

[26] See CBAC, *Population Biobanking in Canada*, table 6.

[27] See H. Rose, *The Commodification of Bioinformation: The Icelandic Health Sector Database* (London, UK: Wellcome Trust, 2001).

[28] M. Levitt, 'Public consultation in bioethics. What's the point of asking the public when they have neither scientific nor ethical expertise?', *Health Care Analysis*, 11, 1 (2003), 15–16.

[29] Einsiedel, *Whose Genes*, 6–9.

public consultation is successful, it may be questioned as to exactly why further consultation is required. If the core ethical questions concerning participation in biobanks focus on informed consent, then it may be suggested that once the participant is sufficiently informed, the individual has sufficient autonomy to decide for himself or herself whether to participate or not. Each individual draws upon her or his own lifeworld competencies and understandings in order to make clear her or his personal stance towards genetic science.

In the light of this comment, public consultation processes may be seen as at worst marketing or PR exercises, promoting the biobank project to an otherwise equivocal or apathetic public, or, put slightly more sympathetically, that the role of public consultation is to generate political legitimacy for the project. As typically state-funded projects, biobanks can be expected to require significant state funding over long-term periods of time. UK Biobank, for example, required £60 million over its first seven years. The Medical Research Council (MRC), in providing evidence to a review of its funding of UK Biobank, noted that: 'A project of the scale and nature of the UK Biobank cannot succeed without widespread support from the public and a wide range of stakeholders, including the NHS and potential users of the resource.'[30] In criticising the process of consultation, the House of Commons Science and Technology Committee (HCSTC) concluded that: 'It is our impression that the MRC's consultation for Biobank has been a bolt-on activity to secure widespread support for the project rather than a genuine attempt to build a consensus on the project's aims and methods. In a project of such sensitivity and importance consultation must be at the heart of the process not at the periphery.'[31] Crucially, the Committee suggested that the MRC was insufficiently prepared to respond to the feedback generated by public consultation, and to modify the project in the light of that feedback.[32] Such a criticism may be coherent with the argument that the MRC shared a fundamental scepticism about the possibility of public participation in UK Biobank, understood as a scientific project. At best, public consultation may thus be seen to perform a purely instrumental role, of ensuring sufficient public participation in the project to make it successful and sustainable.[33]

[30] House of Commons Science and Technology Committee, *The Work of the Medical Research Council.* Third Report of Session 2002–03, HC 132 (London: Stationery Office, 2003), para. 61.
[31] *Ibid.*, para. 65.   [32] *Ibid.*, para. 63.   [33] Einsiedel, *Whose Genes*, 19–21.

A less cynical view of public consultation, and presumably the view that the HCSTC wishes to be taken of it, would entail that the public consultation process serves to generate the normative framework within which the scientific work is conducted. Consultation could, thus, serve to set acceptable standards for informed consent and confidentiality.[34] Different national approaches to, for example, the issue of informed consent may be interpreted as reflecting broader communal values and concerns.[35] The contention here, however, is that, perhaps more profoundly, it is only through public consultation that the hermeneutic and normative implications that the biobank project holds for social groups could be explored. A basic argument against leaving informed consent at the level of individual autonomy may be grounded in a recognition of the implications that genetic information has for collectives. It may be suggested that only if these collectives can come to understand and thus articulate the implications that genetics has for their sense of identity can the project acquire genuine public legitimacy. More precisely, it will be argued that public consultation can provide a focus, through which an implicit or otherwise inchoate sense of identity can be articulated and brought to consciousness. On such an account, the mere aggregation of individual views – which is to say, the aggregation of each individual's subjective act of drawing upon their personal lifeworld resources – would be insufficient. The articulation of an explicit sense of collective identity presupposes intersubjective processes of debate between individuals, within the community.

Something of the importance of public consultation can be seen in the case of genetic research carried out with respect to specific communities, be these aboriginal groups, religious or cultural communities (such as the Amish), or communities brought into existence by a common burden of disease (such as HIV/AIDS sufferers). Weijer *et al.* explore this, by reviewing a series of protocols that have been drawn up to protect such communities in medical research. They note that communities are granted similar rights and protections, at the level of the collective, as individuals are typically accorded. These include informed consent, the right to withdraw from the research at any point, a right to compensation for the costs of involvement, and the right to information about the outcomes of the research.[36] Communities are typically

---

[34] See UK Human Genetics Commission, *Public Attitudes.*
[35] Maschke, 'Ethical patchwork', 542.
[36] C. Weijer, G. Goldsand and E. J. Emanuel, 'Protecting communities in research: current guidelines and limits of extrapolation', *Nature Genetics,* 23 (1999), 277–8.

accorded a more active part in the design and conduct of the research, not least in so far as their distinctive worldviews (or 'epistemologies') are recognised,[37] and members of the community are enrolled into the research project.[38] Importantly, though, Weijer *et al.* recognise that a community is not a homogeneous entity. Individuals within the community will disagree about involvement in the research, and possibly on fundamental grounds, such as disputed understandings of what the identity of the community is.[39] While this point is not developed, it is suggested that communities with recognised and stable political structures (and thus recognisable and legitimate community leaders), and stable cultural traditions, are easier to deal with. They note that the 'HIV community is more dispersed and diverse [than, say, Australian aboriginal communities], having fewer shared traditions and lacking politically legitimate institutions'.[40] This leads to differing views about how much protection such a diverse group should be given. But such points are crucial, for they highlight the tension that may exist between the genetic or biological definition of a group or community (in terms of a shared genetic heritage, or merely a genetic propensity to a specific disease), and its cultural definition and contested self-understanding. The mere sharing of biological information neither determines individuals' recognition of themselves as members of a common collective, nor does it determine how that membership, if acknowledged, is understood. Public consultation must therefore engage precisely at that cultural level, and the interpretation of the biological. But at the same time, it is important to recognise not merely that the identity of the groups is internally contested, but also that any given individual may be a member of multiple communities. Weijer *et al.* note that aboriginal groups are frequently geographically isolated. A biological distinctiveness is thus compounded by geographical and cultural distinctiveness. However, in complex, multi-cultural societies, communities merge geographically and culturally, with the individual contesting her or his communal identity, not merely with other members of that community, but also in interaction with and opposition to the individuals and communities with which they rub shoulders on a daily basis. A model of public consultation must engage with this. The contention here is that a consideration of Habermas's political philosophy offers some relevant guidance.

<hr>

[37] *Ibid.*, 277.   [38] *Ibid.*, 278.   [39] *Ibid.*, 277.   [40] *Ibid.*, 279.

The Habermasian public sphere

The experience of Iceland and Estonia, that the initiation of biobanks generated significant public debate albeit without the formal mechanisms of public consultation, is indicative of the potential importance of the public sphere in guiding the political regulation of biobanks (and genetic research in general). The public sphere may be understood as being composed of those social institutions that facilitate open and rational debate between members of a community, and thus the formation of public opinion. The debate can be conducted in face to face discussion, through letters and internet exchanges, through journals, newspapers and electronic mass communications. Jürgen Habermas's concern with the public sphere dates back to his first published monograph,[41] in which he traced the history of the European public sphere, principally since the Enlightenment. The early public sphere emerges as a mechanism through which the bourgeois can exert pressure on government. This begins to articulate a model of government that makes debate, rather than voting, central to democracy. The public exerts pressure on its elected government, not merely at the moment of the elections, but through the government's critical responsiveness to public opinion. Much of Habermas's subsequent work may be understood as an attempt to explicate the political and moral philosophies and philosophy of language and argumentation, as well as epistemology, that lie behind this understanding of the polity, and thereby articulating of the importance and nature of the public sphere in a healthy and politically open society.

At the core of the Habermasian approach lies a recognition of the importance of open argumentation, such that disputes, between individuals as much as within the public sphere as a whole, are resolved purely through the force of better argument. In his analysis of the early eighteenth-century public sphere, he documented a growing openness in public debate, facilitated through the emergence of coffee houses and learned societies, the exchange of letters and, perhaps most crucially, the development of modern journalism and the circulation of periodicals.[42] However, this openness was compromised by the restriction of the public sphere to the bourgeoisie (and indeed largely to bourgeois men). Thus, Habermas's key point is that the eighteenth-century public sphere contained an image and anticipation of something better, albeit that

---

[41] J. Habermas, *The Structural Transformation of the Public Sphere: An Inquiry into a Category of Bourgeois Science* (Cambridge: Polity Press, 1989).

[42] Habermas, *Structural Transformation*, 31–43.

the reality is compromised by political and economic inequality. This, in effect, sets something of the agenda for Habermas's subsequent analyses of public discussion and argument. Habermas is as much concerned to offer a critical tool, through which those political distortions can be recognised, as a positive account of dispute resolution or decision making. It is this critical tool that can be developed for application to debates about the exploitation of genetic information. Already, and unsurprisingly, discussions of public consultation processes stress the importance of identifying all relevant stakeholders, and ensuring that an appropriate range of voices is heard.[43] But, as the comments above on the competing and complementary natures of scientific and lay expertise highlight, the way in which stakeholder contributions should be handled is rarely self-evident. A scepticism about the ability of non-scientific contributors to understand the grounding science may lead to those opinions being suppressed.

Habermas's theory of communicative action underpins his understanding of the public sphere, and thus of the normative structures that ought to govern political debate within an open and democratic society. Briefly, his contention is that, in principle, any utterance that a speaker or correspondent makes can be challenged at four possible levels, that correspond to basic assumptions that the speaker has made. The challenger raises what Habermas terms 'validity claims'.[44] Firstly, an utterance entails, implicitly or explicitly, ontological assumptions about the external world. This is what Habermas terms the validity claim to truth. If somebody makes an observation about the world, even as trivial as a comment on the weather, an explicit reference is made to the world. The assertion may be incorrect, simply on the grounds that the world is not actually like that. (It is, for example, not raining.) If one person asks another to buy them a beer, the person making the request assumes that there is such a thing as beer in the world, and more importantly, that it is possible to buy it, and to buy it locally, and thus assumes the existence of vendors, the availability of money, and so on. Disputes over any validity claim can be resolved through what Habermas terms 'discourse'.[45] That is to say that, for as long as necessary, the exchange of substantive utterances is suspended, to allow speakers the opportunity to establish the validity

[43] See Einsiedel, *Whose Genes*, 39–40.
[44] J. Habermas, *Communication and the Evolution of Society* (Boston, MA: Beacon Press, 1979), 1–67.
[45] J. Habermas, *On the Pragmatics of Social Interaction: Preliminary Studies in the Theory of Communicative Action* (Cambridge: Polity Press, 2001), 99–100.

or otherwise of the questionable utterance. It is at this moment, in the case of the validity claim to truth, that the very nature of relevant experience, evidence and reasoning can be debated. The experience necessary to establish whether or not it is raining is clearly of a different order from that required to establish that climate change is occurring. The return to normal discussion occurs only once there is agreement between all parties to the exchange.

All utterances raise a second validity claim, to rightness. This is the moral or normative dimension of an utterance, principally grounded in the speaker's right to say what they have said. In imparting knowledge, the speaker's right to speak might be challenged on the grounds that they lack suitable experience, training or expertise. The person who said it is raining may not have bothered to look out of the window to check. The opponent of climate change may lack the appropriate training and expertise in climatology. Similarly, one's right to request (let alone order) another person to buy a beer for you may be challenged due to one's lack of formal or informal authority. The speaker may be too young, depriving them perhaps both of the cultural right to make demands of their elders, and the legal right to consume alcohol. The validity claim to rightness most clearly raises questions of power. The example of requesting beer presupposes some commonly agreed customary or legal framework. If a person makes a request or enforces an order purely by appealing to the threat of physical or other force, then it may be assumed, at least within the context of an open and democratic society, that they have no right to make that utterance. More problematically, the appeal to a customary or legal framework may not wholly resolve the dispute. If the framework is imbued with unquestioned political biases, as for example in a highly patriarchal society, then that very framework may itself be problematic. But further, if the bias goes unrecognised, then the right to challenge a speaker may not be recognised. The recipients of the utterance may be unaware of the possibility of making such a challenge. Thus, the right of men to control women may go unchallenged, precisely because those subject to that power have internalised, and thereby come to accept, the spurious legitimacy of patriarchal authority as if it was legitimate. The framework may be seen, for example, as part of a natural or divinely appointed order, that is by its very nature beyond challenge.

The third validity claim is to what Habermas terms 'truthfulness'. In respects that lie at the core of the present argument, this is the most ambiguous and contested of the four validity claims in Habermas's theory. In his mature work on communication, Habermas treats truthfulness simply in terms of the speaker's sincerity or fidelity. Unlike the other validity claims, the distrust of a speaker's sincerity is resolved, not typically by more speech (for the speaker may simply continue to lie), but by observing the coherence or otherwise between their utterances and their actions. Thus, one finds out if a person was sincere in promising to pay for the beers when those beers actually turn up. In his earliest formulations of the theory, Habermas was still somewhat under the influence of psychoanalytic theory.[46] Truthfulness, in this context, took on the aspect of repression, such that a speaker, rather than deliberately lying, could be unaware that they were deceiving not just others but themselves. In effect, truthfulness then becomes a problem of the very subjectivity and autonomy of the speaker, and one that can only be resolved through some form of self-reflection and therapy. Potentially the therapeutic dialogue of psychoanalysis replaces the discourse through which other validity claims are established. In more recent writings, Habermas began to link the notion of truthfulness to that of self-expression. This allows a certain recognition of the role of the arts, broadly conceived, in articulating an individual's or community's view of their world and of themselves.[47]

The final validity claim, and superficially the simplest, concerns the meaning of the utterance. The listener may simply not understand the words used, and thus requires them to be glossed or translated, or the speaker may have articulated themselves poorly, and the utterance needs to be repeated more carefully. However, and again in the light of psychoanalytic theory and still more pertinently ideology critique, the validity claim to meaning can take on a more complex aspect. Certain forms of language use may overtly or covertly privilege the expression of certain opinions or perspectives. If, for example, debates over government regulation of genetic science are expressed wholly within the language of the natural sciences, then the moral, cultural and religious perceptions that non-scientists bring to the debate may be rendered inexpressible. Thus, a power bias towards the natural sciences may express itself, not in the overt suppression of counter views, but more subtly in the rendering of those views meaningless.

In summary, Habermas's account of validity claims suggests that processes of public consultation may be distorted by power differentials. Such differentials may express themselves overtly, for example with the

---

[46] J. Habermas, 'On systematically distorted communication', *Inquiry*, 13 (1970), 205–18; J. Habermas, 'Towards a theory of communicative competence', *Inquiry* 13 (1970), 360–75.

[47] J. Habermas, *Postmetaphysical Thinking: Philosophical Essays* (Cambridge, MA: MIT Press, 1992), 205–27.

exclusion of non-scientific contributions in general, or specific stake-holders in particular, from the consultation process. It may be suggested that current approaches to public consultation are increasingly aware of such exclusions, and seek to correct them. More subtly, power differentials may express themselves implicitly, through the various ideological distortions in the normative framework that governs participation in debate, or in the language that allows the articulation of positions and arguments. In so far as ideological distortions infuse the lifeworld, they may become constitutive of the very participants in the debate. As the seemingly natural or taken for granted background of social life, they go unquestioned. The final sections of this chapter will seek to sketch points at which such implicit power differentials are present in public discussion of genetic information.

Genetic information and the DNA mystique

Complexity

An argument for the status of genetics as either a golem science or a reflex-ive historical science has been sketched above. If genetics is placed in either of these categories, it follows it has a complexity that at once defies any simple appeal to the expertise of the scientific community, and yet equally defies any simple public involvement in the policy debate. In terms of the Habermasian validity claims, it may be suggested that this entails a tension between truth and rightness. The scientific community overtly focuses on issues of truth. But, to neglect the contestability of the scien-tists' claim to speak, as the sole experts, on issues of the public regulation and funding of research is to neglect the validity claim to rightness that is implicit in any scientific utterance. More importantly, if this normativ-ity is neglected at the level of public policy formation, then the scientific community risks a fundamental loss of public support and legitimacy. Conversely, if the centrality of scientific expertise is not recognised in the determination of matters of truth, for example by throwing questions of regulation and funding open to a potentially ill-informed public debate, and thus presenting them as merely normative problems, then rigorous scientific and technological progress is put at risk. In order to analyse this problem further, Collins and Evans's account of the history of the sociol-ogy of science and knowledge may be drawn upon, precisely because this account allows an articulation of the tension that exists between validity claims to truth and to rightness in the debate over genetics.

Collins and Evans propose that there have been three waves in the development of the sociology of science and knowledge. The first wave, covering the 1950s and 1960s, presupposed a broadly positivist view of science. As such, the scientist is presumed, thanks to their training, to be in a uniquely authoritative position with respect to any decisions about science, including those of the political structures within which science operates.[48] While Collins and Evans present this as a position that has been superseded within sociology, Levitt suggests that a similar approach underpins a continuing model of public consultation. Such a 'deficit' model presupposes that the 'lay' public are largely ignorant of science, and thus that the role of public consultation is principally to identify gaps in public understanding, and to devise public education programmes that will allow some public participation. As Levitt implies, the scientist is assumed to have been trained to be a rational and objective observer of their material.[49] In terms of the Habermasian model, it is assumed that the scientists' right to say and do what they do is largely beyond challenge. Public consultation focuses upon issues of truth, with the assumption that once the 'lay' public understands the truth established by science, then the scientists' public legitimacy, and thus any doubts about the rightness or justice of their actions, will be removed.

The second wave in sociology of knowledge rejects positivism, in large part through the influence of the Kuhnian account of paradigms,[50] replacing it with 'social constructivism'. Science is understood as a social activity. As such the expertise of the science ceases to be understood as something self-evidently grounded in the objectivity of scientific methodology. Rather, 'expertise' comes to be seen as a socially contested category, worked out within political structures and social and cultural conventions.[51] Levitt's second model of public consultation mirrors this stage of sociology. In this model, the 'lay' public is recognised to have an expertise that is different from, and yet complementary to, that of the scientist. Thus, while the first model sought merely to educate the public, the second model opens up the possibility of genuine dialogue.[52] As

---

[48] Collins and Evans, 'The third wave of science studies', 239.
[49] Levitt, 'Public consultation', 17.
[50] In his history of science, *The Structure of Scientific Revolutions* (University of Chicago, 1962), Thomas Kuhn presents paradigms as the working theories or world views which make possible the activity of science. The paradigm encapsulates the orthodox methods of scientific inquiry, as well as broad assumptions about the nature of the objects of scientific inquiry.
[51] Collins and Evans, 'The third wave of science studies', 239–40.
[52] Levitt, 'Public consultation', 18–19.

Levitt presents this: 'The aim of consulting the public is to find out what the participants think is important and what they feel.'[53] Normative questions, and thus the validity claim to rightness, are brought to the fore. It is recognised that science is not a value-free activity, but rather one shaped by its own values and normative assumptions. Such assumptions may be at odds with those of the wider public.

Within such an approach, the Habermasian argument initially highlights the necessity of ensuring a public dialogue over values, and therefore that this should not be carried out as the mere soliciting (and aggregation) of individual views. Only through open and rational dialogue will the biases of individual viewpoints be challenged, and irrational and unsupportable positions eliminated. Public consultation methods that encourage debate are thus preferred. Yet, already this begins to suggest a divergence from a more extreme or radical second wave approach to the sociology of science. Because, from that radical perspective, the expertise of the scientist loses any privileged status, scientific knowledge is not clearly demarcated from any other form of knowledge or belief. In contrast, the Habermasian position strongly suggests that some positions are rationally more defensible than others. This is to suggest that within both the normative positions of scientists and non-scientists, certain assertions may be indefensible because they are logically incoherent, or grounded in spurious evidence. Crucially, the privileged epistemological position of the scientist cannot then be ignored. It is precisely with this challenge that Collins and Evans's proposed third wave in the sociology of science and knowledge engages. As Collins and Evans present this, the problem of the third wave is not a descriptive one, of how science came to be given a privileged status as knowledge, but rather a normative one, of what sort of science should have that privileged status.[54] It is precisely this question that Habermas focuses on by separating the validity claims of truth and rightness. Yet, it is crucial to go beyond Habermas, by recognising the different status of truth claims in normal, golem and reflexive science, precisely in so far as that recognition at once retains a notion of truth, but acknowledges the complexity of discursively establishing the truths of the golem and reflexive sciences. This is done without resorting to an account of objective and universal scientific methodology, characteristic of the positivism of the first wave.

The third wave has implications for public consultation, for it entails that consultation can only work if the non-scientific participants are

<hr />

[53] Ibid., 19.   [54] Collins and Evans, 'The third wave of science studies', 241.

aware of the current state of scientific research, in terms of both its (pro-visional) discoveries and its methodology (of dispute and contest). It is insufficient to engage merely with non-scientists' values. Similarly, in so far as the core aim of this third model of consultation is dialogue, scientists must be able to engage with non-scientific perceptions and cultural frameworks. Thus, the process of engagement requires what Collins and Evans term 'interactional' experts, capable of translating between the scientific and non-scientific communities.[55] These will include journalists, teachers and artists, and as such, the key figures of any vital public sphere. Yet, it is precisely at this point that the critical engagement with science goes beyond mere questions of methodology and research priorities, towards the very language within which scientific and lay understandings of the research are couched. This is to propose a shift from questions of truth and rightness to those of meaning and truthfulness. It is to suggest that the process of translation is neither neutral nor even simply creative, but must also be critical, pursuing the ideological distortions that inhibit understanding and the articulation of opposition. It is at this point, in genetics, that critical translation engages with what, following Nelkin and Lindee,[56] may be termed the 'mystique' of genetics.

Mystique

Nelkin and Lindee write of the 'DNA mystique'. The term 'mystique' is not strictly defined, but it may be taken to embrace the manner in which ideas and images of DNA have percolated through much of Western culture. They are present in advertising and popular culture as much as in science and science journalism, and have become a focus for certain artists. Nelkin and Lindee note that 'DNA appears in stairways, Lego toys, and origami kits as well as on the usual souvenir T-shirts, bracelets, and coffee mugs'.[57] The word play of genes/jeans may be used by the advertisers of clothes.[58] The importance of inheriting 'good genes' is exploited metaphorically to highlight product design. Clothes, cars and even magazines can have inherited DNA, and a 'genetic advantage' over their competitors.[59] In car advertisements, with car design articulated in terms of a metaphorical evolution, a play on the notion of cloning emphasises that a

---

[55] *Ibid.*, 257–8.
[56] D. Nelkin and M. S. Lindee, *The DNA Mystique: The Gene as a Cultural Icon*, 2nd edn (Ann Arbor, MI: University of Michigan Press, 2004).
[57] *Ibid.*, xv.   [58] *Ibid.*, 13.   [59] *Ibid.*, 97.

new car design is not a clone of another car.[60] In popular drama and talk shows, genetic ties between father and child can become the focus of storylines, not least in terms of the tension between issues of biological and social parenting.[61] Genealogy becomes a principal organising theme of television biography. Yet, the notion of 'DNA "activation" jewelry'[62] suggests also an incorporation of the scientific image of DNA into more fanciful conceptions of human life, more readily associated with New Age thinking. The extreme example of this is perhaps the Raëlian cult's claim, in December 2002, to have cloned a human child.[63] DNA and the language of genetics are therefore something that is freely reinterpreted and reimagined within popular culture, the discipline of its scientific origins being readily abandoned.

A 'mystique' is, therefore, not necessarily an accurate (or scientifically justifiable) conception. Mystique disregards truth, and it does so in favour of something more expressive, but also thereby something potentially more sinister. Nelkin and Lindee suggest that DNA is 'something we think with'[64] (borrowing the notion from Turkle).[65] This is not to argue that we simply think about DNA, but rather to suggest that more or less freely imagined notions of DNA are used to articulate our understanding of and engagement with everyday life. It 'provides ways of talking about identity, spirituality, social relations, and the commodification of life'.[66] DNA and its associated talk of genetics provides a resource through which we can make sense of, for example, family relationships, our family and group histories, and the interrelationships between groups, within a society and even globally.

The appeal of DNA, and thus its richness and force as something to think with, is indicated by noting that it has come to serve as a substitute for the grand narratives that were the bedrock of the modernist conception of Western culture. Post-modernism calls into question the legitimacy of any single or over-arching historical narrative. In the face of the babel of fragmentary and contested little narratives that then emerge, biology offers a point of security and stability. Nelkin and Lindee illustrate this by noting that, whereas in the past most US university students would have studied an elementary course on 'Western civilization', now they are more likely to have studied an introduction to biology. Biology

---

[60] *Ibid.*, xv.   [61] *Ibid.*, xxi.   [62] *Ibid.*, xv.   [63] *Ibid.*, xxiv.

[64] Nelkin and Lindee, *The DNA Mystique*, 16.

[65] S. Turkle, *Life on Screen: Identity in the Age of the Internet* (New York: Simon and Schuster, 1995).

[66] Nelkin and Lindee, *The DNA Mystique*, xvi.

offers a way of thinking through questions of identity, ethnicity and history that is potentially more manageable and satisfying, for most people, than whatever is offered in post-modern humanistic thought.[67] As such, genetic and religious imagery readily merge. Michelangelo's God and Adam are now connected, at least on a cover of the journal *Nature*, by strands of DNA,[68] and DNA begins to take on the aspect of something divinely bestowed (and to meddle with DNA becomes heresy).

The mystique of DNA is thus potentially, and perhaps predominantly, an image of genetic determinism or essentialism (whereby the complexity of human cultural life is reduced to its genetic foundations). Appeals to the gene strip away the uncertainty of contested cultural meanings, and offer a foundation in the 'divine', the 'natural' or the 'real'. Thus, within the DNA mystique, biological parenthood may be taken to trump social parenting and, perhaps more problematically, social structure itself is seen to reflect fundamental biological divisions, so that social inequalities, between classes, genders or ethnic groups, are explained in terms of a genetic essentialism that is beyond challenge.[69] The DNA mystique thereby comes to function as an ideology, precisely in so far as it reifies social relationships into natural ones, and thereby places them beyond rational challenge and debate, threatening to make the changing of them, quite literally, unthinkable.

If Nelkin and Lindee are correct in their analysis, then the DNA mystique threatens to distort the possibility of public discussion, and thus public consultation, with respect to genetics. This distortion is not merely a product of a lay misunderstanding of science. Nelkin and Lindee suggest that scientists themselves promote the DNA mystique. The exaggeration of the potential of genetic research, and the simplification of the complex genetic mechanisms that technology can exploit, may serve science in securing funding and public support.[70] Crucially, in terms of the Habermasian validity claims, the meaningfulness of any utterance within the public discussion and consultation becomes problematic. On the one hand, the suggestion is that the dialogue is distorted by economic and political issues. Public understanding of genetics may be counterproductive to science, precisely because the technological and therapeutic promise of, for example, the HGP would be exposed as being highly questionable. On the other hand, it may also be suggested that the public reimagination of genetics, within the DNA mystique, is symptomatic of a need to manage the otherwise overwhelming uncertainties and confusions of

---

[67] *Ibid.*, xvi–xvii.   [68] *Ibid.*, xix.   [69] *Ibid.*, 16.   [70] *Ibid.*, iii; 6–7.

post-modern society. DNA offers an illusion of certainty and stability in an otherwise highly fluid and ever contested cultural landscape. The role of the translator in public consultation, proposed by Collins and Evans, therefore requires the expertise to decode such distortions, and to recognise where the dialogue has become meaningless, and why.

Conclusion

In 2001, the artist Mark Quinn produced a portrait of Sir John Suston, which the UK National Portrait Gallery describes as 'a sample of sitter's DNA in agar jelly mounted in stainless steel'.[71] If Quinn is taken as an example of an interactional expert, an artist translating between the spheres of science and the everyday, then this work can be seen as beginning to perform the critical function of translation. By following the logic of genetic essentialism to its extreme, reducing the traditional portrait to the mere presence of DNA, then the sinister implications of the DNA mystique begin to be laid bare.

Knoppers has suggested that the last decade of the 20th century marked a move from the belief that 'DNA is just biological stuff', to 'DNA is the person'.[72] Quinn's portrait exploits this move, and Quinn also highlights how problematic the phrase 'DNA is the person' is. While Knoppers is making an ethical point about the need to respect DNA, the claim, taken boldly, is difficult to interpret. Either personality is being attributed to DNA (taking the 'is' to be the 'is of predication'), or personality is the same as DNA (reading an 'is of identity'). At worst this implies essentialism, stripping from the person everything but their DNA. In terms of the Habermasian validity claims, it may be argued that such thinking inhibits the possibility of truthfulness, precisely because it inhibits the possibility of authentic reflection upon the self. The consequence for public consultation is that the very agent who would participate as disputant in that consultation is damaged. Akin to the neurotic or hysterical psychoanalytic patient, an important aspect of agency is reified and put beyond autonomous, linguistically mediated interrogation. As Nelkin and Lindee suggest, the DNA mystique, precisely in so far as it legitimates an appeal to biology as the grounding and determination of behavioural traits and personal qualities, serves to undermine pre-genetic notions of

[71] M. Quinn, *Sir John Sulston* (2001), http:www.npg.org.uk/; see also Nelkin and Lindee, *The DNA Mystique*, xvii.
[72] Knoppers, 'DNA Banking', 382.

autonomy and personal responsibility.[73] At the collective level, the group
is similarly defined by its biology. A group seems to be comprehensible
only as a biological entity, and the humanistic question of what it is to
be human is rendered inexpressible, as is the intersubjective contestation
of different individual interpretations of what membership of that group
means. The necessary process of interpreting and indeed freely accepting or rejecting the biological foundations for communal identity plays
no part in the DNA mystique. There is no genetic knowledge beyond the
mere assertion of genetic information. Certain conceptions of human
agency, responsibility and identity are rendered meaningless, placed
beyond the possibility of articulation, as effectively as any articulation of
the political and economic structures that govern the debate are rendered
impossible.

The notion of the 'DNA mystique' presents an extreme picture of the
penetration of a certain form of genetic essentialism into non-scientific
and scientific culture. Essentialism is contested. Yet, its pervasiveness is
potentially of a degree and nature that it does come to distort certain
forms of communication. By offering a ready tool through which to think
certain complex social and moral problems, short-circuiting difficulties,
it is at once attractive and dangerous. It is dangerous not merely in blocking off topics from overt discussion, but also by forming the taken-for-
granted background of that communication, so that its insidious effect
cannot easily be raised to consciousness. The role of the interactional
expert, on this account, is therefore not one of simple translation between
the scientist and non-scientist. Indeed, such translation may be problematic, as the sole language that the two sides might share may be that of the
DNA mystique, given its role in the public promotion of science. Rather,
the task of the interactional expert is akin to that of the psychoanalyst,
initiating a dialogue that penetrates the mystique, exposing its blind
spots and distortions.

[73] Nelkin and Lindee, *The DNA Mystique*, 79–101.

9

Harmonisation and standardisation in ethics and governance: conceptual and practical challenges

RUTH CHADWICK AND HEATHER STRANGE

> Due to the proliferation of ... databases, the question of international coordination and organization arises, both on a scientific and ethical level ... harmonization has therefore become a priority, although it poses significant challenges.[1]

Calls for harmonisation in ethics and law are becoming increasingly common. Our focus here is on harmonisation in ethics, including ethics as a governance tool: what does it mean and is it possible and desirable? How does harmonisation relate to standardisation? The *Concise OED* definition explains harmonisation as the process of making a system consistent.[2] In ethics, this is typically understood in terms of the production of a system of concepts/principles that may be universally/globally applied.

But why the focus on harmonisation? Harmonisation may be sought by people with different meta-ethical commitments: both by those who subscribe to a notion of moral truth to be discovered, and by those who think morality is to be established by agreement. There may, however, be different immediate prompts for the search. One is a direct response to the process of globalisation, broadly understood; or to a particular aspect of this, namely concern about the global impact of developments in technoscience – arising out of concerns, for example, that attempts to regulate such developments in one society will be useless if they can be carried out with impunity elsewhere. Specifically, we are concerned here with calls for harmonisation in relation to a particular development

---

[1] A. Cambon-Thomsen, E. Salleé Raal-Sebbag, and B. M. Knoppers, 'Populational genetic databases: is a specific ethical and legal framework necessary?' *GenEdit* 3, 1 (2005), 6.
[2] C. Soanes and A. Stevenson (eds.), *The Concise Oxford English Dictionary*, 11th edn (Oxford University Press, 2006).

in biotechnology: the networking of different national initiatives in biobanking and biological resources.

The mission of the European BBMRI project is to prepare to construct a pan-European Biobanking and Biomolecular Resources Research Infrastructure (BBMRI), building on existing infrastructure, resources and technologies, properly embedded into European ethical, legal and societal frameworks. One task of the project is to examine the possibility of harmonisation of these ethical frameworks. But what we have to say relates not only to harmonisation within Europe but with the wider question of harmonisation globally. It would surely be a mistake to ignore the context exterior to Europe when examining the possibility of harmonisation within it.

The argument for the need for harmonisation in the biological resource context presupposes, of course, that such developments have the potential to provide an important social benefit:

> High quality Biological Resource Centres (BRCs) are intended to be a crucial element of sustainable scientific infrastructure which is necessary to underpin successful delivery of the benefits of biotechnology, whether with the health, industrial, or other sectors, and in turn assure that these advances help drive growth.[3]

From that starting point, the argument proceeds to claim that it is necessary to have an international infrastructure, which in turn requires investigating the requirements of international networking, including harmonisation at the level of ethical, legal and social issues.

Is harmonisation in ethics possible?

Where harmonisation in ethics is understood in terms of establishing universally applicable values or principles, it is hard to overestimate the practical challenges: a further question, however, is whether it is in fact possible. We are not going to try to resolve the debates about ethical relativism, but it is important to note that one's meta-ethical position will affect the answer given to this question. If there are in fact moral truths to be discovered, then the establishment of universal values is in principle possible; likewise if ethics is the result of human decisions and

[3] Organisation for Economic Cooperation and Development (OECD), OECD Workshop on 'The global biological resource centres network – networking the networks' (Paris: OECD, 2007), 1.

agreements, then again harmonisation in ethics is in principle possible. The status of the results will of course be different.

A fortiori, if harmonisation is possible in ethics *tout court*, it should be so in specific contexts with particular purposes, but this only draws our attention to the fact that those purposes are themselves ends about which disagreement is possible. We want to suggest, however, that in some cases at least, where we have achieved apparent harmonisation in ethics, what we have is not harmonisation but standardisation. A standard is produced which makes cooperation easier because it enables us to rely on others observing certain sorts of behaviour. Depending on the kind of behaviour, different standards can co-exist. Larry Busch gives the context-relative example of driving: the standard in the USA is driving on the right; in the UK the standard is that people drive on the left.[4] To introduce the same standard in both countries would require a huge effort.

There are some aspects of ethics, we want to argue, that can be dealt with by standards. The HUGO Ethics Committee, in its *Statement on Benefit Sharing*, recommended as a standard that profit-making entities should donate between 1% and 3% of their net profits to humanitarian causes.[5] In the biological resources context, also, there may be aspects of informed consent procedures, mechanisms for feedback and so on, for which standards can be established, without full-blown harmonisation in ethics. The important question is which, if any, of these are analogous to driving on the left, and which would require a common standard.

In relation to harmonisation, it is helpful to bear in mind that harmony is a musical concept, and that voices in harmony are not the same as voices in unison. The harmony of different voices is an important aim. We want to argue that in ethics generally and in the BBMRI in particular, standardisation is not sufficient: it is important to strive for harmonisation in ethics, but this should not be interpreted as seeking a single voice. In this we take our inspiration from this entry in the *Oxford Companion to Music*:

> It seems natural and right that music which is ... harmonious, should be highly regarded in civilized societies ... there is a clear correspondence

---

[4] L. Busch, 'Measuring up: how standards shape our lives: a public lecture by Larry Busch', ESRC Genomics Policy and Research Forum Edinburgh (10 May 2007).
[5] Human Genome Organisation (HUGO) Ethics Committee, *Statement on Benefit Sharing* (2000), www.hugo-international.org/Statement_on_Benefit_Sharing.htm.

between the concept of society as a mutually supportive commonwealth, and those manifestations of concert and theatre music which attract the collective approbation 'civilized'. Collective performance, as in singing the same text to different but interdependent vocal lines, can be regarded as the musical correlate of civilized democracy.[6]

In the idea of different voices singing the same text to different vocal lines, there is an important clue to viewing harmonisation as a process. We want to suggest that seeking harmonisation as a goal, to attain in order that the scientific endeavour can progress, is a mistake. Standards can be established, providing a 'text', but the process of harmonisation needs to continue. First, however, we shall examine other approaches to harmonisation.

Approaches to harmonisation

Threefold typology

There has been considerable discussion in the bioethics literature, in the last ten years or so, of the possibilities of a global bioethics. We want to take as our starting point Samuel Fleischacker's typology of three different methods for producing universal ethical agreement: the human rights model, the necessary conditions model and the cultural dialogue model.[7] He approaches universality in ethics from a pragmatic point of view, being primarily concerned with establishing a method for reaching universal agreement on ethics, rather than uncovering a set of objective truths: 'the best agreements about ethical practice precisely do *not* depend on agreement about ethical truth'.[8] He wishes to stress that this position does not necessarily lead to cultural or moral relativism: 'I make no claim that moral terms are meaningless, or that moral sentences have no truth value, outside of a cultural context.'[9] His theory is concerned with the development of a broad universal ethics that is to be enriched by culturally specific morality. His commitment to this point of view leads him to reject both the human rights model and the necessary conditions model, as he sees those as presuming a 'universal truth about ethics'[10] (this is arguable but we shall put this aside for present purposes).

---

[6] A. Whittall, 'Harmony', in A. Latham (ed.), *The Oxford Companion to Music* (Oxford University Press, 2002), 561.
[7] S. Fleischacker, 'From cultural diversity to universal ethics: three models', *Cultural Dynamics*, 11 (1999), 105–28.
[8] *Ibid.*, 106.   [9] *Ibid.*   [10] *Ibid.*

His 'assumption that moral norms tend to be inextricable from cultural ones'[11] leads to an endorsement of the cultural dialogue model. Only this model, he claims, moves away from the production of thin, vague and abstract universal norms towards an incorporation of 'thick' cultural moral values that are evident in ethics at a practical level:

> Individuals in fact tend to guide their decisions much more by the rich, specific way of life embodied in the cultures in which they were raised than by the vague abstractions promoted by universalist moral philosophies.[12]

Necessary conditions model

Before examining in detail the cultural dialogue model, it is worth looking at the other two models in Fleischacker's typology, and exploring the extent to which they might be helpful in relation to international biological resources. The necessary conditions model is philosophical rather than legal or political: like the human rights model it 'tends towards abstract principles'.[13] However, it benefits from the fact that principles are viewed as being descriptive rather than prescriptive. The method consists in examining the features of, and conditions necessary for, ethical life, selecting those that exist cross-culturally, and extracting a set of universal ethical features from the results. Fleischacker claims that many of the values arrived at through the use of this method 'have worked poorly as grounds for universal ethics'.[14] Principles such as the 'well-being or the equal worth of every person are prone to cultural bias':[15] while the method aims towards producing descriptive claims, it 'smuggles in normative presuppositions'.[16] Fleischacker does recommend the use of this method to a limited extent: by asking what principles or practices a society must 'maintain in order to claim the status of *being* a culture',[17] two genuinely universal ethical principles may be established. He argues that a 'universal interest in some minimal conditions of justice and peace'[18] exists across all cultures and communities. The universality of justice is extracted from the fact that, only if every individual has freedom of choice, can a culture exist through mass moral agreement. The universality of peace is in turn extracted from this: all cultures must 'honor the conditions making it possible for their members to reflect on their cultural allegiances, and maintain, modify, or reject them'.[19]

---

[11] *Ibid.*   [12] *Ibid.*, 107.   [13] *Ibid.*, 112.   [14] *Ibid.*   [15] *Ibid.*, 113.
[16] *Ibid.*, 112.   [17] *Ibid.*, 113.   [18] *Ibid.*, 114.   [19] *Ibid.*

Human rights model

The human rights model, which is perhaps the most visible, is perceived as a 'political and a legal model':[20] its politico-legal nature is exemplified by the many prohibitions and ideals that are supposed to transcend state sovereignty, contained within the international declarations and conventions that form the backbone of this approach. For Fleischacker and other critics human rights declarations provide us with 'an example of precisely how *not* to pursue universal ethics':[21] they frequently fail to provide any genuinely practical moral guidance; 'they have no enforcement mechanism'[22] and there are many 'philosophical problems in the instruments themselves'.[23]

A paradigm case of the declaration approach is of course the UNESCO Universal Declaration on Bioethics and Human Rights.[24] The universal ethics project which led to this was launched in 1997, and the common framework document of 1999 claimed that the great increase in the number of globalised problems, and the resulting increase in worldwide moral uncertainty, necessitated 'coordinated responses transcending cultural differences and national borders';[25] and that a culturally harmonious ethical response could be successfully constructed through the 'recognition of a common substratum of values'.[26] It was suggested that the global 'forces of the techno-scientific economy',[27] in particular, were 'giving rise to ever more complex social, political and moral questions'.[28] The 1999 document further claimed that the increased global desire for a system of universal values reflected the 'growing convergence of views that democracy, development, and respect for human rights and fundamental freedoms are all interdependent and mutually reinforcing'.[29] The idea that any practicable theory must 'integrate diversity and relativity'[30] is incorporated into its practical goals: the specific moral identities of communities and cultures ought not to be sacrificed in the process of harmonisation. UNESCO also held that the enterprise required rejection of the dominant 'western synthesis'[31] based on 'ideas of individualism, rationalism, scientism and teleology of progress'.[32]

More recent documents, apart from the Declaration itself, continue to aim towards harmonisation in the universal sense; the 2008–13 medium

[20] *Ibid.*, 108.   [21] *Ibid.*   [22] *Ibid.*   [23] *Ibid.*

[24] United Nations Educational, Scientific and Cultural Organisation (UNESCO), Universal Declaration on Bioethics and Human Rights (2005).

[25] Y. Kim, *A Common Framework for the Ethics of the 21st Century* (Paris: UNESCO, 1999), III.

[26] *Ibid.*   [27] *Ibid.*, 1.   [28] *Ibid.*, 2.

[29] *Ibid.*, 6.   [30] *Ibid.*, 30.   [31] *Ibid.*, 8.   [32] *Ibid.*, 9.

term strategy is fully supportive of the production of a universal ethic: a primary objective is the promotion of specific 'principles, practices and ethical norms relevant for scientific and technological development'.[33] The ongoing support of a universalist position has become crucial to UNESCO:

> Founded on the principles of universality, diversity and dignity, UNESCO's actions continue to be guided and shaped by a set of commonly shared values that include justice, solidarity, tolerance, sharing, equity, respect for human rights, including women's rights, and cultural diversity, pluralism and democratic principles.[34]

The 2008–13 strategy stresses that the impact of science and technology upon ethics remains an issue of particular and enduring concern: one of its most pressing challenges is 'to ensure the monitoring and analysis of the impact of scientific and technological innovations on human rights through the strengthening of its action on the ethics of science and technology'.[35]

The Declaration itself has attracted well-known criticisms from a number of sources. It has been questioned whether the many foundational ethical concepts and normative values consistently endorsed by UNESCO are truly capable of being cross-culturally applied and understood; it has been asked whether international declarations such as this have been drafted from a culturally inclusive moral perspective rather than a legal and practical one; and it has also been questioned whether the principle-based documents favoured by UNESCO are capable of capturing the true richness of practical ethical reasoning, and whether the harmonisation of ethics may be better served by establishing broad universal foundations that allow for diverse interpretations rather than many specific guidelines or principles.

David Benatar claims[36] that principle-based documents that aspire to universality are necessarily limited to being either minimal or vague. In order to construct universal principles, these documents either employ the process of 'agreeing on the lowest common denominator',[37] ignoring issues about which there is no consensus, or

---

[33] United Nations Educational, Scientific and Cultural Organisation (UNESCO), *Medium Term Strategy 2008–2013* (2008), 23.

[34] *Ibid.*, 7.   [35] *Ibid.*, 22.

[36] D. Benatar, 'The trouble with universal declarations', *Developing World Bioethics*, 5, 3 (2005), 220–24.

[37] *Ibid.*, 221.

choose to avoid conceptual conflict by recommending 'formulations that are sufficiently vague that each person can interpret them consistently with his or her own view'.[38] He points to Article 16 of the UDBHR, which states that 'the impact of life sciences on future generations, including on their genetic constitution, should be given due regard',[39] but what does that mean? It is difficult to envisage what would count as an appropriate standard of regard.

Benatar also argues that universal declarations will inevitably 'reflect one of two kinds of hegemony',[40] because the interests of marginalised parties do not have enough input. So they will be driven either by a dominant group or a dominant viewpoint. The point about marginalised voices is important and one that is taken up in particular by feminist bioethics, which has identified specific areas of weakness in the UNESCO approach. Mary Rawlinson and Anne Donchin have advanced two main criticisms, first of the standard concept of universality endorsed by UNESCO, and second, the overlooking of the huge range of structural inequalities that necessarily affect the provision of global health care.[41] While bioethical problems are not, of course, confined to health care per se, this might be a particularly relevant background point in addressing the biobank issue.

Rawlinson and Donchin criticise the concept of universality as one that emerges directly from Enlightenment philosophy. This is problematic because in Enlightenment philosophy moral agency has been 'marked explicitly as male, white, and European in descent'.[42] Principles derived from this tradition therefore may fail to account for the global range of voices. Feminist bioethics has exposed a bias and theoretical oppression that is extended to many other marginalised groups. In order to produce principles that speak for the whole moral community, UNESCO (and other organisations that adopt this approach to harmonisation) ought critically to examine foundational principles that are assumed to be morally neutral. The abstract principles of equality that obscure actual inequities fail to 'articulate a sense of universality ample enough'[43] to address the power differentials across the globe. UNESCO ought also to concentrate on the many ethical differences, to recognise the great diversity of human perspective and experience that is essential to the production of

[38] *Ibid.*   [39] UNESCO, 'Universal Declaration on Bioethics'.
[40] Benatar, 'The trouble with universal declarations', 221.
[41] M. C. Rawlinson and A. Donchin, 'The quest for universality: reflections on the Universal Draft Declaration on Bioethics and Human Rights', *Developing World Bioethics*, 5, 3 (2005), 258–66.
[42] *Ibid.*, 260.   [43] *Ibid.*

genuinely universal norms, and develop a practical approach that incorporates the full range of global perspectives.

In order to move to such an approach, Rawlinson and Donchin recommend shifting the focus away from the abstract and towards the concrete. By taking a detailed look at diverse practical experiences we may gain a 'contextualised understanding of social relations'[44] that avoid unfair bias. Feminist bioethics has already successfully promoted a revised concept of autonomy, one that includes social relations rather than the individual alone, and this precedent suggests that other concepts may similarly be reformulated in the light of global concerns.

Dialogue approach

Fleischacker endorses the cultural dialogue model as that most appropriate for producing a 'concrete, "thick" global ethic'.[45] The method simply involves members of different cultures discussing moral values, discovering parallel moral norms and making use of such norms when addressing cross-cultural moral concerns. The agents involved are not representatives of states or international organisations: they are 'ordinary agents … who come together for any range of economic, educational, religious or political projects'.[46] Fleischacker points out that 'unpressured, low-level conversation'[47] is a feature common to informal multi-cultural meetings, and such conversations often reveal 'striking similarities'[48] in moral values. He wishes for this process to be used as a model for 'cross-cultural interaction that could be made explicit',[49] one that would naturally result in common ethical values being identified. This approach accepts that some degree of moral conflict will always exist. The production of a universal ethic would be an extremely long, complicated process. He uses the Talmud, that was the result of 'over 500 years of intensive argument',[50] as an example of how a genuinely universal ethic could be constructed. A text that outlines a universal ethic should be nothing less than a 'combination of stories, legal arguments, historical reflections and folk wisdom'.[51] Fleischacker criticised other approaches for being too focused on results: their urgency in the face of global problems 'discourages the carefulness and slow building of mutual respect that a global ethic needs'.[52] The cultural dialogue approach focuses on process rather than result.

---

[44] *Ibid.*, 261.   [45] Fleischacker, 'Cultural diversity to universal ethics', 114.
[46] *Ibid.*   [47] *Ibid.*   [48] *Ibid.*   [49] *Ibid.*   [50] *Ibid.*, 115.   [51] *Ibid.*   [52] *Ibid.*

The cultural dialogue process endorsed by Fleischacker has similarities with the discourse ethics approach as advocated by Karl-Otto Apel in his recommended approach to producing universally valid moral solutions to common problems. Apel suggested that in order for ethics successfully to engage with the irreversible processes of globalisation, a new universal moral system is required: 'globalization, I think, provides a novel and highly urgent challenge to a universally valid type of ethics'.[53] Apel points out that, before globalisation became an issue of international political concern, the need for a 'planetary macro-ethics'[54] had already become well established: the global range and 'risk of the effects and side effects of science and technology'[55] that had emerged during the late twentieth century meant that the existing forms of ethics were no longer practically sufficient. Apel points to the fact that a universally valid ethics is 'presupposed and recognized'[56] by the process of inter-subjective communication that occurs in cultures such as 'the community of scientific investigations':[57] complex discussion that depends on shared values between distinct groups has been occurring successfully for many years, and there is no need to suppose that this process cannot continue and be expanded upon globally. Apel notes that the establishment of a respected system of universal ethics has been hampered by the widespread philosophical assertion that moral norms can have no rational basis. Correspondingly, it is commonly assumed that norms extracted from practice are culture-dependent and cannot therefore be universally applicable. Apel's discourse ethics seeks to include the (hitherto) unheard voices of virtual discourse partners such as the members of the next generation or the poor of less developed countries. The successful functioning of rational discourse ethics depends on the 'acknowledgement of a universal principle of justice',[58] although the theory aims towards establishing only very broad ethical concepts for a minimalist global ethics. With reference to the UNESCO approach, discourse ethics may reveal that some of the principles and norms endorsed are specific to 'mainstream' western culture.

Summary

A key theme to emerge from the above discussion is the importance of a multiplicity of voices, whether this is pursued explicitly in the discourse

---

[53] Karl-Otto Apel, 'Globalization and the need for universal ethics', *European Journal of Social Theory*, 3, 2 (2000), 137.
[54] *Ibid.*, 138.   [55] *Ibid.*   [56] *Ibid.*, 139.   [57] *Ibid.*   [58] *Ibid.*, 143.

approach, or via a feminist ethics urging the giving of a voice to the powerless and marginalised. There is something to be taken from the necessary conditions approach too, however, and that is the point that the ethical values or principles that emerge must be fit for purpose, that is, they will be closely related to the purposes for which harmonisation or standardisation is sought, whether on a global level or in a specific context. It should not be assumed that agreement on this can be taken for granted: this is likely to be in sharper focus in relation to specific initiatives such as the BBMRI, especially in the light of sceptical voices concerning the purported benefits of developments in genomics.

Standards

This is an appropriate point at which to turn fully to the context of transnational biomolecular resources. To what extent is harmonisation here necessary, and how much can be dealt with by standards? While there are multiple definitions of the term 'standard', in this context a standard is a rule established to have action-guiding force. Busch points out that an important (ethical) dimension here is who has the power to set the standards.[59] If we look at another context the issues of power become obvious: in pictures of G8 meetings, we can see that despite the different cultural backgrounds of the participating leaders, a common standard of dress has been adopted: the western business suit. What does this say about power to define standards? Where one leader adopts a different style of dress, it really stands out: what sort of statement is being made? In some contexts, where power lies to set the standards may not be traceable: in the context of governance of biomolecular resources, however, transparency has been recognised as a prerequisite.

We suggest that in relation to setting up the international biological resource, three areas for standard setting need to be considered: standards relating to consent to participating in the resource, guidance on access and feedback, and standards on privacy. The question arises as to whether any of these could be dealt with in the way that driving on a particular side of the road is dealt with – it is possible to cope with variation between societies, but not within. For example, take the issue of providing feedback to participants on individual research results. As it happens, existing biobank initiatives have taken different stances on this. But would it matter if different societies participating in a pan-national

---

[59] Busch, 'Measuring up'.

enterprise had a different standard? And what about informed consent procedures?

This is where a discussion of the overall purposes needs to take place – there is a preliminary question as to what extent the purposes of the resource could be achieved with different standards in different countries, and to what extent common standards are required. Even were this possible, however, given agreement about the overall purpose of the resource, it would not be sufficient from an ethical point of view. To approach the topic in this way appears to be a necessary conditions approach – to what extent are common ethical standards necessary for the purposes of the initiative?

It is beyond the scope of this discussion to go into detail on each of the three areas we have mentioned, but we want to illustrate the kinds of questions that need to be asked in relation to standard setting and harmonisation. First let us mention one very important aspect and that is the retrospective/prospective dimension. The consent issues will clearly be different for those giving future consent to a pan-European biobank from those relating to the integration of pre-existing collections. People who have consented to belong to a national initiative may feel very differently about the prospect of transnational research.

That being said, the extent to which variation in standards is possible will depend on the interests at stake in relation to the standard, and whether perception of variation may itself be unlikely to undermine public acceptance of the value of the initiative. We want tentatively to suggest that the three examples, of consent, feedback and privacy, fall into different categories regarding the possibilities of standardisation and the desirability of harmonisation as an ongoing process.

(i) *Consent* If there is no common standard on initial consenting and reconsenting, then there is a danger of a reaction against the initiative by those who feel their opportunity to consent is not quite so good – in an obvious way their voice has not been given as much weight.

(ii) *Feedback* Where feedback is concerned, it is worth considering whether it would be possible to maintain different standards in different countries. While this might lead to objections, as in (i), the extent to which feedback is a benefit is controversial.

(iii) *Privacy* The most interesting example is privacy, because it is commonly pointed to as an area where robust standards of protection are necessary, and yet where promises of protection are not possible.[60]

[60] J. Lunshof, R. Chadwick, D. B. Vorhaus and G. Church, 'From genetic privacy to open consent', *Nature Reviews Genetics*, 9 (2008), 406–11.

A common standard here might be possible, but would arguably be a mistake, precisely because the whole area needs to be rethought, as the following quotation, taken from another context, shows:

> Without minimizing the human and democratic need for privacy, and acknowledging that if only large organizations complied fully with data protection and privacy legislation many ... problems would be reduced, we insist that those problems deserve to be approached in other ways.[61]

The example of privacy shows the ways in which it is important to maintain the interplay of different voices in relation to the 'text' of a standard approach to privacy. Consent, of course, has also come under a great deal of scrutiny in the context of population genomic research in particular, but in the case of privacy the issue is arguably more pressing if promises are being made which it is not, in fact, possible to keep.

Conclusion

We have suggested that in the context of BBMRI what is commonly intended by the term 'harmonisation' in ethics, namely common values, might better be regarded as the establishment of common standards. However, that is not sufficient. A prerequisite is agreement on the ethical credentials of the initiative itself. Beyond that, harmonisation is indeed necessary but not as an end point – rather as an ongoing process – the interplay of different voices in relation to the 'text' of the standards in question. The voices in question must include voices less often heard.

In relation to the wider question of global ethics, the important point to emerge from the discussion of different approaches was, again, the necessity for a multiplicity of voices. Ethics is not a static field: it evolves as science evolves and ongoing dialogue as a process is required. But there is also something to be taken from the necessary conditions approach – analogous to the purpose of the BBMRI in the specific context, dialogue must focus on the overall problem to be solved and purpose to be achieved.

Acknowledgement

The support of the ESRC is gratefully acknowledged. This work is part of the research programme of the ESRC Genomics Network at Cesagen.

---

[61] Surveillance Studies Network, *A Report on the Surveillance Society* (Surveillance Studies Network, 2006), para. 4.2.2, www.surveillance-studies.net/?page_id=3.

BIBLIOGRAPHY

Academy of Medical Sciences, *Personal Data for Public Good: Using Health Information in Medical Research* (London: AMS, January 2006).

Agar, N., *Liberal Eugenics, in Defence of Human Enhancement* (Oxford: Blackwell Publishing, 2004).

Alvarez-Castillo, Fatima, 'Limiting factors impacting on voluntary first person informed consent in the Philippines', *Developing World Bioethics*, 2, 1 (2002), 21–7.

Anderson, D. W., Melanson, S. J. and Maly, J., 'The evolution of corporate governance: power redistribution brings boards to life', *Corporate Governance*, 15, 5 (2007), 780–2.

Apel, Karl-Otto, 'Globalization and the need for universal ethics', *European Journal of Social Theory*, 3, 2 (2000), 137–55.

Argenti, J., *Your Organization: What Is It For?* (New York: McGraw Hill, 1993).

Backing for Organ Donor Overhaul, BBC News Online (16 January 2008) http://news.bbc.co.uk/1/hi/uk_politics/7190168.stm.

Balsamo, A., *Technologies of the Gendered Body* (Durham, NC: Duke University Press, 1999).

Barker, J., 'The Human Genome Diversity Project: "Peoples", "populations" and the cultural politics of identification', *Cultural Studies*, 18, 4 (2004), 571–606.

Baxi, U., *Human Rights in a Posthuman World* (New Delhi: Oxford University Press, 2007).

Benatar, D., 'The trouble with universal declarations', *Developing World Bioethics*, 5, 3 (2005), 220–4.

Berle, A. and Means, G., *The Modern Corporation and Private Property* (New York: Macmillan, 1932).

Beyleveld, D., 'Conceptualising privacy in relation to medical research values' in S. A. M. McLean (ed.), *First Do No Harm* (Aldershot: Ashgate, 2006), 151–64.

'Medical research and the public good', *Kings Law Journal*, 18, 2 (2007), 275–89.

Beyleveld, D. and Brownsword, R., *Consent in the Law* (Oxford: Hart, 2007).

Beyleveld, D. and Histed, E., 'Betrayal of confidence in the Court of Appeal', *Medical Law International*, 4 (2000), 277–311.

Boyd, P., 'The requirements of the Data Protection Act 1998 for the processing of medical data', *Journal of Medical Ethics*, 29 (2003), 34–5.

Brazier, M., 'Do no harm – do patients have responsibilities too?' *Cambridge Law Journal*, 65 (2006), 397–422.

Brennan, G. and Hamlin, A., 'On political representation', *British Journal of Political Science*, 29 (1999), 109–27.

Brock, Dan W., 'Genetics and confidentiality', *American Journal of Bioethics*, 1, 3 (2001), 34–5.

Brown, W. A., 'Inclusive governance practices in nonprofit organizations and implications for practice', *Nonprofit Management and Leadership*, 12, 4 (2002), 369–85.

Brownsword, R., 'The cult of consent: fixation and fallacy', *Kings College Law Journal*, 15 (2004), 223.

'Happy families, consenting couples, and children with dignity: sex selection and saviour siblings', *Child and Family Law Quarterly*, 17 (2005), 435–73.

'Making people better and making better people', *Journal of Academic Legal Studies*, 1 (2005), online.

'The ancillary-care responsibilities of researchers: reasonable but not great expectations', *Journal of Law, Medicine and Ethics*, 35 (2007), 679.

'Informed consent: to whom it may concern', *Jahrbuch für Recht und Ethik*, 15 (2007), 267.

Rights, Regulation and the Technological Revolution (Oxford University Press, 2008).

Buchanan, A., 'Trust in managed care organisations', *Kennedy Institute of Ethics Journal*, 10, 3 (2000), 189–212.

Buchanan, A., Daniels, N., Wikler, D., and Brock, D. W., *From Chance to Choice: Genetics and Justice* (Cambridge University Press, 2000).

Burgess, J. and Chilvers, J., 'Upping the ante: a conceptual framework for designing and evaluating participatory technology assessments', *Science and Public Policy*, 33, 10 (2006), 713–28.

Burgess, M., O'Doherty, K. and Secko, D., 'Biobanking in British Columbia: discussions of personalized medicine through deliberative public engagement', *Personalized Medicine*, 5, 3 (2008), 285–96.

Burley, J., 'Bad genetic luck and health insurance' in J. Burley (ed.), *The Genetic Revolution and Human Rights* (Oxford University Press, 1999), 54–61.

Busch, L., 'Measuring up: how standards shape our lives: a public lecture by Larry Busch', ESRC Genomics Policy and Research Forum, Edinburgh (10 May 2007).

Cahill, L. S., 'Genetics, commodification and social justice in the globalization era', *Kennedy Institute of Ethics Journal*, 11 (2001), 221–38.

Cajete, G., *Native Science: Natural Laws of Interdependence* (Santa Fe, NM: Clear Light Books, 2000).

Cambon-Thomsen, A., Salleé Raal-Sebbag, E. and Knoppers, B. M. 'Populational genetic databases: is a specific ethical and legal framework necessary?', *GenEdit*, 3, 1 (2005), 1–23.

Campbell v. Mirror Group Newspapers [2004] UKHL 22.

Campbell, A. V., 'The ethical challenges of biobanks: safeguarding altruism and trust' in S. A. M. McLean (ed.), *First Do No Harm* (Aldershot: Ashgate, 2006).

'The ethical challenges of genetic databases: safeguarding altruism and trust', *King's Law Journal*, 18 (2007), 242.

Carroll, A. B., 'The pyramid of corporate social responsibility: toward the moral management of organizational stakeholders', *Business Horizons* (July-August, 1991).

Caudfield, T., Upshur, R. E. G. and Daar, A., 'DNA databanks and consent: a suggested policy option involving an authorization model', *BMC Medical Ethics*, 4, 1 (2003), www.biomedcentral.com/1472–6939/4/1.

CBAC, *Population Biobanking in Canada: Ethical, Legal and Social Issues* (2003), http://cbac-cccb.ca/epic/site/cbac-cccb.nsf/en/ah00589e.html#1.

Chadwick, D., Bock, G. and Whelan, J. (eds.), *Human Genetic Information: Science, Law and Ethics* (Chichester: John Wiley, 1990).

Chadwick, R. and Wilson, S., 'Genomic databases as global public goods?', *Res Publica*, 10, 2 (2004).

Chambers, S., 'Deliberative Democratic Theory', *Annual Review of Political Science*, 6 (2003), 307–26.

Chevalier, J., *Stakeholder Analysis and Natural Resource Management* (Ottawa: Carlton University, 2001), http://http-server.carleton.ca/~jchevali/STAKEH2.html.

Chilvers, J., 'Deliberating competence: theoretical and practitioner perspectives on effective participatory appraisal practice', *Science, Technology & Human Values*, 33, 3 (2008), 421–51.

Collins, H. and Evans, R., 'The third wave of science studies: studies of expertise and experience', *Social Studies of Science*, 32, 2 (2002), 235–96.

Council of Europe, *Convention for the Protection of Human Rights and Dignity of the Human Being with Regard to the Application of Biology and Medicine: Convention on Human Rights and Biomedicine CETS No 164* (Oviedo, Spain, 1997), http://conventions.coe.int/treaty/en/treaties/html/164.htm.

European Convention on Human Rights (Rome, 4 November 1950), www.hri.org/docs/ECHR50.html.

Daniels, N. and Sabin, J., 'The ethics of accountability in managed care reform', *Health Affairs*, 17, 5 (1998), 50–64.

Setting Limits Fairly: Can We Learn To Share Medical Resources? (New York: Oxford University Press, 2002).

Data Protection Act 1998, www.hmso.gov.uk/acts/acts1998/19980029.htm.

Davies, P. L., *Gower and Davies' Principles of Modern Company Law*, 7th edn (London: Sweet & Maxwell, 2003).

Davis, D., *Genetic Dilemmas: Reproductive Technology, Parental Choices, and Children's Futures (Reflective Bioethics)* (New York: Routledge, 2001).

Davis, J. H., Schoorman, F. D. and Donaldson, L., 'Towards a stewardship theory of management', *Academy of Management Review*, 27, 1 (1997), 20–47.

Deakin, S., 'The coming transformation of shareholder value', *Corporate Governance*, 13, 1 (2005), 11–18.

Dekkers, F., Laurie, G. and Kent Shalev, C., *Genetic Databases. Assessing the Benefits and the Impact on Human and Patient Rights* (European Partnership on Patients' Rights and Citizens' Empowerment, A Network of the World Health Organisation Regional Office for Europe, 2003).

Dickenson, D., 'Commodification of human tissue: implications for feminist and development ethics', *Developing World Bioethics*, 2, (2002), 55–63.

Dickson, D., 'Patent study urges R&D boost for neglected diseases', *SciDev.Net* (2006), www.scidev.net/en/news/patent-study-urges-rd-boost-for-neglected-disease.html.

Donaldson, T. and Preston, L. E., 'The stakeholder theory of the corporation: concepts, evidence and implications', *Academy of Management Review*, 20, 1 (1995), 65–91.

Doukas, David J. and Berg, Jessica W., 'The family covenant and genetic testing', *American Journal of Bioethics*, 1, 3 (2001), 2–16.

Dretske, F., *Knowledge and the Flow of Information* (Cambridge, MA: MIT Press, 1981).

Naturalizing the Mind (Cambridge, MA: MIT Press, 1995).

Du Bois, F. G., 'Rights trumped? Balancing in constitutional adjudication', *Acta Juridica* (2007), 155–81.

Dworkin, R., *Sovereign Virtue* (Cambridge, MA: Harvard University Press, 2000).

Egorova, Y., Pattison, S. and Edgar, A., 'The meanings of genetics: accounts of biotechnology in the work of Habermas, Derrida and Baudrillard', *International Journal of the Humanities*, 5, 3 (2006), 97–103.

Einsiedel, Edna, *Whose Genes, Whose Safe, How Safe? Publics' and professionals' Views of Biobanks* (Ottawa: Canadian Biotechnology Advisory Committee, 2003).

European Parliament and Council, Directive 95/46/EC on the protection of individuals with regard to the processing of personal data and on the free movement of such data (24 October 1995).

Directive 2004/23/EC on setting standards of quality and safety for the donation, procurement, testing, processing, preservation, storage and distribution of human tissues and cells (31 March 2004).

Evan, W. M. and Freeman, R. E., 'A stakeholder theory of the modern corporation: Kantian capitalism' in T. L. Beauchamp and N. Bowie (eds.), *Ethical Theory and Business*, 3rd edn (Englewood Cliffs, NJ: Prentice Hall, 1988).

Feinberg, J., 'The child's right to an open future' in J. Feinberg, *Freedom and Fulfillment. Philosophical Essays* (Princeton University Press, 1992), 76–97.

Fleischacker, S., 'From cultural diversity to universal ethics: three models', *Cultural Dynamics*, 11 (1999), 105–28.

Franklin, S., 'Making miracles: Scientific progress and the facts of life' in S. Franklin and H. Ragone (eds.), *Reproducing Reproduction* (University of Pennsylvania Press, 1998), 102–17.

Fraser, N., 'After the family wage', *Political Theory*, 22, 4 (1994).

Freeman, R. E., *Strategic Management: A Stakeholder Approach* (Boston: Pitman, 1984).

'The politics of stakeholder theory: some future directions', *Business Ethics Quarterly*, 4, 4 (1994), 409–21.

Freeman, R. E. and Evan, W. M., 'Corporate governance: a stakeholder interpretation', *Journal of Behavioural Economics*, 19, 4 (1990), 337–59.

Freeman, R. E. and McVea, J., 'A stakeholder approach to strategic management', in M. A. Hitt, R. E. Freeman and J. S. Harrison (eds.), *The Blackwell Handbook of Strategic Management* (Oxford: Blackwell Publishing, 2001), 189–207.

Gamble, A. and Kelly, G., 'Shareholder value and the stakeholder debate in the UK', *Corporate Governance*, 9, 2 (2001), 110–17.

Gewirth, A., *Reason and Morality* (University of Chicago Press, 1978).

Gilligan, C., *In a Different Voice: Psychological Theory & Women's Development* (Cambridge, MA and London: Harvard University Press, 1982).

'Reply by Carol Gilligan', *Signs*, 11, 2 (1986), 324–33.

Gitter, D., 'Ownership of human tissue: a proposal for federal recognition of human research participants' property rights in their biological material', *Washington & Lee Law Review*, 61 (2004), 257–345.

Glover, J., *Causing Death and Saving Lives* (Penguin, 1977).

Godard, B., Marshall, J. and Laberge, C., 'Community engagement in genetic research: results of the first public consultation for the Quebec CARTaGENE Project', *Community Genetics*, 10 (2007), 147–58.

Godard, B., Marshall, J., Laberge, C. and Knoppers, B. M., 'Strategies for consulting with the community: the case of four large-scale genetic databases', *Science and Engineering Ethics*, 10, 3 (2004), 457–77.

Goldworth, A., 'Informed consent revisited', *Cambridge Quarterly of Health Care Ethics*, 5 (1996), 214–20.

Goodin, R., *Reasons for Welfare: The Political Theory of the Welfare State* (Princeton University Press, 1998).

Goodjik, R., 'Partnership at corporate level: the meaning of the stakeholder model', *Journal of Change Management*, 3, 3 (2003), 225–41.

Gould, C. C. and Scholz, S. J. (eds.), *Journal of Social Philosophy*, Special Issue on Solidarity, 38, 1 (Spring, 2007).

Greely, Henry T., 'Human genomics research: new challenges for research ethics', *Perspectives in Biology and Medicine*, 44, 2 (2001), 221–9.

Grice, H. P., 'Meaning', *Philosophical Review*, 66 (1957), 377–88.

Groenhout, R. E., *Connected Lives: Human Nature and an Ethics of Care (Feminist Constructions)* (New York: Rowman & Littlefield, 2004).

Guidance Notes to Human Tissue Act 2004, www.opsi.gov.uk/acts/acts2004/en/ ukpgaen_20040030_en_1.

Habermas, J., 'On systematically distorted communication', *Inquiry*, 13 (1970) 205–18.

'Towards a theory of communicative competence', *Inquiry*, 13 (1970), 360–75.

Communication and the Evolution of Society (Boston, MA: Beacon Press, 1979).

The Structural Transformation of the Public Sphere: An Inquiry into a Category of Bourgeois Science (Cambridge: Polity Press, 1989).

Postmetaphysical Thinking: Philosophical Essays (Cambridge, MA: MIT Press, 1992).

On the Pragmatics of Social Interaction: Preliminary Studies in the Theory of Communicative Action (Cambridge: Polity Press, 2001).

The Future of Human Nature (Cambridge: Polity Press, 2003).

Haddow, G., Laurie, G., Cunningham-Burley, S. and Hunter, K., 'Tackling community concerns about commercialisation and genetic research: a modest interdisciplinary proposal', *Social Science and Medicine*, 64, 2 (2007), 272–82.

Harris, J., 'The rationing debate: maximising the health of the whole community. The case against: what the principal objective of the NHS should really be', *British Medical Journal*, 314 (1997), 669–72.

'Scientific research is a moral duty', *Journal of Medical Ethics*, 31 (2005), 242–8.

Harris, J. and Keywood, K., 'Ignorance, information and autonomy', *Theoretical Medicine*, 22 (2001), 415–36.

Harrison, J. S. and St John, C. H., 'Managing and partnering with external stakeholders', *Academy of Management Executive*, 10, 2 (1996), 46–60.

Hayton, D. J., *The Law of Trusts* (London: Sweet & Maxwell, 1998).

Henderson, M., 'Ministers will rethink Bill that could block stem-cell experiments', *The Times*, 22 January 2008, 2.

Hillman, A. J. and Keim, G. D., 'Shareholder value, stakeholder management, and social issues: what's the bottom line?', *Strategic Management Journal*, 22, 2 (2001), 125–31.

Holm, S., 'There is nothing special about genetic information' in A. K. Thompson and R. F. Chadwick (eds.), *Genetic Information – Acquisition, Access, and Control* (New York: Plenum Press, 1999), 97–103.

Holm, S. and Takala, T., 'High hopes and automatic escalators: a critique of some new arguments in bioethics', *Journal of Medical Ethics*, 33 (2007), 1–4.

House of Commons Science and Technology Committee, *The Work of the Medical Research Council*. Third Report of Session 2002–03, HC 132 (London: Stationery Office, 2003).

Human Fertilisation and Embryology Bill 2007–08.

Human Genome Organisation (HUGO) Ethics Committee, *Statement on Benefit Sharing* (2000). www.hugo-international.org/Statement_on_Benefit_Sharing.htm.

  Statement on Human Genomic Databases (2002), www.hugo-international.org/Statement_on_Human_Genomic_Databases.htm.

Human Tissue Act 2004.

Human Tissue (Scotland) Act 2006.

Hummels, H., 'Organizing ethics: a stakeholder debate', *Journal of Business Ethics*, 17, 13 (1998), 293.

Husted, J., 'Autonomy and a right not to know' in R. Chadwick *et al.* (eds.), *The Right To Know and the Right Not To Know* (Aldershot: Ashgate, 1997).

Hutton, W., *The State We're In* (London: Jonathan Cape, 1995).

Intergovernmental Working Group on Public Health, Innovation and Intellectual Property, *Elements of a global strategy and plan of action* (2006), www.who.int/gb/phi/PDF/phi_igwg1_5-en.pdf.

Irwin, A., 'Constructing the scientific citizen: science and democracy in the biosciences', *Public Understanding of Science*, 10 (2001), 1–18.

Jablonka, E., 'Information: its interpretation, its inheritance and its sharing', *Philosophy of Science*, 69 (2002), 578–605.

Jensen, M. C. and Meckling, W. H., 'Theory of the firm: managerial behaviour, agency costs and ownership structure', *Journal of Finance Economics*, 3 (1976).

Johnston, C. and Kaye, J., 'Does the UK Biobank have a legal obligation to feedback individual findings to participants?', *Medical Law Review*, 12 (2004), 239–67.

Jones, P., 'Human rights, group rights and peoples' rights', *Human Rights Quarterly*, 21, 1 (1999), 80–107.

  'Group rights and group oppression', *Journal of Political Philosophy*, 7, 4 (1999), 353–77.

Kakabadse, N. K., Rozuel, C. and Lee-Davies, L., 'Corporate social responsibility and stakeholder approach: a conceptual review', *International Journal of Business Governance and Ethics*, 1, 4 (2005), 277–302.

Kay, L. E., *Who Wrote the Book of Life? A History of the Genetic Code* (Stanford University Press, 2000).

Kiarie, S., 'At crossroads: shareholder value, stakeholder value and enlightened shareholder value: which road should the United Kingdom take?', *International Company and Commercial Law Review*, 17, 11 (2007), 329–43.

Kim, Y., *A Common Framework for the Ethics of the 21st Century* (Paris: UNESCO, 1999).

Kittay, E. F., 'Human dependency and Rawlsian equality' in Diana T. Meyers (ed.), *Feminists Rethink the Self* (Boulder, CO: Westview Press, 1997).

Knoppers, B. M. (ed.), *Human DNA: Law and Policy* (The Hague: Kluwer Law International, 1997).

Knoppers, B. M., 'Who should have access to genetic information?' in J. Burley (ed.), *The Genetic Revolution and Human Rights* (Oxford University Press, 1999), 39–53.

'DNA banking: a retrospective-prospective', in J. Burley and J. Harris (eds.), *A Companion to Genethics* (Oxford: Blackwell, 2002).

'Of genomics and public health: building public "goods"?', *Canadian Medical Association Journal*, 173, 10 (8 Nov 2005).

Knoppers, B. M. and Chadwick, R., 'Human genetic research: emerging trends in ethics', *Nature Reviews Genetics*, 6 (2005), 75–9.

Koenig, B. A., 'Why not grant primacy to the family?', *American Journal of Bioethics*, 1, 3 (2001), 33–4.

Kolk, A. and Pinkse, J., 'Stakeholder mismanagement and corporate social responsibility crisis', *European Management Journal*, 24, 1 (2006), 59–72.

Kuhn, T., *The Structure of Scientific Revolutions* (University of Chicago Press, 1962).

Langtry, B., 'Stakeholders and the moral responsibilities of business', *Business Ethics Quarterly*, 4, 4 (1994), 431–43.

Laurie, G., *Genetic Privacy: A Challenge to Medico-Legal Norms* (Cambridge University Press, 2002).

Laurie, G., Bruce, A. and Lyall, C., 'The roles of values and interests in the governance of the life sciences: learning lessons from the "Ethics+" approach of UK Biobank', in C. Lyall, J. Smith and T. Papaioannou (eds.), *The Limits to Governance: The Challenge of Policy-making for the New Life Sciences* (Aldershot: Ashgate, 2009 *forthcoming*).

Legal Guidance to Data Protection Act (DPA) 1998, www.ico.gov.uk/upload/documents/library/data_protection/detailed_specialist_guides/data_protection_act_legal_guidance.pdf.

Lehrman, S., 'US drops patent claim to Hagahai cell line', *Nature*, 384, 6609 (1996), 500.

Levitt, M., 'Public consultation in bioethics. What's the point of asking the public when they have neither scientific nor ethical expertise?', *Health Care Analysis*, 11, 1 (2003), 15–25.

'UK Biobank: a model for public engagement?', *Genomics, Society and Policy*, 1, 3 (2005), 78–81.

Levitt, M. and Weldon, S., 'A well placed trust? Public perceptions of the governance of DNA databases', *Critical Public Health*, 15, 4 (2005), 311–21.

Lindemann Nelson, H. and Lindemann Nelson, J., *The Patient in the Family* (Routledge: London and New York, 1995).

Lipton, P., 'Genetic and generic determinism: a new threat to free will?' in D. Rees and S. Rose (eds.), *The New Brain Sciences – Perils and Prospects* (Cambridge University Press, 2004).

Low, C. and Cowton, C., 'Beyond stakeholder engagement: the challenges of stakeholder participation in corporate governance', *International Journal of Business Governance and Ethics*, 1, 1 (2004), 45–55.

Low, L., King, S. and Wilkie, T., 'Genetic discrimination in life insurance: empirical evidence from a cross sectional survey of genetic support groups in the United Kingdom', *British Medical Journal*, 317 (1998), 1632–5.

Lunshof, J., Chadwick, R., Vorhaus, D. B. and Church, G., 'From genetic privacy to open consent', *Nature Reviews Genetics*, 9 (2008), 406–11.

MacLean, S. and Burgess, M. M., 'Biobanks: informing the public through expert and stakeholder presentations', *Health Law Review*, 16, 4 (2008), 6–8.

Manson, N. C., 'What is genetic information and why is it significant?' *Journal of Applied Philosophy*, 23, 1 (2006), 1–16.

'Consent and informed consent' in R. Ashcroft, A. Dawson, H. Draper and J. McMillan (eds.), *Principles of Health Care Ethics*, 2nd edn (London: John Wiley, 2007), 297–304.

Manson, N. C. and O'Neill, O., *Rethinking Informed Consent in Bioethics* (Cambridge University Press, 2007).

Martin, J., *The Meaning of the 21st Century* (London: Transworld Publishers, 2007).

Maschke, K. J., 'Navigating an ethical patchwork – human gene banks', *Nature Biotechnology*, 23, 5 (2005), 539–45.

Mason, C., Kirkbride, J. and Bryde, D., 'From stakeholders to institutions: the changing face of social enterprise governance theory', *Management Decision*, 45, 2 (2007), 284–301.

Mauro, F. and Hardison, P., 'Traditional knowledge of indigenous and local communities: international debate and policy initiatives', *Ecological Applications* (2000), 1263–9.

McConkie-Rosell, A. and Spiridigliozzi, G. A., '"Family matters": a conceptual framework for genetic testing in children', *Journal of Genetic Counselling*, 13, 1 (2004), 9–29.

McHale, J. V., 'Regulating genetic databases: some legal and ethical issues', *Medical Law Review*, 12 (2004), 70–96.

McKibben, B., *Enough: Genetic Engineering and the End of Human Nature* (London: Bloomsbury, 2003).

Metcalfe, C. E., 'The stakeholder corporation', *Business Ethics*, 7, 1 (1998), 30–6.

Mill, J. S., *On Liberty*, E. Rapaport (ed.) (Indianapolis, IN: Hackett, 1978).

Millikan, R., *Language, Thought and Other Biological Categories* (Cambridge, MA: MIT Press, 1984).

Mitchell, Gordon R. and Happe, Kelly, 'Informed consent after the human genome project', *Rhetoric and Public Affairs*, 4, 3 (2001), 375–406.

Morsing, M. and Schultz, M., 'Corporate social responsibility communication: shareholder information, response and involvement strategies', *Business Ethics: A European Review*, 15, 4 (2006), 323–38.

MRC and Wellcome Trust, *Biobank UK: A Question of Trust: A Consultation Exploring and Addressing Questions of Public Trust* (London: People Science & Policy Ltd, 2002).

Mullen, C., 'Sustaining life, enabling activity and inflicting death: what risk and physical harm caused by transport is morally defensible?', unpublished PhD thesis, University of Manchester (2004).

Murphy, Timothy F., 'Mapping the human genome', in H. Kuhse and P. Singer (eds.), *A Companion to Bioethics* (Oxford: Blackwell, 1998).

Murray v. *Express Newspapers plc* [2007] EWHC 1908 (Ch).

NARC (National American Research Council) *Model Ethical Protocol for Collecting DNA Samples* (1999), www.stanford.edu/group/morrinst/hgdp/protocol.html.

Nelkin, D. and Lindee, M. S., *The DNA Mystique: The Gene as a Cultural Icon*, 2nd edn (Ann Arbor, MI: University of Michigan Press, 2004).

Noddings, N., *Caring: a Feminine Approach to Ethics and Moral Education* (Berkeley, CA: University of California Press, 1984).

Nozick, R., *Anarchy, State and Utopia* (Oxford: Blackwell, 1974).

Nuffield Council on Bioethics, *The Ethics of Research Related to Healthcare in Developing Countries* (London: Nuffield Council on Bioethics, 2002).

    Human Tissue: Legal and Ethical Issues. Response from the Nuffield Council on Bioethics to the Human Tissue Bill (London: Nuffield Council on Bioethics, 2004), www.nuffieldbioethics.org/fileLibrary/pdf/NCOB_response_-_HT_bill.pdf

    The Forensic Use of Bioinformation: Ethical Issues (London: Nuffield Council on Bioethics, 2007).

    Public Health: Ethical Issues (London, Nuffield Council on Bioethics, 2007).

Okin, S. M., *Is Multiculturalism Bad for Women?* (Princeton University Press, 1999).

    '"Mistresses of their own destiny": group rights, gender and realistic rights of exit', *Ethics*, 112 (2002), 205–30.

O'Neill, O., 'Some limits of informed consent', *Journal of Medical Ethics*, 29 (2003), 4–7.

Organisation for Economic Co-operation and Development (OECD), OECD Workshop on 'The global biological resource centres network – networking the networks' (Paris: OECD, 2007).

Oyama, S., *The Ontogeny of Information. Developmental Systems and Evolution*, 2nd edn (Durham, NC: Duke University Press, 2000).

Oyama, S., Griffiths, P. E. and Gray, R. D., *Cycles of Contingency. Developmental Systems and Evolution* (Cambridge, MA: MIT Press, 2001).

Papineau, D., 'The status of teleosemantics, or how to stop worrying about swamp-man', in *Australasian Journal of Philosophy*, 79, 2 (2001), 279–89.

Parker, M., 'Confidentiality in genetic testing', *American Journal of Bioethics*, 1, 3 (2001), 21–2.

Parker, M. and Lucassen, A., 'Genetic information: a joint account?', *British Medical Journal*, 329 (2004), 165–7.

Parliamentary Office of Science and Technology, 'Data protection and medical research', *Postnote*, 235 (2005), www.parliament.uk/documents/upload/postpn235.pdf.

'The UK Biobank', *Postnote*, 180 (2002), www.parliament.uk/post/pn180.pdf

Pattinson, S. D., *Medical Law and Ethics* (London: Sweet and Maxwell, 2006).

Pettet, B., *Company Law*, 2nd edn (Harlow: Pearson Education Limited, 2005).

Philips, J. and Firth, A., *Introduction to Intellectual Property*, 4th edn (London: Butterworths, 2001).

Pimbert, M. and Wakeford, T., 'Deliberative democracy and citizen empower-ment: an overview', *PLA Notes*, 40 (February 2001), 23–8.

Pitkin, H., 'Representation and democracy: an uneasy alliance', *Scandinavian Political Studies*, 27, 3 (2004).

Property Regulation in European Science, Ethics and Law Project, www.propeur.bham.ac.uk.

Quinn, M., *Sir John Sulston* (2001), www.npg.org.uk/live/search/portrait.asp?search=sp&sText=sulston&rNo=0.

R v. Department of Health, ex parte Source Informatics Ltd [1999] 4 All ER 185; [2001] QB 424 (CA).

Rachels, J., 'Why privacy is important', *Philosophy and Public Affairs*, 4, 4 (1975), 323–33.

Rawlinson, M. C. and Donchin, A., 'The quest for universality: reflections on the Universal Draft Declaration on Bioethics and Human Rights', *Developing World Bioethics*, 5, 3 (2005), 258–66.

Rawls, J., *A Theory of Justice* (Cambridge, MA: Harvard University Press, 1971).

Political Liberalism, new edn (New York: Colombia University Press, 1996).

Reddy, M., 'The conduit metaphor: a case of frame conflict in our language about language' in A. Ortony (ed.), *Metaphor and Thought* (Cambridge University Press, 1979), 284–324.

Rees, D. and Rose, S., (eds.), *The New Brain Sciences – Perils and Prospects* (Cambridge University Press, 2004).

Reiman, J. H., 'Privacy, intimacy, and personhood', *Philosophy and Public Affairs*, 6, 1 (1976), 26–44.

Roberts, J., 'Agency theory, ethics and corporate governance', paper prepared for the Corporate Governance and Ethics Conference, Macquarie Graduate School of Management (Sydney, Australia, 28–30 June 2004), www.le.ac.uk/ulsm/research/cppe/levinas/pdf/roberts2.pdf.

Rose, H., *The Commodification of Bioinformation: the Icelandic Health Sector Database* (London, UK: Wellcome Trust, 2001).

Rose, N., *The Politics of Life Itself* (Princeton University Press, 2007).

Runciman, D., 'The paradox of political representation', *Journal of Political Philosophy*, 15, 1 (2007), 93–114.

Sarkar, S., 'Biological information: a sceptical look at some central dogmas of molecular biology', in S. Sarkar (ed.), *The Philosophy and History of Molecular Biology: New Perspectives* (Dordrecht, Netherlands: Kluwer, 1996), 187–232.

Scully, J. L., 'Drawing a line: situating moral boundaries in genetic medicine', *Bioethics*, 15, 3 (2002), 189–204.

Shakespeare, T., 'Disability, genetics and global justice', *Social Policy and Society*, 4 (2005), 87–95.

Shapshay, S. and Pimple, K. D., 'Participation in biomedical research is an imperfect moral duty: a response to John Harris', *Journal of Medical Ethics*, 33 (2007), 414–17.

Shea, N. 'Representation in the genome, and other inheritance systems', *Biology and Philosophy*, 22 (2007), 313–31.

Sheremata, L., *Population Biobanking in Canada: Ethical, Legal and Social Issues*, report for the Canadian Biotechnology Advisory Committee (2003).

Shiva, V., *Biopiracy: The Plunder of Nature and Knowledge* (Cambridge: South End Press, 1997).

    Protect or Plunder? Understanding Intellectual Property (London: Zed Books Ltd, 2001).

    Earth Democracy: Justice, Sustainability and Peace (London: Zed Books Ltd, 2005).

Silver, L., *Remaking Eden: Cloning and Beyond Brave New World* (New York: Avon Books, 1997).

Smeeth, L. *et al.*, 'Measles, mumps, and rubella (MMR) vaccine and autism', *British Medical Journal*, 323 (2001), 163–9.

Smerdon, R., *A Practical Guide to Corporate Governance*, 2nd edn (London: Sweet & Maxwell, 2004).

Smith, J. M., 'The concept of information in biology', *Philosophy of Science*, 67 (2000), 177–94.

Soanes, C. and Stevenson, A. (eds.), *The Concise Oxford English Dictionary*, 11th edn (Oxford University Press, 2006).

Solbakk, J. H., Holm, S. and Hofmann, B. (eds.), *The Ethics of Research Biobanking* (Springer, 2009, *forthcoming*).

Weijer, C., Goldsand, G. and Emanuel, E. J., 'Protecting communities in research: current guidelines and limits of extrapolation', *Nature Genetics*, 23 (1999), 275–80.

Westin, A., *Privacy and Freedom* (New York: Atheneum, 1967).

Whittall, A., 'Harmony', in A. Latham (ed.), *The Oxford Companion to Music* (Oxford University Press, 2002), 560–3.

WHO Advisory Committee on World Health, *Genomics and World Health* (World Health Organisation, 2002).

Widdows, H., 'Genetic challenges to ethics', paper presented at EACME conference, Barcelona, August 2005.

'Conceptualising the self in the genetic era', *Health Care Analysis*, 15 (2007), 5–12.

'Reconceptualising genetics: challenges to traditional medical ethics' in C. Lenk, N. Hoppe and R. Andorno (eds.), *Ethics and Law of Intellectual Property: Current Problems in Politics, Science and Technology* (Farnham: Ashgate, 2007), 159–73.

'Moral neocolonialism and global ethics', *Bioethics*, 21, 6 (2007), 305–15.

Williams, M. S., *Voice, Trust and Memory* (Princeton University Press, 1998).

Wilson, J., 'Is respect for autonomy defensible?', *Journal of Medical Ethics*, 33 (2007), 353–6.

Wilson, S. E., 'Social perspectives and genetic enhancement: Whose perspective? Whose choice?', *Studies in Ethics, Law, and Technology*, 1, 1 (2007), www.bepress.com/selt/vol1/iss1/art3.

'The ethic of care and Rawlsian social justice: critique and reinterpretation', unpublished PhD thesis, Lancaster University (2003).

Winickoff, D. E., 'Governing population genomics: law, bioethics, and biopolitics in three case studies', *Jurimetrics*, 43 (2003), 187–228.

'Partnership in UK Biobank: a third way for genomic property?', *Journal of Law, Medicine & Ethics*, 35, 3 (2007), 440–56.

Winickoff, D. E. and Neumann, L., 'Towards a social contract for genomics: property and the public in the "Biotrust" model', *Genomics, Society and Policy*, 1, 3 (2005), 8–21.

INDEX